OSCAR ROSE JUNIOR COLLEGE
LIBRARY

D0290397

A1 0000 54654

The Chinese Military System

The Chinese Military System

An Organizational Study of the Chinese People's Liberation Army

Harvey W. Nelsen

Westview Press
Boulder, Colorado

Thornton Cox Publishers
London, England

This volume is included in Westview's Special Studies on China and East Asia.

All rights reserved. No part of this publication may be reproduced or transmitted in any form or by any means, electronic or mechanical, including photocopy, recording, or any information storage and retrieval system, without permission in writing from the publisher.

Copyright © 1977 by Westview Press

Published in 1977 in the United States of America by
  Westview Press, Inc.
  1898 Flatiron Court
  Boulder, Colorado 80301
  Frederick A. Praeger, Publisher and Editorial Director
Published in 1977 in Great Britain by
  Thornton Cox Publishers
  3 Colebrook Court
  Sloan Avenue
  London SW3 3DJ

  ISBN (U.K.): 0-902726-24-2

Library of Congress Cataloging in Publication Data
Nelsen, Harvey, 1939-
  The Chinese military system.

  (Westview special studies on China and East Asia)
  Bibliography: p.
  1. China (People's Republic of China, 1949-   ). Chung-kuo jen min chieh
fang chün. I. Title.
UA837.N44   355'.00951   76-54157
ISBN 0-89158-221-5

Printed and bound in the United States of America

Contents

Tables, Charts, and Maps

Abbreviations

CB	*Current Background*, U.S. Consulate General, Hong Kong
CCP	Chinese Communist Party
CMC	Central Military Commission of the Chinese Communist Party
CNA	*China News Analysis*, Hong Kong
CNS	*China News Summary*, Hong Kong
DRV	Democratic Republic of Vietnam
FBIS	*Foreign Broadcast Information Service, Daily Report; People's Republic of China*, Washington, D.C.
GPCR	Great Proletarian Cultural Revolution
GPD	General Political Department
GRSD	General Rear Services Department
GSD	General Staff Department
ICBM	intercontinental ballistic missile
IRBM	intermediate range ballistic missile
JCP	Japanese Communist Party
JMJP	*Jen-min Jih-pao* (People's Daily), Peking
JMP	jen-min-pi, standard Chinese currency
JPRS	Joint Publication Research Service, U.S. Department of Commerce
LAD	*Chieh-fang Chun-pao* (Liberation Army Daily), Peking
MND	The Ministry of National Defense
MRBM	medium range ballistic missile
NCNA	New China News Agency
NDIO	National Defense Industries Office
NDSTC	National Defense Science and Technology Committee
PAD	People's Armed (Forces) Department
PCC	Production-Construction Corps
PKI	Indonesian Communist Party
PLA	People's Liberation Army
PLAAF	People's Liberation Army Air Force
PLAN	People's Liberation Army Navy
PRC	People's Republic of China

PWNL   People's Wars of National Liberation
SCMM   *Selections from Chinese Mainland Magazines,*
          U.S. Consulate General, Hong Kong
SCMP   *Survey of China Mainland Press,* U.S. Consulate
          General, Hong Kong
SEATO Southeast Asia Treaty Organization
SPRCP *Survey of People's Republic of China Press,* U.S.
          Consulate General, Hong Kong
URS   *Union Research Service,* Hong Kong

Preface

The purpose of this book is to fill a gap in scholarship in Chinese organizational studies. Although fine works have been written in the last decade on the Chinese Communist Party and governmental organizations (two of the most prominent are Franz Schurmann, *Ideology and Organization in Communist China,* and A. Doak Barnett, *Cadres, Bureaucracy and Political Power in Communist China*), recent writings on the military bureaucracy are few or scattered in periodical literature. The two most important works are John Gittings, *The Role of the Chinese Army,* and General Samuel B. Griffith, *The Chinese People's Liberation Army,* both researched in 1965–66 and dealing mostly with the history and development of the People's Liberation Army (PLA). Much has happened to the PLA since that time, and equally important, much has been learned concerning its organizational forms and how they function in peacetime. This writing attempts to begin the study of the Chinese military system where Professor Gittings and General Griffith ended theirs—on the eve of the Great Proletarian Cultural Revolution—continuing through mid–1976 when research was completed.

A topical approach is used in order to best explain how the various parts of the system operate and are interrelated. This method sacrifices a continuous historical chronicle; however, several "recent history" sections have been appended to the organizational discussions. Hopefully the book will provide the reader with a general understanding of how the PLA functions internally and how it performs its role in Chinese society and politics.

A minimum of Chinese military leaders are mentioned herein—only top level military officers are identified, and then only for key organizations. It is my purpose to provide information regarding the responsibilities and authority of military organizations, regardless of who occupies the positions. Moreover, this is a period of generational transition in China; thus, leadership lists will quickly be outdated. There is a good deal of military capabilities information included; more than I had originally intended. However, the information was readily available, so I incorporated it even though such material is much more perishable than the organizational information.

Researching this volume proved to be a mixture of scholarship and journalism. A standard academic approach served well for exploring the events of the Cultural Revolution, due to the abundance of Red Guard materials. However, when dealing with more recent events and present military capabilities, journalistic practices were used. Lengthy discussions with the Defense Liaison staff of the American Consulate General in Hong Kong and the Defense Attaché Office of the U.S. Embassy in Taipei provided many insights and much new information.

At the Institute for International Relations in Taipei, I was allowed free access to the library which contained many classified Ministry of Defense studies on the PLA. These proved very valuable for providing organizational information. Since they were not intended for public distribution, they were free of propaganda and accurate. There would be little use in citing specific works since they are available only in classified Chinese Nationalist libraries. However, Western scholars can arrange to do research at the Institute for International Relations simply by writing in advance of their arrival in Taiwan. (The address is 64 Wan-shou Road,

Mucha, Taipei.) When using overt Chinese Nationalist sources and right wing newspapers, such as the *Hsing-tao Jih-pao* of Hong Kong, I have assiduously attempted to separate fact from propaganda. My own background assisted me greatly since from 1965 to 1970 I was employed by the U.S. Departments of Defense and State analyzing the role of the PLA in the Cultural Revolution.

In the words of I. F. Stone, "all governments are liars." The People's Republic of China is no exception; Peking propagandizes some aspects of the People's Liberation Army into half-truths while keeping remarkably well guarded most information on the military. Therefore, although I spent a decade working on the subject prior to the concentrated research and writing efforts in 1974–76, this book is not definitive. Some of the data are soft, and my analyses and interpretations occasionally probe the limits of the available evidence. For this I beg the reader's understanding; it is better to risk error than to write nothing at all.

In the researching and writing of this book, I have been assisted by many organizations and individuals. Those organizations to which I owe a special debt of gratitude are the Joint Committee on Contemporary China of the Social Science Research Council, New York City, and the Sponsored Research Program of the University of South Florida for funding my work in Hong Kong and Taiwan. The Universities Service Centre, under the able guidance of Martin Whyte and John Dolfin, provided vital facilities and resources in Hong Kong, as did the Institute for International Relations in Taipei.

My tenure at the Universities Service Centre fortunately coincided with that of Harlan Jencks who was then researching his doctoral dissertation on the People's Liberation Army for the University of Washington. I owe much to discussions with him and am especially grateful for permission to use his unit organization charts herein. At the U.S. Defense Liaison Office, Col. Richard E. Gillespie and Major William McMurdy read and made valuable comments on my first draft. Lt. Col. John Boswell, the U.S. Army attaché in Taipei, performed the same service. Others who have read and commented on draft versions include Professors Parris Chang of Penn State, Thomas Robinson of the University of Washington, and Mr. Glenn Dick. Finally I wish to thank *The China Quarterly* for permission to reprint the tables on unit movements and takeovers, drawn from my article, "Military Forces in the Cultural Revolution," CQ, no. 51, July–September 1972.

1

An Overview of the Military System

This army is powerful because of its separation into two parts;
the main forces and the regional forces with the former
available for operations in any area whenever necessary, and
the latter concentrating on defending their own localities and
attacking the enemy there in cooperation with local militia.
— *Mao Tse-tung*

This chapter is written partly for those readers who are
seeking general information and partly as an introduction to
those who have little previous knowledge of the People's
Liberation Army (PLA). Organizations mentioned here are
described in greater detail and with more documentation in
ensuing chapters.

Size and Strength

The term PLA encompasses China's ground, naval, and
air forces. The leadership chooses not to reveal its size, thus
there are only approximations on how large the force is and
how it is apportioned among the branches and service arms;
recently published estimates range from 2.9 to over 4 million.[1] Rather than attempting to give precise figures, it is
wiser to describe the PLA in order of magnitude: the military numbers somewhat less than 4 million men including
ground, air, and naval forces, but excluding the paramilitary

militia and production-construction corps. Over 3 million men are in the ground forces, while air and naval forces are estimated at 300,000 and 200,000 respectively.[2]

The above figures seem impressively large, or even ominous. However, the PLA may be smaller than the Soviet forces.[3] China's ground forces are undoubtedly the world's largest, but that is partly an attempt to compensate for the relative weakness of the air and naval forces. On a per capita basis, the armed forces' size is only about one-half the international average. Most importantly, the PLA is organized and equipped as a defensive force with scant ability to project its armies to areas distant from China's borders. The ground forces are equipped with reliable conventional weapons, mostly of Russian design. Infantry forces are not motorized, have poor strategic mobility, and, unit for unit, have less artillery and tanks than Western or Soviet forces. There are four to six divisions designated as "airborne," but that is not a real figure since it is unlikely that there are enough transports and helicopters in all of China to put even one division of paratroopers in the air.

The PLA Air Force has perhaps 100 obsolescent medium bombers, a few hundred obsolete light bombers, and about 500 new fighter-bombers. Rather than an aerial striking force, the Chinese choose to emphasize air defense with about 3500 fighter/interceptor aircraft including a new model nearing production. They also spent a significant portion of the air force budget in the 1960s developing an improved air-defense radar system and expanding production of surface-to-air missiles.

The PLA Navy is a coastal defense force, lacking any cruisers or aircraft carriers. It has a fleet of almost sixty diesel-powered submarines which have not been known to leave China's coastal waters. Many of the surface vessels are patrol craft, including some modern guided-missile boats which provide an inexpensive coastal defense against warships. The navy has made no effort to build troop transports, much less to develop an amphibious strike force.

The acquisition of nuclear weapons should also be viewed as primarily defensive. China has had the atom bomb since 1964 and the hydrogen bomb since 1967. Already deployed are about 100 medium-range and intermediate-range ballistic missiles (MRBM: 700-1000 mile range; IRBM: 1500-3500 mile range). These are under the control of the Second Artillery—the PLA's equivalent to the Soviet Strategic Rocket forces. The navy also has a nuclear submarine under development. While not nearly equalling the strategic striking power of the U.S. or USSR, China is, even now, a fully fledged member of the nuclear club. However, to use those weapons in a war of aggression would be to invite annihilation; the oft-repeated Chinese pledge never to be the first to use nuclear weapons in case of war is common sense and almost certainly a genuine commitment. Like other major powers, China views its nuclear capacity as a deterrent to would-be attackers.

Despite the fact that the PLA is behind other major armies in technical sophistication, mobility, and heavy equipment, students of the PLA agree that the Chinese military is quite capable of defending its homeland against invasion by conventional forces. This defensive credibility is due partly to sheer size but more to the high morale of the troops and the way in which the ground forces are structured.

Two major components make up the infantry. The first of these are the 37 or 38 "main force" corps (often referred to as "armies"). Each is normally composed of 3 divisions and smaller support units (about 50,000 men at full strength), having most of the artillery, armor, and heavy equipment. The remainder of the army's main forces are armor, artillery, and railway divisions, and signal and engineer regiments which, in wartime, would be used in conjunction with the 37 corps. The regional forces, the second major component of the infantry, are equipped with lighter weapons and have fewer troops than the equivalent echelons of the corps. Most of the regional forces are independent regiments and battalions, although there are some divisions. Unit echelons and estimated personnel are listed on the following page. The figures for subordinate units do not total the sum of the next higher echelons because, for the sake of simplicity, all support elements are omitted here. See chapter 4 and the Appendix for more detailed tables of organization and equipment.

		Main Forces	Regional Forces
corps	50,000		---
division	12,000	(3 divs./corps)	10,000
regiment	3,000	(3 reg./div.)	2,800
battalion	800	(3 batt./reg.)	750
company	160	(3 comp./batt.)	130
platoon	37	(3 plat./comp.)	37
squad	12	(3 sqd./plat.)	12

Defensive Strategy

Were China to be invaded, the main forces, which include the air and naval units, would carry the battle to the enemy. If the enemy penetrated deeply into China, some of the regional forces would defend their own localities and mobilize the militia to act as guerilla units behind the enemy lines, while other militia and regional units would keep the main forces supplied and provide personnel replacements and intelligence on enemy movements. In peacetime, the militia and production-construction corps serve China's domestic economic needs and spend only part of their time in military training. They are the Chinese "minutemen," numbering in the tens of millions. In Mao Tse-tung's concept of defensive warfare, the invader would become bogged down, the PLA forces would surround and eventually defeat him, or compel the intruding force to withdraw.

The following 1969 quotation from Mao Tse-tung sums up both the defensive orientation of the PLA and the strategy to be adopted were an invasion to occur:

> If the enemy should invade our country, we would refrain from invading his country. As a general rule, we do not fight outside of our own borders. I say we should not be provoked into doing so, not even if you send us an invitation. But if you should invade our country, then we will deal with you. We would see if you want to fight a small war or a big war. If a small war, we would fight at the border. If a big war, I propose that we make some

room for that. China is a vast country. I presume the
enemy would not come without the prospect of gaining
something from it. We want the whole world to see that
in fighting such a war, we would be on logically sound
and advantageous grounds. As far as I can see, *if he
enters our country, we shall have the advantage* . . .
making it a good war to fight and making the enemy a
victim of the quagmire of the people. As to such
weapons as aircraft, tanks, and armored cars, numerous
experiences have shown it is within our competence to
deal with them.[4]

The emphasized clauses reveal China's greatest defensive
weakness. The force structure is best prepared against conventional invasion—a course of action which few, if any, of
Peking's potential enemies would be apt to adopt. Rather
than attacking the greatest strength of the PLA, opponents
could be expected to challenge the technologically deficient
air and naval forces. Their weaknesses are such that a highly
modern force could harass and intimidate China from the air
and sea with either conventional or nuclear weapons. Of
course, it would be extremely unwise to resort to nuclear
weapons unless the attacker's homeland and allies lay
outside the range of the PLA's retaliatory IRBM force.

Command and Control

The 1975 Chinese constitution stipulated that the commander in chief of the armed forces is the chairman of the
Chinese Communist Party, a position which is currently
held by Mao's successor, Hua Kuo-feng. He controls the
military through a concurrent appointment as chairman of
the Central Military Commission (CMC) of the Central
Committee, Chinese Communist Party. Beneath the CMC,
the military is managed through three major channels, each
having its own communications network and specific missions: the Chinese Communist Party political apparatus;
the military command channels; and the administrative
functions such as logistics, military pay, and medical support. There is some overlap among the three networks which

explains why some organizations appear in each of the first
three organizational charts in this chapter (Charts I, II, and
III). The eleven military regions, for example, are the top
level organizations for dealing with military affairs in the
provinces. They 'have political, command, and administrative responsibilities.

Political Control

The Chinese Communist Party (CCP) reigns supreme in
the military as in other segments of society and government.
Virtually all persons holding positions of responsibility are
Party members, but the political control apparatus does not
simply rely on that fact. An elaborate structure has been
created which permeates all levels of the PLA and oversees
virtually all of its manifold activities. At the pinnacle of the
bureaucracy is the CMC. Its size is variable, but the six to
twelve men who form its core, the Standing Committee, are
without doubt the men who control the PLA—politically,
militarily, and, indirectly, administratively. Under the CMC
is its political arm, the General Political Department (GPD).
It supervises a pyramid network of Party committees and
political commissars in service branches and arms, all units,
and regional, provincial, and local military headquarters.
Every organization in the PLA down through regimental
level must have a Party committee. Battalions and companies have Party "branches" which serve the same function. The leaders of these groups are usually political
commissars who serve as secretaries of the Party committees,
countersign military orders, and are responsible for personnel matters, morale, and discipline. In peacetime, the Party
committees lead the PLA and the political commissars lead
the Party committees.

Command Structure

In terms of military orders, the top of the pyramid is again
the CMC. Its command arm is the General Staff Department
(see Chart IV), which has an elaborate communications
system capable of relaying orders not only to the service

CHART I - MAJOR LINES OF POLITICAL CONTROL

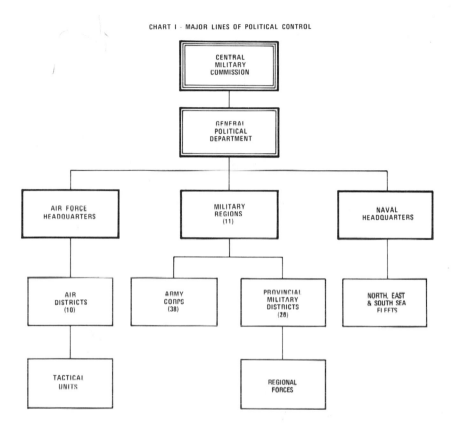

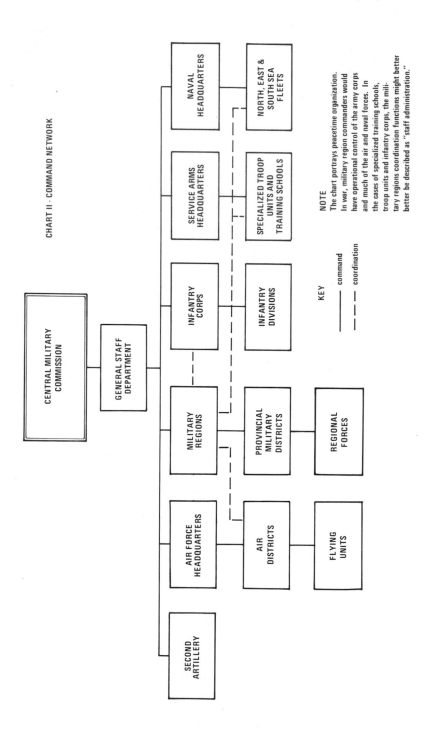

CHART II · COMMAND NETWORK

KEY

——— command

– – – coordination

NOTE

The chart portrays peacetime organization. In war, military region commanders would have operational control of the army corps and much of the air and naval forces. In the cases of specialized training schools, troop units and infantry corps, the military regions coordination functions might better be described as "staff administration."

CENTRAL MILITARY COMMISSION

GENERAL STAFF DEPARTMENT

SECOND ARTILLERY

AIR FORCE HEADQUARTERS

MILITARY REGIONS

INFANTRY CORPS

SERVICE ARMS HEADQUARTERS

NAVAL HEADQUARTERS

AIR DISTRICTS

PROVINCIAL MILITARY DISTRICTS

INFANTRY DIVISIONS

SPECIALIZED TROOP UNITS AND TRAINING SCHOOLS

NORTH, EAST & SOUTH SEA FLEETS

FLYING UNITS

REGIONAL FORCES

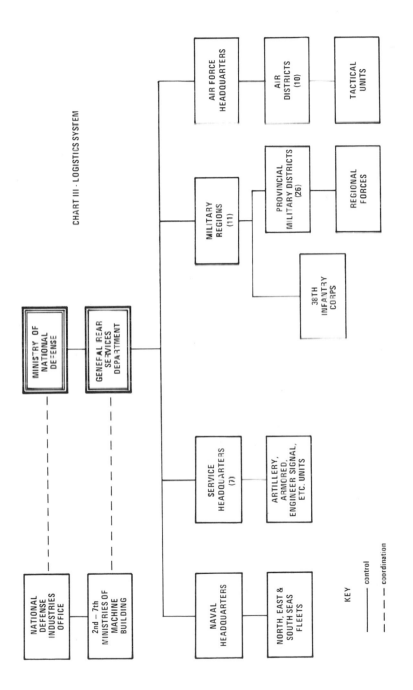

CHART III - LOGISTICS SYSTEM

branches and arms and military regions, but also directly to main force troop units down to regimental level. The only forces of any size with which the General Staff cannot deal directly are the regional units, who are given orders via the eleven military regions, three urban garrison commands, and twenty-six provincial military districts. In case of hostilities, the military regions are converted into operational war zones and the regional commanders take over tactical command of all forces in their areas.[5] However, in peacetime, the military region commander does not have operational control over the main force units stationed in his geographic jurisdiction. The army corps get their operational orders from the General Staff—usually routed through the military region headquarters to avoid confusion. The air force and navy get their orders from their own headquarters via the ten air districts and the three naval fleet commands. Liaison officers from air and naval forces are stationed in most military regions to minimize the potential mix-ups inherent in the multiple command channels.

Logistics and Administrative Network

Most of the PLA's needs can be lumped under the general term "logistics." The organization responsible for logistics, military pay, and medical care is the General Rear Services Department (see Chart V). It supplies the air force and navy through their respective commands which have rear services (quartermaster) headquarters. The administrative chain continues down at least as far as naval and air base levels. The army is supplied through the military regions which, in this case, are responsible for all ground forces stationed in their jurisdictions. The rear services administrative pyramid has its own communications network.[6]

At the national level there are also seven specialized forces, i.e., artillery, second artillery, armor, signal, anti-chemical warfare, railway, and engineering troops. These service headquarters are primarily administrative rather than command elements. Most of the specialized ground force units are integrated into the main force army corps, although a few score are "independent" in the sense of being unattached to

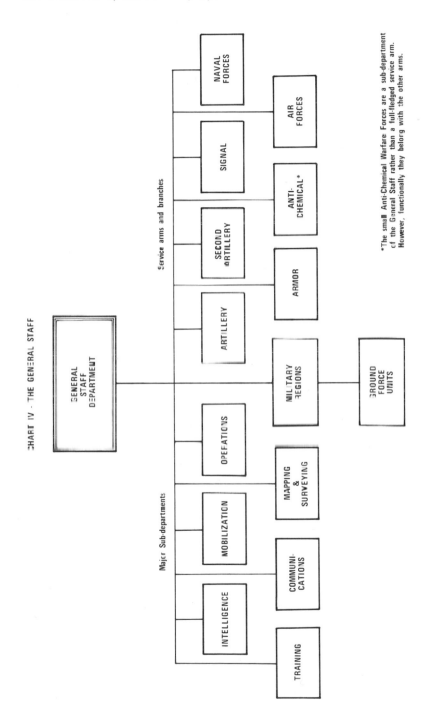

CHART IV - THE GENERAL STAFF

GENERAL STAFF DEPARTMENT

Major Sub-departments

INTELLIGENCE

MOBILIZATION

OPERATIONS

TRAINING

COMMUNI-CATIONS

MAPPING & SURVEYING

Service arms and branches

ARTILLERY

SECOND ARTILLERY

SIGNAL

NAVAL FORCES

ARMOR

ANTI-CHEMICAL*

AIR FORCES

MILITARY REGIONS

GROUND FORCE UNITS

*The small Anti-Chemical Warfare Forces are a sub-department of the General Staff rather than a full-fledged service arm. However, functionally they belong with the other arms.

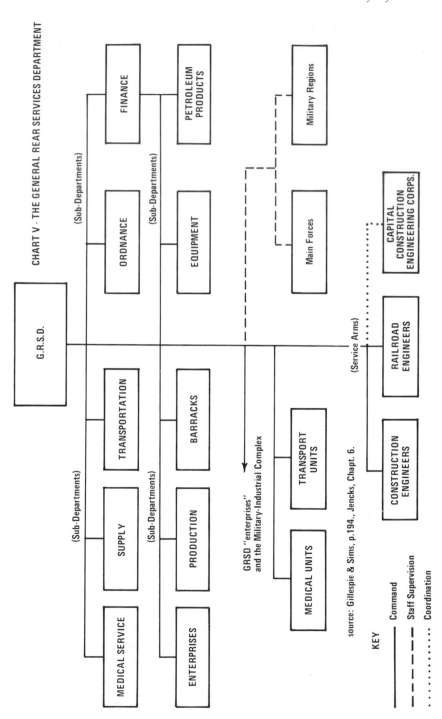

CHART V - THE GENERAL REAR SERVICES DEPARTMENT

G.R.S.D.

(Sub-Departments)

MEDICAL SERVICE | SUPPLY | TRANSPORTATION | ORDNANCE | FINANCE

(Sub-Departments)

ENTERPRISES | PRODUCTION | BARRACKS | EQUIPMENT | PETROLEUM PRODUCTS

GRSD "enterprises" and the Military-Industrial Complex

MEDICAL UNITS | TRANSPORT UNITS

Main Forces | Military Regions

(Service Arms)

CONSTRUCTION ENGINEERS | RAILROAD ENGINEERS | CAPITAL CONSTRUCTION ENGINEERING CORPS.

source: Gillespie & Sims, p.194., Jencks, Chapt. 6.

KEY

——— Command

– – – Staff Supervision

·········· Coordination

other units. The national headquarters provides specialized equipment and training, and ministers to the unique needs of those forces. Because they have limited operational responsibilities, the ground forces service arms are omitted from the command system diagram (Chart II). With a few exceptions the independent units, such as armored and artillery divisions, are under the operational control of the General Staff, not the service headquarters.

Military Budget

The PLA is one of the least expensive per capita military systems in the world. Troops grow up to one-half of their own food and even run some small-scale local industries geared to meet their needs. Only about one-third of the military budget is spent on operating costs—the rest goes for weapons procurement and military research and development. Recently, about 7 percent of the gross national product has been devoted to defense, but that figure will rise somewhat as additional nuclear forces are deployed. Estimates of the defense budget dollar value are little better than educated guesses, due to the difficulty of calculating equivalent purchasing power and the absence of data. However, recent estimates range from about $10 to $15 billion.[7] This gives China the third largest defense budget in the world, but it trails far behind those of the U.S. and USSR which are now approximately $100 billion. China's defense expenditures are much closer to those of West Germany and France than to those of the super powers.

The Ministry of National Defense (MND) manages the military budget, but only after the figures have been decided upon by the top Party leaders in the Politburo of the Central Committee. The MND also handles conscription and demobilization, as well as coordinating defense production with the National Defense Industries Office of the State Council.

Organizational Assessment

The organizational system provides for checks and balances and specialization of function, and has a great deal of flexibility in accommodating modernization. The communications networks are adequate, although much of the equipment at low echelons is clumsy. It might seem that three separate communications/control networks would be too cumbersome, that there would be an inherent danger of paralysis should the commander and political commissar of a unit come into disagreement. Under actual conditions, this rarely happens. In peacetime the political commissar is ultimately in charge, while in battle the commander's views prevail. Moreover the system is advantageous in that the checks and balances within the PLA make it difficult for unstable or politically dangerous officers to threaten the national leadership and the public safety. Military regions, while powerful, do not command the largest and best equipped units within their geographic jurisdictions; hence, the regions do not serve to decentralize national power beyond the bounds desired by the leadership. Under no circumstances, short of complete national political collapse, could a military region headquarters create a geographic power base in defiance of Peking's authority.

At the center, the General Staff has extensive operational powers, but could do virtually nothing to mobilize the armed forces for political purposes without the concurrence of the General Political Department. In the extremely unlikely case that both the GPD and General Staff were to collude in some politically nefarious scheme, word would likely get back to the Politburo from the General Rear Services Department or the air force and navy. On the surface it would appear that the Central Military Commission has the power to be politically dangerous, but from 1935 until his death, Mao Tse-tung was the CMC chairman, and most of the vice-chairmen are Politburo members of the highest political standing. Moreover, there has been a CMC Control Group formerly made up of the president, premier, and first Party secretary, which supervised the CMC. A similar control group may again be in operation.

Control has not been totally effective. The regional PLA disobeyed instructions in 1967, and the Lin Piao affair of 1971 involved much of the high command in a power struggle with civilian leaders. The current post-Mao succession struggle can be expected to again put the command/ control network to the test. Yet, because of its institutional safeguards, China is probably in less danger of sliding into a military dictatorship than most of the world's nations.

2

The Military Administration in the Provinces and Regional Forces

In the period since the founding of the People's Republic, China has been at peace for all but about five years. It is the regional forces and their controlling bureaucracy which are the heart of the peacetime army. The provincial military districts and subdistricts are in constant touch with the responsible civilian Party officials. The military headquarters take orders from the Party secretaries and committees concerning the work of the provinces. The equivalent army-Party echelons are as follows:

provincial military districts = provincial Party committees
military subdistricts = special district Party committees
people's armed forces departments[1] = county and municipal
                                                    Party committees

Regional troop units may be assigned to major construction projects, assisting with planting and harvesting, providing additional security, or any other task which the provincial leadership deems suitable for the locally controlled military.

    The closeness of the equivalent civil-military administrative echelons is organizational as well as functional. At provincial level, first Party secretaries usually serve concurrently as the first political commissars of the military districts. It may well be that secretaries of the special districts also serve as political commissars of the subdistricts. Conversely, district commanders have often served in concurrent provincial government and Party posts. Thus the PLA and Party in China's provinces have formed a single web which still exists, although much has happened to it in the past dozen years.

In addition to tasks laid on by the local political leadership, there are three basic responsibilities assigned to the provincial and local military administration. First, the annual recruitment and demobilization of PLA personnel; second, the military training of regional forces; and finally, the training and organizational strengthening of the militia. Each function deserves separate treatment.

Recruitment/Demobilization

There is a unique system of military conscription in China. The problem is not getting young men into the army, but rather selecting the best recruits from the millions that are eager to join every year, since the PLA is one of the most attractive ladders of success in Chinese society. Living conditions are better in the army than on the rural communes and families of recruits get special treatment while their sons or daughters are serving their country. Upon release, PLA veterans are usually assigned higher paying or more responsible jobs than the average citizen can obtain. This is due in part to the training received in the PLA, but status also plays a role in this favored treatment. There is a much higher percentage of Party members in the PLA than in society at large; if a young recruit acquits himself well and is selected for reenlistment, he has a chance of becoming a Party member. Membership continues after discharge, which means instant entrée to the local elites and limitless possibilities for advancement. Understandably, there is fierce competition to enter the ranks of the PLA; the military draft has become as much an elimination as an induction process.

Every year an annual quota is set, probably by the Ministry

of National Defense, for the total number of men needed to replenish PLA manpower. The figure is then divided among the provinces in proportion to their populations, and then divided again among the military subdistricts which handle most of the actual recruitment processing. Following the harvest, local people's armed forces departments begin the screening of young men who have reached the draft age of seventeen to twenty-one, have excellent political, academic, and work records, and who appear to be in perfect health. A new selection technique is to encourage fellow workers or neighbors to recommend candidates. Very few youths are now allowed to enter the PLA directly from middle school; they must first have work experience. The candidates are sent to the military subdistrict headquarters where an extremely strict medical examination greatly reduces the number. Perfect vision is required, and men have been refused enlistment on such grounds as having hemorrhoids or too many fillings in their teeth. Those who pass the medical exam are further tested and screened politically in order to pare the number down to quota level. Naturally, no one is taken who does not wish to serve, and a small percentage of the quota is reserved for women—about 1 or 2 percent.

While the overwhelming majority of the recruits are middle school graduates, the level of education is less important than politics. Some who can neither read nor write Chinese are inducted, especially minority peoples.[2] Minority recruits frequently receive special training after enlistment, often becoming Party cadres in their home regions following demobilization and usually serving in their local areas. For example, in 1973 it was revealed that 23.6 percent of regimental and battalion cadres and 63 percent of company officers in the Liangshan Yi Autonomous Chou were of the Yi nationality.[3] Minority military cadres are often assigned to militia duty, a practice which seems to serve the dual purpose of improving civil-military relations and further ensuring government political control in minority areas.[4]

Minimum terms of service are now two to four years for the army, three to five years for the navy, and four to six years for the air force, depending upon the amount of specialized training received, but many of the men are allowed to reenlist.[5] The retirement age is flexible; unit commanders in their fifties and early sixties are common. Minimum terms of service were shortened in the mid-1960s to enable a larger percentage of China's youth to have PLA experience. Even so, only about 10 percent of the eligible males are inducted.[6] In addition to its defense functions, the military serves as a great political training ground: it builds dedication to the nation, discipline to Party orders, and a revolutionary enthusiasm much sought after by Mao Tse-tung.

Throughout most of the history of the Chinese Communist movement, its leadership has sought to transfer the revolutionary élan and dedication of the soldiery to the civilian sectors:

> In many aspects, servicemen and demobilized veterans have occupied a special position in Chinese society. Veterans have been seen not only as a group requiring special attention because of the problems of reintegration into civilian life, but also as an active political support group; a progressive force which, if mobilized properly, could itself have a major impact on changing society in the desired directions.[7]

The most consistent method adopted to achieve these political aims has been the control of the demobilization process. Therefore, the responsibilities of the military districts, subdistricts, and armed departments during demobilization are seen as at least as important as their recruitment duties. This demobilization work is done by the people's armed departments and the provincial Party apparatus through "veteran's allocation offices"[8] which determine where the ex-military men are to be sent and assign them jobs.

Many of the veterans are not returned to the homes they left, but are instead resettled in areas where their skills are needed and jobs are available. Since 1949, about 15 million men have been released from the PLA and good jobs have been found for most of them. One striking example was provided by the Kiangsi Province Post and Telecommunications Bureau. In 1956-57, 1407 PLA veterans were hired, which amounted to 42 percent of all new personnel. Of those, 52 percent became technical specialists and 22 percent assumed leadership positions. Fully 61 percent of the veterans hired were Party members.[9] Such hiring practices have caused occasional friction with local civilian cadres who would rather give choice appointments to friends and relatives than to PLA outsiders.[10] China has an annual national campaign to strengthen the bonds between the PLA and civilian society and solve any existing problems. One unpublicized issue is the civilian complaint that too many of the best jobs are being skimmed off the top by discharged PLA vets (whose numbers now run about 500,000 per year) who have come to expect special treatment and are quick to protest when occasionally they don't receive it.[11] Recently, national attention has been focused on demobilized cadres who accepted menial rural job assignments. However, these difficulties should not be overstressed. If veterans had received shabby treatment or found themselves at loggerheads with local civilian cadres, they would have begun showing up among the refugees in Hong Kong. This writer can attest that they were not to be found there in 1974.

Military Training of the Regional Forces

The regional force troop units under the command of the military regions and provincial military districts are an integral part of the PLA. However, under normal peacetime conditions they are not maintained at a high level of readiness but are widely dispersed. For example, an independent regiment is normally attached to a military subdistrict command, its subordinate battalions and companies scattered over several counties engaged in public security, militia work, or assisting in civil construction. This provides scant opportunity for large unit training.

In 1972, Mao Tse-tung revealed that prior to the Cultural Revolution, "military training among the troops" took five to six months of each year.[12] He was probably referring to main force units, unless one counts the time devoted to militia instruction as training for the regional forces as well. In any case, for at least five of the last ten years, the local troops have had scant opportunity to concern themselves with military readiness.[13]

During the late 1960s and early 1970s, regional forces were almost totally absorbed in Cultural Revolution activities and their aftermath. The Chinese dubbed those duties the "three supports and two militaries." The three supports referred to PLA assistance to industry, agriculture, and the "revolutionary left"—i.e., the Maoist mass organizations who were attacking the Party bureaucracy. The two militaries were military control—which at times approximated martial law—and military training in the schools. The regional forces first undertook those duties and they continued to bear the brunt of the work in the early 1970s. The mainforce units were assigned to help out in the strife-torn period of 1967-68 but were gradually returned to their regular duties at the end of the decade. At present, such terms as "military control" are no longer to be found in the Chinese press, but the regional PLA is still deeply involved in local government and public security. Although evidence is lacking, it may be that most regional force troops have had no large unit training since 1966.

Militia Training

Militia work has long been divided into three basic categories: organization, politics, and military training. Theoretically, the Party leadership looks after both organization and politics, while the regional PLA provides military training. In case of war, the militia would come under military control. In fact, such a transfer of control occurred from 1967 to 1971. The peacetime division of responsibilities is occasioned by the nature of the militia. Militiamen and women are ordinary civilian workers and not part of the PLA.

A small proportion, about 7 to 9 million, make up to so-called armed militia, used to supplement PLA border patrols and to help with internal security. Typically, they receive three to six weeks of military training annually following the harvest, provided by the regional PLA with some assistance from locally stationed main force units. Because their duties are arduous and time consuming, armed militiamen receive some additional remuneration.

The basic militia (sometimes called the backbone militia) is a much larger segment of the Chinese population— perhaps 15-20 million. They receive a few days of training each year but do not ordinarily possess arms and are not given paramilitary duties in peacetime. The ordinary or common militia is the largest group of all, but it is very loosely organized and controlled. Estimates range from 40 to 250 million, but something around 100 million seems more probable. The ordinary militia includes men and women of all ages from late teens to old age. They receive no significant military training.

For the purposes of this chapter, only the armed and basic militia categories need be considered. The training given the armed militia includes weapons firing, hand grenade throwing, mine laying, and frequently familiarization with mortars and light antitank guns. This sort of activity is not easily done on the communes, so the armed militia are brought to military bases for training. The basic militia can be trained at their places of employment since they receive little in the way of weapons firing, and the duration of their training is much shorter. This instruction still requires considerable time and effort because there are at least twice as many basic as armed militia.

During the Cultural Revolution, militia training ceased. However, since the clashes on the Sino-Soviet border in 1969, militia preparedness has been taken very seriously. For example, in 1973-74 there was a drive to strengthen and expand the basic and armed militia in the cities. Their role in wartime would be civil defense, and supplementing the PLA's antiaircraft defenses against low-altitude bombing attacks. The militia training responsibility is a heavy burden which falls primarily on the regional PLA. In this work, just as in recruitment/demobilization duties, the regional forces and the Party are interdependent.[14]

Recent History of the Regional Forces

Party-Army Relations, 1960-65

Beginning in the early 1960s, the regional PLA was closely tied to the civilian Party apparatus in the provinces. Central Military Commission directives in 1961 ordered the provincial military districts and subdistricts to "act like staff members and assistants for Party committees."[15] In 1966, the director of the General Political Department, Hsiao Hua, stated: "The system of dual leadership by the military command and the local Party committees, under the unified guidance of the Party Central Committee, must be enforced."[16] Such statements were more than mere exhortation: dual Party-army leadership in the provinces was a reality prior to the Great Proletarian Cultural Revolution (GPCR), 1966-69.

As mentioned in the preceding section, the duties of the military districts and subdistricts in militia work, recruitment/demobilization, and internal security are all interconnected with the responsibilities of the Party committees. The conjoining of Party and regional PLA was successful. It served domestic political and economic needs, and in case of war, Party-army coordination would be necessary to develop local defenses and mobilize the militia.

The Background and Development of the Cultural Revolution

The development of the GPCR caused grave damage to the Party-regional PLA relationship which had been so carefully nurtured in the preceding years. For readers unfamiliar with the GPCR, a brief summary is in order. The roots of the GPCR began in the late 1950s when China, under Mao Tse-tung's leadership, attempted a shortcut to modernization through massive mobilization of manpower and thorough-going collectivization of industry and agriculture. The failure of this daring effort not only caused severe economic hardship, it also weakened Mao Tse-tung's political power and led China away from strict socialist economic policies. There was a concomitant decline in revolutionary enthusiasm within the populace and the Party. The pursuit of personal self-interest became flagrant and the commitment to ideological goals suffered according-ly. The one major exception to this general malaise was the PLA: its strong political motivation did not interfere with its ability to handle technical problems—it was both "red and expert." Beginning in 1964, Mao launched a "learn from the PLA" campaign in which he attempted to transfer PLA experience to the Party and government organizations, without marked success.

Following other unsuccessful efforts to rejuvenate the government and society of China and to regain the political power which he had earlier lost, Mao Tse-tung determined that more drastic measures were needed. With the help of his supporters in Shanghai and the military newspaper *The Liberation Army Daily*, Mao launched a political attack on "bourgeois" writers, journalists, and educators. In early 1966, this was expanded into criticism of ranking Party officials, culminating in the dismissal of a Politburo mem-ber who was then the mayor of Peking.[17] This signal victory strengthened the hand of the Maoists, and in August 1966 they were able to convene a Plenary Session of the Party Central Committee. There is much concerning that meeting which remains mysterious, but apparently Mao was able to exclude many political opponents and pack the session with his supporters—notably PLA leaders. The Plenum then reshuffled the Politburo giving much stronger political power to the PLA and to its leader, Defense Minister Lin Piao.

Also in the summer of 1966, Mao was able to establish the Red Guards, very loosely organized groups of student politi-cal activists of both sexes, aged nine to eighteen, drawn from schools throughout China. In the months following the Central Committee Plenum, Mao and other leaders "re-viewed" about 11 million Red Guards in giant parades staged in Peking. They were sent back to their home provin-ces with a political mission: to expose, criticize, and elimi-nate "bourgeois" and "antirevolutionary" practices wherev-er such tendencies might be found—including the Party leadership. The GPCR became a giant mass movement involving tens of millions of people, adults as well as students, mostly in the urban areas. This was an unprecedented, almost incredible development for a communist nation. The authority of the Party leadership was openly challenged by immature youths at the direction of the one man who had done more than any other to bring the Chinese Communist Party to power. The Party leaders resisted the movement, using all the political tools at their disposal to mobilize conservative forces within the society against the Red Guards. Street violence in the cities became widespread and the Party leaders seemed to be gradually gaining the upper hand at the end of 1966.

In order to save a deteriorating situation, Mao Tse-tung escalated the GPCR in January 1967. He ordered the Red Guards, which by this time included many adult "revolutionary rebels," to seize power in the provinces—i.e., actually take control of government and Party offices at local and provincial levels. At the same time, he ordered the PLA to assist by establishing military control throughout China as a sort of holding operation until the revolutionaries, along with Party officials who had proven themselves acceptable to the Maoist leadership, could form new organs of political power, completely displacing the former political system in the provinces.

Events proved it was much easier to destroy the political system than to rebuild it. Rivalries among the Maoist mass organizations became severe and violence grew much worse in 1967. The PLA was caught in the middle and itself became a target of political attacks. New governments were gradually formed at province level, but the pace was leaden and conflicts at local levels remained mostly unresolved throughout 1967 and much of 1968. Finally at the end of July 1968, Mao Tse-tung ordered the PLA to impose governments from above, and the great revolutionary mass movement was ended. Red Guard type–organizations were disbanded and millions of youth were sent out of the cities to live in rural communes or work in production-construction corps under PLA command.

This brief summary of events should suffice to provide an overview and to allow an analysis of the regional PLA role in the GPCR. Ensuing chapters examine in some detail the parts played by other components of the PLA.

The Regional Forces in the Cultural Revolution

The GPCR in its first year (November 1965 to December 1966) did not greatly affect the regional PLA. An internal PLA Cultural Revolution was begun in the spring of 1966, but it was then nothing more than another in a long series of political "rectification" campaigns. After the christening of the Red Guards in August, the military districts, subdistricts, and garrisons were required to send out numerous cadres from their political departments to serve as propagandists and chaperones to the disorganized teenagers. Main force units also dispatched some political officers to make contact with local Red Guard organizations.[18] This sort of activity was not a novelty to the regional PLA and did not seem to create serious problems.[19]

The pace picked up markedly on December 31, 1966 when the PLA was ordered to give "short term military and political training" to Red Guards in schools throughout China.[20] Such training was categorized as militia work, and hence the responsibility of the regional PLA. Although the size of such a task was enormous, the job itself was within the established missions of the regional PLA and did not threaten the political status quo. As usual, the civilian Party officials were represented on the militia training committees at military region and district levels which supervised the PLA work in the schools.[21]

The GPCR took a dramatic turn in the last half of January 1967. It was only then that the Maoist leadership in Peking took steps to establish the PLA (especially the regional administrative structure) as an independent political power base. Party resistance to the mass movement and the levels of street violence were so great that the PLA had to play a far more active role or the GPCR might have collapsed. On January 14, a major step was taken to strengthen the military administration at the expense of the Party leadership in the provinces. A national directive ordered the PLA to take over the civilian Party communications system along with Party archives. At the same time the PLA also assumed control of the public telegraphic and postal systems.[22] The directive specified that the transfer was to be made to "military organs." In other words, the military regions, districts, and subdistricts took charge of the Party communications systems in the provinces. This was an unprecedented event: the regional PLA suddenly monopolized the normal political control system in every area of China. The local Party committees were isolated from each other and prevented from communicating with their superiors and subordinates except with the permission of the military organs.

An even more far-reaching directive to the PLA was issued on January 21. The military was ordered to support the revolutionary left—i.e., the Red Guards and Maoist adult mass organizations.[23] The PLA was to take an active role in the GPCR on the side of the Maoists who were then attacking the civilian Party apparatus. On the following day, *People's Daily* issued a nation-wide call to seize power from the Party committees in the provinces and cities of China.[24] The military was to assist in the takeovers. Once again, the regional PLA was given the job.[25] Except for a relatively few political cadres from the navy, air force, and army corps who were already involved in Red Guard liaison work, the main forces did not then become involved in the GPCR.

Following a short period of confusion, a standard formula for political rebuilding was set which became effective at the end of January. Once the power seizures were completed, the PLA, Red Guards, and approved Party cadres were to coalesce together in the so-called triple alliances. The next step was to set up new governments in the provinces called "revolutionary committees." It was to be a revolution from below in the sense that the civilian representatives on the revolutionary committees would emerge from the mass movement rather than being appointed by the Peking leadership. However, the establishment of provincial and special district revolutionary committees required national level approval, and military representatives on the committees were appointed. This blueprint for reconstruction encountered many unforeseen difficulties which are discussed below.

Originally, military involvement in the political take-

overs and rebuilding was to be sharply limited. In addition
to restricting the GPCR involvement to the regional PLA,
the Peking leadership also made the Party machinery within
the military the locus of activity. Party committees of military regions, districts, and subdistricts made the decisions
regarding relations with Red Guard groups,[26] and the
military leaders of the few provincial revolutionary commit
tees formed early in 1967 were all political commissars.
Table 1 illustrates that pattern.

Why was the regional PLA ordered to enter the political
arena in January while the army corps and regional and
district commanders were largely kept out of important new
political posts in the provinces? Military presence was
needed because the revolutionary left was too weak to seize
power from the Party leaders. The "real" revolutionary
rebels were too few and too disorganized—a common slogan
of that time was "win over the majority." Armed forces
intervention was a necessity if the power seizures were to be
successful. One reason for not involving the main forces and
the regional commanders was a desire to preserve intact
China's strategic defenses. Also, there was no need of massive
military power against the unarmed Party committees.
Token forces sufficed to impose military control within the
government offices. Finally, there is evidence that some PLA
leaders had been reluctant to approve military involvement
in the GPCR;[27] after the involvement was forced, such
leaders would have sought to minimize the extent of the
commitment. In January-February 1967, it was the political
system within the regional military which bore the responsibilities. However, the attempt to keep the command
system out of politics failed. The requirements for troop
presence grew as the GPCR widened, and by the spring of
1967, commanders as well as commissars were given positions of political responsibility.

The regional PLA had a dual role relative to the power
seizures. First, they were to protect the vital services, public
buildings, transport, and communications against disruptions. This was done expeditiously throughout China in the
form of "military control committees" which also served as
interim governments at local and provincial levels. By April

Table 1

Concurrence of Political Commissars and Revolutionary Committee Chairmen, January–March 1967

Revolutionary Committee	Date founded	Chairman	Previous regional position	Concurrent positions following establishment of Revolutionary Committee
Heilungkiang	31 January 1967	P'an Fu-sheng	1st party secretary, Heilungkiang Province.	1st political commissar, Shen-yang Military Region, and Heilungkiang Military District.
Kweichow	13 February 1967	Li Ts'ai-han	Deputy political commissar, Kweichow Military District.	1st political commissar, Kweichow Military District; deputy political commissar, Kunming Military Region.
Shanghai	5 February 1967	Chang Ch'un-ch'iao	(2nd?) secretary, Shanghai Municipal Party Committee.	1st political commissar, Nanking Military Region and Shanghai Garrison Command.
Shansi	18 March 1967	Liu Ko-p'ing	Vice-governor, Shansi.	1st political commissar, Shansi Military District; deputy political commissar, Peking Military Region.
Shantung	3 February 1967	Wang Hsiao-yü	Vice-mayor, Tsingtao Municipality.	1st political commissar, Tsinan Military Region and Shantung Military District.

1967, military control committees were to be found through-out China in government, in economic enterprises, and in the educational system. This entailed an immense drain on military manpower, as virtually all of the regional units were committed to this work.[28] The military districts and subdistricts were so absorbed in GPCR duties that conscriptions and demobilization were cancelled until 1969, and militia training stopped. Despite the obvious strain, the military control committees were rapidly established and run without insurmountable problems. Maintaining order came naturally to the regional forces: that had been one of their primary duties since 1949.

The regional PLA was also called upon to carry out a second major mission in the GPCR, and this mission caused real trouble. The military administration in the provinces was ordered to support the left and to defend this minority against attacks from conservative mass organizations masquerading as genuine "revolutionary rebels." Many of the conservative groups had been organized or supported by the local Party leadership prior to the military takeover in January. This engendered great confusion because, while everyone waved the red book of Mao's thoughts and claimed to support the new revolution, a wide political spectrum was represented. It was up to the regional PLA to identify the real leftists and support them politically while suppressing rightist opposition. To this end, garrison and district head-quarters were given complete authority over mass organizations.[29]

The military districts and garrisons were not organizationally or politically suited for the job of supporting the left and eradicating all influences of the former provincial and municipal Party committees. Indeed, except for what became the "model provinces" of Heilungkiang, Shantung, Kweichow, and Shansi, the regional forces failed in their efforts to implement the order of January 21. The new revolutionary committee form of government did not appear, and most of the power seizures were not recognized by the Peking leadership, who suspected conservative forces of putting up a sham performance. Conservative mass organizations were not won over to the left; more often they were supported by the garrisons and districts. Many revolutionary groups which were later vindicated as genuine were suppressed by the PLA in the first months of 1967.[30]

From the standpoint of the Maoist leadership in Peking, the regional forces had performed miserably from January through March 1967. Why had they so behaved? Partly it was a national leadership failure. Peking did not try to separate the regional PLA from its ties with the Party bureaucracy until it was too late to be effective. At a Party Central Committee work conference (probably in September 1965), Mao Tse-tung criticized "nominal political commissars" of the PLA, meaning the civilian Party secretaries who, through their concurrent political commissar positions, kept one foot in the regional PLA.[31] However, no action was taken during 1966 to replace those men with career commissars from the PLA. Quite likely, the requirement to do this was not foreseen and the Maoist leadership may then have been too weak to take effective action in any case. By the end of 1966, it was clear that leaders of provincial committees were targets of the GPCR. Yet, as mentioned above, when the PLA was ordered to give militia training in the schools, the directive included a leadership role for the Party committees. The Maoist leaders apparently failed to realize until mid-January 1967 that the PLA would have to be used as an independent source of political power in the GPCR. This realization came little more than one week before the military intervention order.[32]

Quite apart from leadership myopia in the early stages of the GPCR, the 1960-66 program to tie together the military and Party provincial administrative systems had been a distinct success. The quotes below are taken from 1967 statements by military district officials recalling the techniques used by Party leaders to enlist the support of the military district commands against the revolutionaries:

> The [Party leaders] said . . . that the provincial military district was not a part of the national defense army, and that its task was mainly concerned with the localities and its principal leadership was the provincial Party committee.[33]

At that time [during Red Guard attacks on the Party], we were in a very difficult position and in a complex frame of mind. . . . The provincial Party committee . . . restricted us with the so-called club of discipline. They ruled that "differences are to exist internally; unity is to be obeyed; opinions are to be reserved." Many times they asked us to have "uniform caliber" with them. What should we do under these circumstances?[34]

When . . . the people of Heilungkiang rose to rebel . . . the first thing [the provincial Party officials] did was to attempt to seize control of the army. In the name of the provincial committee, they asked us to consider the so-called question of "protecting the safety of the Party committee. . . . [T]he Party, when surrounded ring upon ring by the masses, begged us of the provincial military district to give them shelter.[35]

Similar examples are available for subdistricts and "people's armed departments" (the militia control organs). Clearly the civilian Party leaders did not lack the bonds to tie and levers to move the regional PLA administration.

The regional PLA was as distant from the revolutionary rebels as it was close to the Party apparatus. In the words of one district commander:

Some comrades of the PLA complain: "the revolutionary masses pay no heed to what you say;" "those of the left also make mistakes;" "the revolutionary masses are not pure;" "the organizations of various factions have both merits and demerits;" "the royalists are concerned with production but the rebels are not;" "I do not understand the situation."[36]

No wonder so few military districts and garrisons supported the left wholeheartedly. The surprising thing is that in four provinces—the "model" provinces of Heilungkiang, Shansi, Kweichow, and Shantung—the military did tear themselves away from their local Party ties in early 1967 and established provincial revolutionary committees which were approved by Peking.

Under the weight of military control, the momentum of the GPCR slowed to a near halt in February-March 1967. To counter this, Peking undertook two measures to weaken the political power of the PLA. First, the legal authority of the military district and garrison commands was constrained. A directive of April 6 forbade mass arrests and declared that the regional PLA on its own authority could not declare specific mass organizations to be illegal.[37] Second, the Maoist leadership punished the regional PLA leadership with a political purge. The following areas experienced the removal, suspension, or transfer of commanders in the spring of 1967: Chengtu, Peking, Sinkiang, Lanchow, and Inner Mongolia Military Regions; Liaoning, Kirin, Honan, Shansi, Kiangsu, and Chekiang Provincial Military Districts.[38] Dismissals and transfers of PLA administrators in the provinces were not unusual prior to the GPCR, but never on such a large scale.

Involvement of Main Force Units

Although the removal of many high ranking PLA provincial leaders was a stern measure, an undertaking which was to have more serious repercussions began in the first quarter of 1967. Peking ordered about sixteen of the army corps to intervene in the GPCR.[39] These corps were sent to trouble spots and used as a source of power and authority under central control, not subject to the commands of the districts and garrisons. They were popularly known as "central support for the left troops."

Officers of the main force units which entered the GPCR—including some air and naval units—were not assigned important political positions in the provinces at that time. The main forces were to remain the centrally controlled fist and not become part of provincial politics, a role which had been reserved for the regional forces. Despite obvious qualms in Peking, military regions and districts still carried the major political-military responsibilities in the spring of 1967. However, there must have been a deep sense of unease, because involving the main force units in domestic affairs weakened China's defensive posture at a time of international crises. Independent units served side by side with their newly arrived "big brothers." There was a geographical division of labor, each unit being allocated an area where it was responsible for military control and "support the left" work.

The Wuhan Incident and Its Aftermath

The Wuhan Incident of July 1967 nearly destroyed what remained of Peking's confidence in the regional PLA. On July 19, an independent division of the Wuhan Garrison Command aided in the kidnapping of two members of the Central Committee Cultural Revolution Group. The conservative mass organization which carried out the actual seizure enjoyed the support of the Wuhan Garrison and its superior, the Wuhan Military Region Headquarters. Peking used main force units to break this "mutiny," as it has been flamboyantly called. At least one division, Unit 8199 of the 15th Corps, stationed just outside the urban complex, was ordered into the tri-city area. East Sea Fleet warships were dispatched up the Yangtze River, and locally stationed air force units gave additional assistance. Mao's envoys were safe by July 22, and the Wuhan Military Region, Wuhan Garrison, and independent division leaders were under lock and key in Peking no later than July 26.[40]

Wuhan was the worst case of many showing poor political reliability in the regional PLA. Independent units, garrisons, and military districts had been involved in too many actions which contravened the GPCR. After the Wuhan Incident, Peking decided to exert more strict control at the expense of the regional forces. In the weeks which followed, main force units were ordered to seize control of several military districts and run them directly. Taken over in August were one military region and about ten provincial military districts.[41] In other provinces, leaders of main force units were added to established revolutionary committees or "preparatory groups"[42] for revolutionary committees. Main force units were also involved in takeovers of administrative areas below the province level. In brief, there was a sweeping trend of politicizing main forces units and leaders who had previously served in narrowly military functions. It would be only slight overstatement to say that, in their new positions, they served as representatives of the central leadership in Peking.

The use of centrally controlled units to supplant the administrative roles of the regional PLA was Mao's final trump card in his efforts to keep developing the GPCR. Initially, the Party had stymied the revolution from below in 1966. The first half of 1967 had revealed that the regional forces were also inclined to preserve what they could of the status quo. The main forces have always been the ultimate base of national power in China, and August 1967 saw them committed to an overt political role for the first time since the early 1950s. The game would be lost unless those units were able to further the task of political reconstruction, guiding the mass organizations and approved Party cadres. Otherwise, the GPCR would have to cease short of a full political victory. Later events were to prove that the main forces were unable to reshape the GPCR into a Maoist mold. While such units were not connected with the old Party machinery, they were almost as unsuited for dealing with factionalism and power struggles in the provinces as were the regional forces.

National policy vacillated following the Wuhan kidnapping. It now appears that the takeovers by main force units was meant as a prelude to a thorough housecleaning of the regional forces. On July 22, the Central Committee Cultural Revolution Group issued a call to "drag out the handful of capitalist roaders in the army." When those same terms were used earlier to describe enemies in the Party, it was the beginning of full-scale attacks on the Party apparatus. So it was in the late summer of 1967 for the regional PLA. A short-lived but disastrous program of arming Red Guard factions was begun, also in late July. The levels of violence climbed sharply.

In August, Defense Minister Lin Piao ordered the Red Guards to "teach the cadres of military regions, districts, and militia departments who have made mistakes."[43] Physical assaults and kidnappings of PLA leaders reported during the period apparently stemmed from Lin's directive. Note that the targets were exclusively in the regional military administration. Main force units were supposed to be exempt from attacks, although the nicety of that distinction was lost on the armed revolutionaries. Lin Piao also virtually paralyzed the military region headquarters by ordering them to take no actions regarding mass organizations without central approval.[44]

With a large part of the PLA under political attack, and mass organizations having become gun-toting bands, August 1967 saw the apogee of strife and destruction in the GPCR. Peking wisely and abruptly changed its military policies at the end of August. Madam Mao, who then was a leader of the Central Committee Cultural Revolution Group, made a speech September 5, ordering the revolutionaries to stop "stealing" arms and revealing that the PLA was authorized to retaliate if attacked. Peking had decided to heal the wounds within the military. Mao Tse-tung succinctly summed up the policy reversal as follows:

> The handful of persons within the Party taking the capitalist road should not be lumped together with the group of people taking the capitalist road in the military. We should mention only the handful in the Party and strive to make the military a success. There must be no chaos in the army.[45]

The new policy quickly reduced the level of disorder and defused the destructive forces which had been placed under the regional PLA administrative structures.

Study classes for PLA cadres from regions, districts, militia departments, and independent units were begun in Peking and in the military regions. In September, Mao mentioned the problems of the regional forces. He revealed that an independent unit from Inner Mongolia had abruptly terminated a meeting with Premier Chou En-lai by smashing the furniture! However, Mao sanguinely added that "an independent division can change for the better after some training."[46]

Military Factionalism

After September 1967, the regional PLA was no longer a target of the GPCR. However, that did not mean an end to the PLA's difficulties. Factional rivalries developed between regional and main forces in at least seven military regions, districts, and garrisons.[47] There were almost certainly additional rivalries at local levels, the news of which was apt to remain unreported. Intra-PLA struggles generally took the form of supporting rival mass organizations. These were "proxy battles," not armed clashes among military units, although the contending military factions occasionally launched open political attacks.[48] In those disputes between the regional PLA and the main forces, the stakes involved were high—political power in the provinces.

What caused the widespread dissidence between main force and regional units? Some bad feelings were built into the situation: the army corps were to correct mistakes made by provincial forces. If a military district had supported Red Guard group X and had fallen under a political cloud, the centrally dispatched units would naturally support Red Guard group Y. There was also ill feeling by local PLA leaders against uninvited outsiders who were threatening or usurping their jobs. The psychology of "the haves versus the have-nots" also probably contributed to the rancor. Independent units had always been the stepchildren of the PLA, carrying out dull and tedious labor projects and receiving no priority in resource allocation. The officers of such units had been in dead-end careers. Few, if any, of the top echelon military leaders were from independent units. Last, but not least, following the summer of 1967, regional and main forces were rivals in filling the political power vacuum in the provinces.

In order to cope with the factionalism, Peking undertook policy shifts, organizational measures, and ideological training from the latter part of 1967 through much of 1968. A major policy shift was made in September 1967 when army units were ordered to "support the left but no particular faction." In other words, the military was to disengage itself from the mass movement. PLA leaders were spared the responsibility of determining the political coloration of mass organizations for the first time since January 21, 1967. If fully implemented, such a disengagement would have meant an end to the PLA proxy battles in the provinces. Unfortunately, the factionalism among the mass organizations and within the PLA was too deep and the earlier battle lines too well drawn to allow for even-handed military treatment of the Red Guards.

In terms of training, the "Mao Tse-tung Thought" study meetings also began in September. These served as platforms for airing grievances, resolving differences, and receiving new instructions. While ameliorating the situation, such military meetings did not eliminate the root causes of the disputes.

Two organizational measures were also taken. First, early in 1967, "joint service liaison committees" were set up at military region and district levels to coordinate PLA functions in the GPCR. The authority of these organizations was reaffirmed in 1968, but without notable results.[49] Second, Peking ordered that the regional forces should, in case of conflict, yield to the judgment of the main forces leadership:

> Party committees at various levels [within the PLA] and the whole body of commanders and fighters must resolutely . . . promote unity between army units assigned from outside areas and local army units and between cadres who come from outside and local areas. . . . Where problems occur, the local units and cadres must take the initiative to bear the responsibility and to examine their defects and mistakes.[50]

These various efforts to eliminate military factionalism proved insufficient. Indeed, the conflicts grew still worse in 1968 because tensions began developing among main force units.[51] The issues were the same as in earlier disputes— military units supporting rival mass organizations. Despite modifications, the GPCR was still a revolution from below. The revolutionary groups could not agree among themselves on an equitable division of political representation in the new governments, resulting in sustained conflict which embroiled the PLA.

Factionalism among the main forces was not a widespread phenomenon, nor were there serious armed clashes among military units. And although much less widespread than difficulties with regional forces, conflict among main forces was of deep concern to the Peking leadership. By late summer of 1967, Mao had committed all of his political resources to the GPCR. The main force units were his final card, and he was counting on them to keep the other institutions "on the rails" or to eliminate those "which no longer met the needs of the revolution."[52] Should those units become generally embroiled in the local struggles over political power and thus lose their usefulness as referees, peace keepers, and mediators, Mao would then lose control. He had no remaining source of power and authority to which he could turn.

The first months of 1968 had made it apparent that internal PLA issues could not be resolved so long as the military was deeply involved in "support the left" work. The timetable for the GPCR was then speeded up, and a deadline of May 1968 was established for all provincial revolutionary committees to be formed. Premier Chou En-lai and the Central Committee Cultural Revolution Group worked even harder than before holding meetings among provincial factions in Peking. Unfortunately the "solutions" agreed upon often dissolved into new conflicts once the delegations returned to their home provinces. The May deadline was not met. June and July brought a hard-line approach—central directives called for a strictly enforced return of social order. The new policy was climaxed by a dramatic predawn meeting between Peking Red Guard leaders and Mao Tse-tung on July 28, 1968. Mao told the Red Guards that they had failed in their revolutionary mission. Revolution from below was terminated. The military was ordered to impose revolutionary committees on provinces where such governments had not been formed and to suppress disturbances wherever they occurred. This task was largely completed within a five-week period, although isolated troubles flared up again in 1969.

With the ending of the GPCR as a mass movement, the major cause of military factionalism was eliminated. Contending mass organizations were dissolved and decisions as to who would hold power in the provinces were made. Increased concern about the continued viability of the PLA as a centrally controlled political instrument was one cause of the rapid denouement of the GPCR. Other important causes were leadership frustration at the continued inability of the mass organizations to work together for political reconstruction, and the increased threat from the USSR as perceived in the troop buildup along China's northern border and the intervention into Czechoslovakia. The so-called Brezhnev Doctrine, announced after the Czech crisis, proclaimed that socialist bloc countries had only limited sovereignty. The USSR took upon itself the right to intervene whenever socialism was threatened by domestic developments in communist countries. The implication for China was obvious—especially in view of the Soviet military buildup in the north.

Military factionalism was also responsible for a new policy announced in April 1968:

Chairman Mao has instructed that military cadres must be transferred to other posts and the armed forces units must also be dispatched to other places.[53]

Prior to the GPCR, units were relocated only for emergencies. In 1969-70, such unit rotations began. First, the tactical units of the air force were moved—without changing the overall deployment pattern. Then reports began filtering out of China regarding the relocation of army corps. Units which had been deeply involved in political difficulties were among the first to be moved.[54] By the mid-1970s, about one-fifth of the thirty-eight army corps had been relocated, and in December 1973, there was a major reshuffle of military region commanders as well.

The Peking leadership had been very reluctant to involve its main forces in the politics of the GPCR. Upon first opportunity they again began to separate those units from such complications, returning them to military duties, some in new areas. As Mao Tse-tung complained in 1971, probably in reference to the main forces:

> In the past military training in the troops absorbed five or six months of the year. Today they do civilian not military work. Our troops have become cultural troops.[55]

By the 1970s, the main forces had been largely withdrawn from the political arena. Should the Peking leadership again require them for some major political crisis in the future, they will be available.

Regional force units do not seem to have been affected by the rotation directive.[56] Many officers of the regional administrative bureaucracy have, however, been assigned new positions. One reason why regional units are not shifted about may be that it would be too harmful to their effectiveness. They are supposed to be intertwined with the local political leadership in order to do their job. Such Party-army interdependence created immense difficulties during the GPCR, but under normal political circumstances it is advantageous.

Instead of relocating regional forces, the Peking leadership has emphasized anew subordination to local civilian Party leadership. The refrain sounds just like the 1960-66 period:

> The armed forces departments at all levels in our provinces are the departments of Party committees for the grasping of militia work. They must bring . . . their . . . activities under the leadership of the Party committees and try to be staff officers of the Party committees in militia work.[57]

> Discipline inspection groups must be formed [in the PLA] and sent to visit local Party and government offices . . . so as to solicit earnestly their opinions.[58]

There was a real need to emphasize the political supremacy of the civilian Party from 1969 to 1972. Party reconstruction in the provinces was very slow, being completed finally in 1972. The authority of the local and regional Party leadership had been destroyed by the GPCR and military men dominated the key positions in the provinces. When new Party committees were finally established, most of the first Party secretaries were still PLA officers. Western scholars began to speculate whether "the Party or the gun" was destined to rule in China. As of now, the Party has carried the day, but only since 1972 after Defense Minister Lin Piao paid with his life for his efforts to delay Party rebuilding and to ensure the political supremacy of himself and his military followers.[59]

This section has discussed at length the problems encountered by the PLA in the GPCR. To conclude this chapter, let us look at the other side of the story. The GPCR and its aftermath was a grueling test of the Chinese military system. Two million men of the PLA were involved in GPCR work and they suffered "hundreds of thousands" of casualties according to Premier Chou En-lai.[60] The military system bent under the strain, but it did not break. With the exception of the Wuhan Incident, discipline was maintained, even though the PLA proved to be a clumsy political instrument in an artificially created revolution. The military was remarkably restrained in dealing with street violence. Although there was bloodshed aplenty, there were no incidents of troops wantonly massacring large numbers of rioting civilians. The PLA was whipsawed for over one and one-half years in a desperate political and ideological campaign in which the military had little vested interest. In many, if not most nations, similar treatment would lead to a coup d'état or mutiny within the ranks. Medals and battle campaign ribbons were not awarded, but the PLA can be proud of its overall performance in the GPCR.

3
The High Command

This chapter is divided into three sections: first, the Communist Party organization within the PLA; second, the military command and support network; and, finally, a recent history of the high command. There are a good many information gaps regarding national level military organizations and their interrelationships; however, it is possible to describe the system in general terms.

Party Leadership Within the PLA

The Central Military Commission

The full title of the Central Military Commission (CMC) is the Military Commission of the Chinese Communist Party Central Committee. (Many English language works translate it as the "Military Affairs Committee.") The CMC is the pinnacle of the PLA pyramid; not only does it set military policy and strategy, it is also involved in budgeting, training, military technology, command of forces, militia work, approving promotions of officers at division level and above, and political indoctrination. Virtually all directives to the PLA as a whole come from the CMC as opposed to the Ministry of National Defense or some lower echelon. Subordinate organizations such as the General Staff and General Political Departments are responsible to the CMC. However, the CMC does not rely solely upon the reports of subordinates; it has a large staff and sends out investigation teams when necessary. Professor Ralph Powell, after studying the captured 1960-61 *Work Bulletins* of the CMC, described the scope of such investigations:

> Members of the Standing Committee of the Central Military Commission have conducted inspections, investigations and studies in the field throughout China. Investigations have included problems such as political reliability of the troops, indoctrination, relations between the troops and the people and between officers and men. The CMC has also investigated morale, combat operations, troop dispositions, military units, schools and factories. While on inspection trips, committee members conduct conferences for cadres, provide guidance, issue directives and write reports.[1]

There is probably no field of activity within the PLA which falls outside the purview of the CMC, and no military echelon is safe from the possibility of direct investigation by the CMC.

Although the organization has at times had different titles, the CMC has been in existence since 1925. Mao Tse-tung was chairman of the body from 1935 to 1976—a fact which was closely related to his political survival over those many years. Mao knew whereof he spoke when he said "political power grows out of the barrel of a gun." In 1975, the new state constitution stipulated that the command of the armed forces is delegated to the chairman of the Chinese Communist Party, Mao Tse-tung. In this immediate post-Mao period, one of the primary keys to power will be the post of Party chairman, since the holder of that office will have a strong influence in the Party and an even stronger control over the military. If the Party apparatus should become bogged down in power struggles, the chairmanship of the CMC could become the most important job in China; even now it ranks among the top four politically.[2]

Beneath the chairman are a small number of vice-chairmen. The Minister of National Defense is normally the First Vice-Chairman who runs the day-to-day affairs of the CMC and takes charge of routine meetings when the chairman is not in attendance. Until recently, the vice-chairmen have been the PLA elders, i.e., men who were senior officers at the time of the Long March (1934-36). Political purges and the grim reaper have combined over the past decade to reduce the veteran vice-chairmen to only three in 1976.[3] Over their long careers, these men gradually developed areas of interest in which they play dominant roles. For many years, Yeh Chien-ying has supervised military training and readiness. Nieh Jung-chen has been in charge of military research and development. Liu Po-ch'eng, until his retirement because of ill health, was the primary strategist. Newcomers have filled the depleted ranks of the CMC; they too will probably develop similar functional specializations or be selected to the CMC because of prior specialized knowledge.[4]

The chairman and vice-chairmen comprise the core of the Standing Committee.[5] The chief of the General Staff Department, who normally serves concurrently as the secretary of the CMC, is another important member. The directors of the General Political and General Rear Services departments have in recent years been included in the Standing Committee. Due to its power, the membership of the Standing Committee is highly political and fluid. Over the past decade, there have been three or four reorganizations which twice saw the committee "packed" for particular political purposes (see the section on recent history in this chapter). The full membership of the CMC includes leaders of the air and naval forces and at least some military region commanders.[6]

Ranking in importance with the Standing Committee is the secret Control Group of the CMC. This organization is composed of the highest civilian leaders in the land, i.e., the Party general secretary, the premier, and, until the abolition of the office, the president.[7] Its presumed function is to serve as a civilian check on the awesome powers of the CMC and its chairman, to supervise the general PLA policy line, and to oversee the implementation of Party decisions on important military matters. Chou En-lai's sole reference to the Control Group made clear that it has important responsibilities in the fields of strategic weapons and military research and development.[8] The Control Group probably has a veto power over the CMC, but it is not likely that it would be involved in the routine activities of the commission. Nothing has been heard of this group since the GPCR, but that does not necessarily mean the organization is defunct; more likely it has been reconstituted and is again operating under tight secrecy.

Beneath the Standing Committee are multiple functional committees, the most important of which is the General Office (known as the Administrative Committee prior to the demise of Lin Piao). It seems to be the CMC's internal executive organ, and at least some other commission organizations report to it. Information on other functional committees is sparse and dated, although Chinese Nationalist analysts have identified an Operations Department which may oversee the work of the General Staff.[9] There has been mention of a Committee for Training and Research, which sounds like an odd juxtaposition of functions; however, the unit has apparently been led by the military technology administrator Nieh Jung-chen, thus the "training" may well refer to advanced weapons rather than mixing infantry sweat with scientists' smocks.[10] There is an Inspectorate Office which probably supervises the many CMC investigations and studies in the provinces; Yeh Chien-ying is almost certainly its director.[11] Literature and art within the PLA merits its own committee, whose last known head was Madam Mao. Another unit oversees the operations of the national military newspaper, the *Liberation Army Daily*.[12] During the GPCR, an important role was played by the Political Work Committee of the CMC.[13] In the early 1960s, mention was made of a Naval Engineering Committee and a Hygiene and Medicine Bureau of the CMC.[14] There is even a special CMC guard unit (Unit 8341) which may be responsible for a range of security functions, including the "secret service" function of providing physical protection for the top leadership.[15] There are undoubtedly other functional committees. Given the diversity of problems and issues with which the CMC deals and its predilection for skipping echelons to investigate affairs in the provinces, the staff must be quite large.

The CMC's powers effectively centralize control over the

PLA. Military region commanders and service arms and branches are all closely supervised by and must report to this body. The CMC probably maintains direct command authority over the seven service arms as well as the two service branches, the naval and air forces.[16] If necessary, orders can be sent directly to units as low as regimental level, bypassing all intermediate echelons.[17] Except for orders to the regional forces, which can be generated at military region and district levels, almost all important military command directives are thought to originate in the CMC, including those which apply to only a few units.[18] Thus, whoever controls the Central Military Commission controls the PLA.

The General Political Department

The functions of the General Political Department (GPD) are relatively well understood; its duties fall into three broad categories: ideology, discipline, and morale.[19] Ideologically, the GPD must ensure Party leadership over the armed forces and see to it that the Party line and regulations are implemented; it is responsible for the ideological condition and political indoctrination of the PLA. General educational, cultural, and recreational activities within the military also fall under GPD control.

Within the general category of discipline, the GPD has broad responsibilities for internal PLA security. It is specifically charged with keeping track of the political and ideological quality of high ranking cadres, although the CMC Guard Unit may share this responsibility. The GPD also keeps track of assignments, promotions, dismissals, rewards, and punishments within the PLA, but in many cases, the decisions on such matters are made elsewhere. For example, the GPD power of appointment is limited by "elections" of officers within units (described in chapter 5). Moreover, the CMC and General Staff have an equal or greater voice over the selection of top-ranking officers. Despite those limitations, the GPD wields a great deal of clout within the PLA as a result of its personnel powers. Military justice is also under its control.

As for morale, the GPD is responsible for the condition of

the soldiery, their dependents, and relations between officers and men. Immensely important to the civil roles of the PLA are close military-Party ties, the prestige of the PLA, and helpful and harmonious PLA-civilian relations, and the GPD spends a large portion of its times handling these matters. In wartime, the GPD is responsible for political warfare against the enemy and for handling all captured enemy soldiers (including the proviso that POWs are to be leniently treated).[20]

The national GPD headquarters includes the following subdepartments: (1) propaganda—general education within the PLA; (2) youth department—the Chinese Communist Youth Corps which serves, within the PLA, as a testing period and recruitment pool for full Party membership; (3) mass work department—civil-military relations; (4) culture department—arts and letters in the PLA under the guidance of the CMC committee of the same name; (5) cadres department—personnel records and officer evaluation (there is also a bureau, perhaps of this department, which looks after the political aspects of recruitment, presumably including background investigations of inductees); (6) organization department—functions unclear, but it may serve as the "catch-all" office.

In order to carry out its many tasks, the GPD has at its disposal a pyramid of Party committees, political departments, and commissars within the PLA, a network reaching to every geographic corner of China and into each minute functional system within the military. The political control net is well described in John Gittings' book, *The Role of the Chinese Army*. He makes clear the separate roles of the Party committees and political departments: the Party committees exist at every level down to regiment, and in many battalions. (There seems to be an intention to have Party committees in all battalions, but the Party membership is often insufficient.) At lower levels, Party "branches" and "small groups" perform functions similar to the committees; even military dependents have their own Party branches.[21]

Despite their importance, the Party organizations are not formally part of the PLA organization, but rather, they represent the Party membership within the PLA. At each echelon the Party committee is normally led by the political commissar who handles routine matters on his own authority and serves as the committee secretary and de facto representative of the GPD; the commander and key staff officers usually round out the committee membership. The Party committees are responsible only to the next higher Party committee and so on up through the GPD and CMC to the Politburo. When PLA directives (as distinct from operational orders) are issued, they normally originate in the CMC and are transmitted through the GPD and down the chain of Party committees. If a directive is important, committee meetings take place to discuss its implementation. The Party committees also make the important policy, planning, and personnel decisions at their own levels. As John Gittings succinctly put it: "They effectively initiate and supervise all important decisions reached at their own and higher levels."[22]

Once the decisions are made, they are then implemented by the political departments. These departments are generally directed by a political officer who handles most of the bureaucratic donkey work and who is of lower rank than the commissar. However, in low echelon units, the political commissar or political officer may serve in both capacities.[23] Unlike the Party committees, political departments are an integral part of the PLA organizational system, attached directly to the headquarters of administrative and troop units as low as the regimental level. At the higher echelons, political departments are subdivided into offices which deal with education, recreation, political warfare, and the like. Political work long ago became a specialization within the PLA. Political staff schools train the officers, most of whom remain in this specialization throughout their military careers.

Taken together, the Party committees and political departments form an effective control apparatus for the GPD and CMC. In the 1950s, efforts were made to further strengthen political dominance within the PLA by attempting to reach a very high level of Party membership within the ranks—about 33 percent,[24] but although Party membership went up, such a high ratio proved unrealistic. The target figure in the 1970s is much lower, but Party membership is far higher proportionately in the PLA than in the populace as a whole. In the civilian sector, for example, only about 5 percent of the populace are Party Members. Figures for the army are not available, but a 1963 directive stipulated that before a Party branch could be formed at company level (140-160 men) there must be at least three Party members within the unit.[25] Since that time, Party membership has risen sharply and the new goal is to have one Party member in each squad. If and when this is achieved, the membership would be about 12-15 percent. Virtually all officers above the company level are Party members; however, it is difficult to attain a high ratio among the enlisted men, because of their youth and the large turnover. Party membership is a high honor and a weighty responsibility which is very reluctantly given to men who have not reached maturity. A much higher percentage of the enlisted men are members of the Chinese Communist Youth League, but only a small portion of those are eventually selected to become full fledged Party members.

Of course, political training in the PLA goes far beyond the process of Party recruitment. Every young soldier receives a thorough indoctrination into the principles, goals, and values of the Republic. In the early 1960s, fully 30-40 percent of training time was devoted to political and educational work. That proportion may be somewhat lower now, but the order of magnitude remains the same. The subject matter includes the "thoughts of Chairman Mao," current Party policies, central directives, the responsibilities and missions of the various military branches and service arms, PLA traditions, and even explanations of the various national days of celebration. Summing up the breadth and importance of political work in the PLA:

> The military recognizes that it has a special responsibility for China's youth, and this responsibility includes socialization into the basic concepts of a centralized communist nation-state as well as the specific responsibilities and missions of the PLA.[26]

Over the past decade or so, the political system within the military has done a fine job. PLA prestige is very high, troop morale must rank among the best in the world, and rank and file discipline was amply demonstrated during the strains of the GPCR. From a political standpoint, the PLA is about as ready as it can be to fight a war or to continue with its peacetime work. Another famine such as China experienced in the early 1960s or crushing defeats at the hands of technologically superior forces would certainly blacken the present rosy picture, but the PLA could be expected to survive enormous strains before crumbling. Of course, not all of this is due to the work of the GPD, but it deserves a share of the credit.

The greatest weakness of the PLA control system is in internal security at high echelons. The GPD and the Guard Unit of the CMC failed to head off breaches of discipline by regional PLA leaders during the GPCR—most notably the kidnapping of Cultural Revolution leaders at Wuhan. The security system also failed to uncover the "Lin Piao plot" of 1971 (discussed in the recent history section of this chapter). It remains to be seen if, in the future, the GPD can better fulfill its charge to keep track of the political and ideological quality of high ranking military cadres.

The Military Command and Support Network

At both national and regional levels, a clear distinction must be made between administrative and operational powers. The CMC virtually monopolizes major operations decisions, leaving to other high level organizations extensive administrative responsibilities—those monumental housekeeping tasks of a huge military system. For example, a troop unit probably would not undertake any activity which entailed a change of status—e.g., relocating subunits or commencing an exercise—without a direct military order from above. Yet the same unit, on a daily basis, might decide on dozens of administrative matters and submit several requests of its own to higher headquarters. All of the organizations described in this section are primarily administrative in nature, although the three "General

Departments"—political, staff, and rear services—have such broad powers that the operational/administrative distinction becomes somewhat blurred.

General Staff Department

The General Staff Department (GSD) is the chief executive of the CMC. Military orders, as opposed to political directives, are issued through it; it is the second step in the command chain, and as such it can generate routine military orders which are deemed too unimportant for CMC attention. The contact point with the CMC is the chief of the General Staff Department who is normally the secretary of the CMC and concurrently secretary of the Party Committee of his own department. He is assisted by several deputy chiefs of staff. The number varies, but there rarely seems to be less than a half-dozen such deputies. The chief of staff must exercise restraint when issuing orders under his own authority lest the CMC perceive it as usurping its authority.

Most of the peacetime work of the GSD is, therefore, administrative in nature. It oversees the military service arms, except for the engineering forces and probably the Railway Troops which are under the General Rear Services Department. Military training of the ground forces is the GSD's responsibility. This includes most, if not all, PLA schools. There are two subdepartments dealing with military schools, one having to do with combat-related training and the other with administrative training. (General education is handled by the GPD.) There is a military operations department (literally "combat department") which very likely operates under guidelines set by the CMC committee of the same name. The mobilization department is in charge of the militia system and keeps track of PLA veterans in case of a national emergency, although China does not have a formal reserve system in the Western sense of the term. An intelligence bureau collects and analyzes information on foreign military forces. Other known offices include an economic and administrative department, communications department, an equipment office, and a military mapping and surveying department. There are undoubtedly other subordinate offices which have not been publicly identified. For example, general staffs usually include military planning functions; in the PLA, there may be a separate planning section, or the function could be carried out by the various specialized departments. In any case, the CMC would certainly retain final decision-making powers over all military planning.

Prior to the GPCR, one of the military service arms—the PLA Public Security Forces Headquarters—was abolished, and now PLA public security functions are performed by the regional forces. There may some coordination of such activities within the General Staff, even though China has intentionally decentralized its security apparatus in order to prevent the rise of a police-state strongman.

The chief of staff is probably acutely aware that the CMC is looking over his shoulder in virtually all matters. His is the difficult job of converting military policy and command decisions made above him into realities to be implemented throughout the military system beneath him. Although the chief of staff has extensive executive powers and considerable latitude in his actions, he remains essentially a man in the middle. Over the past two decades, all incumbents were removed in disgrace, although three of the five were later "rehabilitated" and given less important jobs.[27]

It is at this level of leadership, occupying the key position in the policy transmission belt between the political center and the military machine, that the conflicting pressures from above and below, between political and military priorities, seem to be the most concentrated.[28]

General Rear Services Department

The General Rear Services Department (GRSD) handles military logistics including planning, procurement, and distribution. It supplies fuels, munitions, and a broad range of general commodities, and provides and repairs equipment. PLA equipment testing and improvements are carried out by GRSD technicians. Military transportation is also a

GRSD responsibility. It provides all medical services and facilities for the PLA and serves as the military paymaster as well. In the U.S. army, the nearest equivalent is the Joint Logistics Department of the General Staff, although its responsibilities are considerably narrower.

The GRSD has its own subordinate organizational pyramid within the PLA. At national level, the subordinate offices of the GRSD include medical service, supply, transportation, ordnance, finance, production, barracks (which includes warehouses and general storage), petroleum-oils-lubricants, and equipment.[29] In 1971, mention was first made of an Enterprises Subdepartment,[30] which may oversee and assist the many local PLA sideline production facilities, including agriculture, local arsenals, machine shops, and even some small-scale heavy industrial production. At the next lower echelon, the GRSD is administratively responsible for the engineer troops—not including combat engineer elements attached to infantry units.[31] The signal corps is similarly divided between the GSD and GRSD. Signal regiments—units responsible for constructing and maintaining communications networks—are probably under the GRSD; signal complements attached to various military units would fall under the operational control of the General Staff. Since the GRSD is in charge of military transport, it likely manages the railway engineers and coordinates the forty-two motor transport regiments stationed throughout China.[32]

Naval and air forces have their own logistic systems, but they too are under the general supervision of the GRSD. A similar pattern holds for the specialized equipment needed by the service arms such as the signal corps and anti-chemical warfare forces. At times some service arms have attempted to wrest control of their own logistics away from the GRSD. In the early 1960s, there was competition between the GRSD and the PLA railway forces concerning who should control logistics for that service arm.[33] The railway forces temporarily won the battle, but seem to have lost their newly won gains in the late 1960s when control of rail transport was centralized to cope with the extraordinary demands made upon it during the GPCR.

In early 1967, a national directive established the Capital Construction Engineering Corps as an integral part of the PLA. The order did not reveal the subordination of the new organization nor its precise mission, but it did state that the corps was "drawn from the Ministry of Industry and Communications of the State Council."[34] In the spring of 1968, it was revealed that the State Planning Commission's "industry and communications unit" had been abolished.[35] In late 1968 and throughout 1969, the official media began to mention new production-construction corps being established in several provinces. These were soon placed under the control of the various military regions, then apparently redesignated as "agricultural production divisions" in 1975 and turned over to civilian control. The relationship between the GRSD, the Capital Construction Engineering Corps, and the various special labor brigades in the provinces is a puzzle; however, it would seem a logical possibility that the GRSD at least has a coordination function with the national and provincial production-construction organizations. When one considers the massive war preparations' civil-defense shelter building, and tunnel digging campaign of 1969-74, it would seem imperative that the resources of the national and provincial production-construction corps be committed to the campaign. The Defense Ministry, the Mobilization Department of the General Staff, and/or the GRSD probably had supervisory roles.

The GRSD is also responsible for supplying arms to foreign allies and insurgent groups through its International Equipment Division—often mentioned in meetings with North Vietnamese representatives in Peking. In addition to small arms, ammunition, antiaircraft artillery, and much more supplied to North Vietnam, China has also provided Pakistan with MiG-19 fighter aircraft and T-59 tanks. Tanzania received T-59 and T-62 tanks. Numerous Asian and African insurgent groups have received small arms and training. Over three score fast gunboats and torpedo boats have gone to the navies of Albania, Vietnam, North Korea, Sri Lanka, and Tanzania, with the Communist countries getting the lion's share. North Korea may even have a few Chinese submarines.[36]

Immediately below the national level are the eleven military regions. The rear services departments of each region provide logistical support for all ground forces stationed in their areas. Large infantry units, e.g., corps and divisions, have rear services departments which oversee the distribution of supplies to lower echelons. A good deal of PLA procurement is done locally; the GRSD supplies funds to buy foodstuffs and clothing from local suppliers, which has the advantage of assisting local PLA self-sufficiency as well as reducing bureaucratic foul-ups which inevitably accompany over-centralization. One disadvantage is the increased possibility of cheating and graft on the part of local military leaders.

Ministry of National Defense

The Ministry of National Defense (MND) is the only top-level organization which spans both the military and government bureaucracies. As a ministry, it comes under the "cabinet" organization—the State Council, led by Premier Hua Kuo-feng. In recent times the defense minister has usually held a concurrent appointment as a vice-premier. He has also concurrently served as First Vice-chairman of the CMC and frequently been selected as a vice-chairman of the Chinese Communist Party. Thus the defense minister holds important posts in all three bureaucratic pyramids—Party, government, and military. Despite the apparent power of the post, the defense minister has recently been in a political decline. Following Lin Piao's disappearance in 1971, Yeh Chien-ying was named to the post. The aged Yeh was much less ambitious than Lin and seemed content to work in Chou En-lai's shadow. Following Chou's death and the purge of Teng Hsiao-p'ing, the Hong Kong rumor mill averred that Yeh had resigned or had been forced out. After a mysterious absence from public activity, Yeh reappeared in his normal protocol position in July 1976. Thus the rumors of the Peking Military Region commander, Ch'en Hsi-lien, serving as acting minister of defense are probably false. He is, however, a likely candidate to succeed Yeh.

The functions of the ministry are less clear than those of

other national-level PLA organizations. It seems to have no policy-making or command functions. Since 1959, the defense minister has carried out most of his responsibilities through the CMC. Identifiable MND responsibilities span military-government and military-civilian sectors. There is a conscription department which probably administers the national conscription-demobilization program. The MND handles liaison with foreign nationals within and without China's borders through its Foreign Affairs Bureau.[37] The only other clearly identifiable MND section is the relatively unimportant "reception office" which looks after the needs of PLA personnel and officers visiting Peking.

The titles of the other known offices do not provide any understanding of their functions, thus speculation must suffice in place of data. There is a "general office," one responsibility of which may be the drafting and enactment of military regulations and field manuals. The MND also has seven numbered bureaus whose functions remain well-kept secrets. Possibly they are related to defense production, since there are seven defense related ministries (six machine-building ministries and the Ministry of Petroleum). Civil defense is another possible MND responsibility along with administration of the defense budget after it has been established by the Politburo and the CMC.

Military Production

Most organizations dealing with military production theoretically come under the aegis of the civilian government—the State Council. However, it can be safely assumed that the CMC and GRSD determine what and how much is to be produced, and when and where it is to be delivered. Richard Latham has identified a National Defense Industries Committee of the CMC which seems to be the key policy-making body.[38] Military production is coordinated by the National Defense Industries Office (NDIO),[39] a high level government organization theoretically subordinate to the office of the premier, although in actual fact, the NDIO director is appointed by the minister of defense and is probably responsible to the CMC.[40]

Beneath the NDIO are six ministries of machine building which are responsible for the various sectors of defense production. These ministries are large; some if not all, have personnel numbering in the tens of thousands.[41] In the early 1960s, the CMC decided that armed forces officers who became ministers of machine building would retain their military rank and status;[42] at present, five of six military related machine building ministries are led by PLA officers,[43] and, moreover, a high proportion of the working personnel in the ministries are active-duty PLA men. Despite their civilian government subordination, the defense-related ministries of machine building seem to be adjuncts of the PLA.

There are a total of seven ministries of machine building, of which the second through seventh are military related. The responsibilities of the various ministries are as follows:[44]

1st	machinery and equipment for civilian use
2nd	atomic energy
3rd	aircraft
4th	electronics
5th	ordnance (conventional weapons and equipment)
6th	ship building
7th	missiles

Other ministries have some military production responsibilities; for example, the Ministry of Petroleum Industries has especially close relations with the General Rear Services Department; former leaders of the GRSD have become ministers of petroleum and vice-versa. The Ministry of National Defense has some responsibilities for defense production, but its exact role is not known. Vice-minister Su Yu has been, over the past decade, the leading figure in the field. To what extent he exercises his leadership through the MND or through the National Defense Industries Office is an open question.

Military Research and Development

The top military research and development organization

is the National Defense Science and Technology Commission (NDSTC). It reports directly to the CMC and, in the protocol list, ranks along with the National Defense Industries Office between the three PLA general departments and the military service branches and arms.

The responsibilities of the NDSTC concern all defense research and development projects: to plan and supervise their implementation, allocate funds for them, and audit the use of such funds. Its writ extends to defense related research and development in various civilian institutes, schools, and factories, as well as scientific and technical organizations attached to the military branches, services, and regions, and defense industries. The NDSTC also plans and directs technical and scientific instruction in PLA schools and training programs. It has the power to transfer personnel from PLA units, and various institutes and universities to work in any of the other organs under the NDSTC.

Fourteen research institutes are known to be directly subordinate to the NDSTC and there may be more. These are quite large—over 1600 personnel were employed by the first, second, and third institutes collectively in 1968.[45] Other organizations are civilian in subordination, but much of their work may be military in nature.[46] The system is somewhat similar to the research and development network in the U.S., but the Chinese have no private research firms and the entire system is far more centralized.

Another important organization is the Science and Education Group, formerly known as the National Science and Technology Committee. This is the civilian equivalent to the NDSTC, and it reports to the State Council. A good deal of China's basic research is done under its auspices and in the independent Academy of Sciences. However, once a research discovery is found to have military implications, the NDSTC takes over.

In the case of military hardware, the NDSTC has primary responsibility for the design, building, and testing of prototypes.[47] It also has ties with the ministries of machine building. Apparently, the NDSTC runs experimental factories within the military production ministries.[48] Its responsibilities and those of the General Rear Services Department overlap confusingly in the realm of defense production. The GRSD has scientific institutes of its own which may be in charge of equipment testing and improvement of existing designs.[49] The NDSTC may be responsible for solving production engineering problems even after serial production has begun. This hypothetical division of functions would help explain why the NDSTC has a production research department as well as science and teaching departments.[50]

The General Staff, naval, and air forces also have subordinate research institutes. Presumably, the two service branches use their research and development facilities for their own specialized equipment needs; similarly, at least some of the service arms have technical departments.

Reducing the bureaucratic overlap and complications to a minimum, the overall military research, development, and production cycle in China looks like this:

Requestor	*Developer*	*Producer*	*User*
CMC ———————➤	NDSTC ———➤	National Defense ———➤	PLA troop units
GRSD		Industries Office	and specialized
	research		forces
PLA branches	institutes	2nd-7th Ministries	
and services		of Machine Building	

Service Arms

In addition to the naval and air forces, which constitute separate military branches, there are seven service arms.[51] Six of these—the Artillery, Armored, Signal, Engineer, Anti–Chemical Warfare and Railway Forces Headquarters—support the infantry units and, to a lesser extent, assist the air and naval forces. (The anti–chemical warfare forces are ranked beneath the other services as a subdepartment of the General Staff. However, its functions are similar to a service headquarters, hence it is here treated with the others.) The remaining service arm is the Second Artillery, which seems to be an embryonic version of Russia's Strategic Rocket Forces. These service headquarters are directly subordinate to the CMC in terms of operational command. However, for administrative purposes, the General Staff oversees all service arms except the engineers, railway forces, and probably part of the signal corps, which are attended to by the GRSD.

The service headquarters seem to be administrative rather than operational in nature. They run training schools for their troops and may assist in logistics and specialized equipment development. These headquarters also have some role in personnel matters such as promotions and transfers.

The service arms differ somewhat in terms of their power, prestige, and authority. The signal and anti-chemical warfare troops are mostly integrated with the ground, naval, and air force units.[52] There are about eleven signal and a small number of anti-chemical warfare independent regiments ("independent" in the sense of unattached to other units). These appear to receive operational orders from the General Staff and military regions rather than from their parent service arms. The artillery, armored, and engineering forces also have the bulk of their troops integrated into the infantry corps; however, they have more independent units. Estimates vary, but there are about seven armored divisions and twenty artillery divisions which serve as strategic reserve forces, ready to reinforce the regular infantry corps as needed.[53] Like the smaller signal and anti-chemical warfare forces, these independent units are under the operational control of the General Staff and the military regions. However, the commanders of the artillery and armored forces have been of higher rank and exercise more power than their colleagues in the other service arms.[54]

About eleven divisions of specialized troops comprise the railway forces,[55] independent units which serve military transport requirements and also do a great deal of general-purpose railway construction. Prior to the GPCR, one man served concurrently as commander and political commissar of the railway forces and as minister of railways in the civilian government.[56] He petitioned the CMC to grant him operational control over the railway forces and permission was granted.[57] During the GPCR, he was dismissed from all of his posts; his successor, Chang I-hsiang, has not been granted so much centralized authority. One of the railway maintenance divisions in Kweichow Province was at least temporarily turned over to the control of the Kweichow Military District in 1968.[58] However, at present the Railway Forces Headquarters could still have more operational control than most other service arms.

Of all the specialized forces, the Second Artillery is the most shrouded in mystery. It was formed about 1964 and has been mentioned in official media several times since 1965, ranking just below the Artillery Forces as the second most important service arm. Although its functions have never been revealed, virtually all students of the PLA agree that the Second Artillery is in charge of China's ballistic missile forces. For over a decade, missile units have been involved in troop training. Within the past ten years, medium range (700 mi.) and, more recently, intermediate range (1500-3000 mi.) ballistic missiles have become operational and have been deployed. The missiles have mostly been aimed against the USSR, although a few are deployed to strike Taiwan, South Korea, Japan, and Southeast Asian targets.

It is safe to presume that these forces can do little without a direct order from the CMC; the danger of an unintended launch of a nuclear-tipped missile is a specter which haunts all the major powers. It is possibly significant that no commander of the Second Artillery has ever been officially identified, although political commissars have been. The Second Artillery undoubtedly has more checks on its authority than any of the other service arms. The problem of nuclear arms control was posed by Charles Horner in the following terms:

Whenever one considers nuclear dispersal and large numbers of tactical warheads widely distributed throughout the country, the technical and mechanical problems of command and control become enormous. Under such an arrangement it is impossible to control the actual arming and detonation of a nuclear warhead from a source not physically present on the scene.[59]

How have the Chinese approached this problem of preventing an accidental nuclear launch? There is one clue: most of the men who have been identified in Second Artillery leadership positions are former public security officers. Clearly such men were chosen for their mastery of security techniques rather than technological expertise. It is not known how these men go about keeping the nuclear forces on a tight rein, but obviously they have been completely successful.

Leaving aside the knotty problem of differing degrees of authority, most of the service arms seem to have basic functions common to all. Each has its own specialized training schools, not only at the national level but also within many of the military regions. Each deals to some extent with the military production requirements of its own forces. For example, during the GPCR, the political commissar of the armored forces and a director of the abolished Ordnance Department assisted CMC member Su Yu in supervising national defense industries.[60] In addition to production, the specialized needs of the service arms require close liaison with the GRSD. In personnel matters, the service arms probably recommend for promotion and transfer officers of their specialized commands, but it is clear that they do not make the final judgment in such matters.[61]

Military Effectiveness of Service Arms

The artillery is China's largest and most effective service arm. (This excludes the infantry which is not classified as a service arm in the Chinese military lexicon.) It is equipped mainly with Russian-type artillery ranging in size from small antitank weapons to 152 mm field guns. Many of the larger weapons are in the hands of the twenty artillery divisions (about 6000 men each).[62] The guns are not outmoded; they are indigenously produced and have longer range than equivalent U.S. artillery pieces. Over the past decade, China has turned out large quantities of conventional artillery pieces and now equals the USSR in the number of guns and has a three-to-one advantage over the U.S.[63] Yet, because the infantry is so large, there is still a shortage of artillery on a per unit basis.

For purposes of economy, ease of maintenance, and reliability, China has opted to produce towed guns rather than self-propelled artillery. However, due to a shortage of towing vehicles, the present day PLA artillery forces are hampered by a lack of mobility. This could be especially dangerous if China were fighting a highly mobile army such as that of Russia. Artillery units might find themselves cut off from their infantry protection or unable to move their guns or ammunition rapidly enough to areas of critical need. Improvements are being made, but many guns still cannot be moved at a faster rate than the pace of the draft animals pulling them.

Somewhat different problems confront the armored forces. The main battle tank is the T-59—a Chinese-produced version of the T-54 Soviet medium tank. The Chinese version omits some elaborate equipment and there are newer tanks in the Soviet inventory. Still, it is by no means an obsolete weapon; the simplification of electronics and fire control should make it more reliable in combat.[64] The problem has been that the Chinese have not had enough of them. In the mid-1960s (the latest firm data available) there were only a few tanks for each tank company attached to infantry units. According to an official table of equipment captured at that time, an infantry corps which at that time numbered over 46,000 men had only 96 tanks![65] Like the artillery command, the Armored Headquarters administers independent divisions. There are only seven such units, thus it is clear that China has been woefully short of armor.

However, the situation is rapidly improving. China has at least three tank factories at Harbin, Ta-t'ung, and Loyang, and is now producing a light tank (T-62), an amphibious tank (T-60), and an armored personnel carrier in addition to the T-59. While personnel carriers and light tanks are still in very short supply, the T-59 inventory is now approaching full strength.[66] China has at this writing about 10,000 tanks, i.e., the same number as the U.S.[67] While still badly outnumbered by the USSR, the world's largest armored force with about 40,000 tanks, the expanded Chinese capabilities in this field represent a meaningful deterrent. This is especially true since most Soviet armor is deployed in Europe.

The engineering forces are divided into combat engineers and support units. The former are integrated into infantry corps and divisions. Each infantry corps has about one regiment of combat engineers divided among its three component infantry divisions. Subunits specialize in laying mine fields, constructing defense works and temporary bridges, handling demolitions, and providing camouflage. The support units are nearly all independent forces under the joint control of the military regions and the GRSD. These have various specializations including permanent bridging, general construction, electrical work, and providing potable water.

Western and Chinese Nationalist descriptions of the independent engineer units differ. What the U.S. calls divisions, the Nationalists term regiments. However, since divisions of specialized forces such as the engineers are much smaller than infantry divisions (6000-8000 as opposed to 10,000-12,000), both Western and Nationalist studies appear to be referring to the same units. This assumption is further strengthened since both estimates number the independent engineering units at about 30.[68] Given the nature of the PLA, this is a small force. Engineering units provide much of the military's assistance to the civilian economy and support to the PLA's own sideline production. For purposes of road and bridge construction, water conservancy and reclamation projects, and local military managed arsenals and machine shops, 30 engineering divisions are too few. However, these regular PLA units are supplements by the paramilitary production-construction corps which are much larger but less mechanized. Engineering equipment is mostly of Soviet design dating from the 1950s. However, the Russian equipment at that time is likely to have been the world's best, so obsolescence is not yet a major problem. Domestic production of this equipment, however, is assumed to have been less than optimal in the 1960s, perhaps providing one reason why there are not more engineering units in the PLA.

In the late 1960s, the U.S. had a chance to see Chinese engineering forces in action. Their role was to repair bomb damage and keep open lines of communication in North Vietnam between Hanoi and the Chinese border. The U.S. Air Force will attest to the efficiency of those troops under wartime conditions.

The anti–chemical warfare forces are responsible for protecting the PLA against biological, chemical, and nuclear attack, and for smoke-generated concealment. While there is no indication that the Chinese have an offensive chemical-biological-radiological warfare program, the anti-chemical warfare forces do have one offensive role—they organize the flame throwing troops. These units as well as most other anti–chemical warfare troops are integrated into the large combat units. Such attached units are usually of company size although there is a battalion at the infantry corps level. There are some independent regiments, but their exact number is not known. These regiments may serve as a reserve which could be quickly relocated to any region in order to assist units which had suffered heavy chemical or nuclear attacks.

Defense against doomsday weapons is obviously not very well developed in any army; however, the Chinese have been especially backward. Troop training in the 1960s was poor or totally lacking, equipment was crude or nonexistent, and some units did not have attached anti–chemical warfare troops. In smaller units, the position of anti–chemical warfare defense officer was often vacant.[69] Presumably, the sitution has improved since the 1960s; the PLA has trained under nuclear conditions during some of the atomic and hydrogen bomb tests. In the field of nuclear defense the anti-chemical warfare forces appear to be most highly trained, but here too detection and protection equipment seems crude and/or lacking. The government has apparently opted to rely on China's size and dispersal of forces as the primary defense against nuclear attack, although the many bomb shelters would at least provide some protection against radiation. China is also very vulnerable to biological warfare, especially crop-destroying weapons. However, such an attack would presume a total war situation in which China's nuclear power would serve as a deterrent.

The signal corps plans and operates military communications. The signal forces therefore are mostly integrated with other troop units in order to install, maintain, and operate all forms of communications equipment. However, each military region has an independent regiment which is used to improve and extend the communications network—civil as well as military. Each military district has an independent battalion, and a signal company is located at military subdistrict headquarters. The equipment is rather old and heavy, and there is too much reliance on vulnerable land lines. Yet military communications in China are efficient. The code systems are very sophisticated, and it is virtually impossible for potential enemies to "break" them. The signal corps' capabilities seem to be sufficient to carry out its mission.

Few of the world's armies have railway troops, but they are especially important to the PLA. China as a nation has only about 500,000-600,000 trucks, and relatively few long-distance highways.[70] Apart from the railway system, the PLA ground forces often have to get there by walking. Local roads are common, but usually unsurfaced, and during the rainy seasons, many are impassable by truck. Thus the railways are vital to PLA mobility and logistics. Trains provide a reliable, inexpensive supply and transport system which can move vast tonnages over great distances. There is, however, a fly in the ointment: China does not have enough railroads and rolling stock. The railway forces can be credited with major achievements—the most notable of which was the 1966 completion of the Kunming-Kweiyang rail line through extraordinarily mountainous terrain. However, there are still no rail connections with Tibet and only one line serves most of Northwest China.

Because the PLA is so dependent upon the railroad system and because there are very few alternate rail lines available, the conventional wisdom has held that the PLA would be very vulnerable to air interdiction. However, the experience of the Vietnam War proved otherwise. Only two rail lines lead from China into the Democratic Republic of Vietnam and these were heavily bombed in the late 1960s in an effort to cut off the flow of supplies from China. However, with the help of Chinese engineering and railway forces units, repairs were made with astonishing rapidity. Pontoon bridges replaced destroyed steel spans and where pontoon bridging could not be used, railway cars, or the contents thereof, were ferried across rivers. Despite unlimited U.S. air superiority, the overland flow of supplies was never stopped for long. Except in the case of nuclear attack, the rail-dependent logistics system of the PLA is not as vulnerable as was once believed.

During normal peacetime conditions, the railway forces engage in construction and maintenance. There is a confusing overlap with the work force of the Ministry of Railways. In general, the ministry seems primarily concerned with operating the rail system and producing rolling stock while the PLA force does the engineering work—surveying and building the lines. Given the obvious need for more railroad lines in China, the rate of construction has been none too fast. An effort was made to supplement the eleven railway force divisions with paramilitary engineering units attached to the regular forces, but apparently problems arose regarding discipline and morale.[71] However, it is quite possible that paramilitary forces are still being used to boost construction manpower.

As the tactical mobility of the PLA ground forces gradually increases in coming years with the introduction of more motorized and tracked vehicles, the strategic mobility will decrease.[72] A lightly equipped infantry division can be moved very quickly by a few trains. If the same unit has hundreds of trucks and armored vehicles, several trains will be needed and a much longer time period would elapse before the unit would be ready to fight in its new location. Thus the railroad corps will have a still more difficult job in the years ahead.

Nuclear Capabilities

To evaluate the effectiveness of the Second Artillery requires a discussion of China's nuclear program. The first atomic test was in 1964; the first hydrogen bomb was exploded in 1967. By the end of 1975, China had detonated seventeen test explosions ranging from ten kilotons to three megatons. In 1966, a rocket armed with an atomic warhead was fired over a 700 mile test range into Sinkiang where it successfully exploded. This was a dangerous test; should the rocket have malfunctioned, its flight path was perilously near the Soviet border. The U.S. has never tried such a live nuclear warhead rocket test firing. However, also in 1966, China successfully launched a large number of medium range ballistic missiles (MRBMs). The Chinese MRBM is a copy of a Soviet demonstration model given to China just before the Sino-Soviet split; the 7th Machine Building Ministry has been producing this weapon for over a decade. The large number of firings in 1966-67 indicated that serial production had begun. The only reason for firing so many missiles is to train troops, so by 1967, the Second Artillery had the equipment and the trained manpower; highly secretive deployment may have begun at that time. Since China had relatively few missiles, it was crucial that they not be quickly detected, lest the USSR (or U.S.) feel impelled to destroy China's fledgling nuclear capacity. The secrecy was successful—at least insofar as U.S. intelligence was concerned.

In the early 1970s, China developed two intermediate-range ballistic missiles (IRBMs). The first was a modification of the existing MRBM which extended its range to 1200-1500 miles. The second is a two-stage missile—probably using two modified MRBM rocket motors—which has a range of 2500-3500 miles.[73] This two stage IRBM was tested in the early 1970s and was likely to have been the launch vehicle used to orbit China's earth satellites. It was deployed as an operational weapons system in 1974, giving China the capability of striking targets throughout Russia and most of the Asian Pacific region. Thus far, all of China's strategic rockets use cryogenic liquid fuels which require considerable preparation to launch and are difficult to maintain. Solid-fuel propellants are still in the research phase. Recent testing patterns indicate that China is now engaged in developing a thermonuclear warhead small enough to be used on the MRBM/IRBMs.[74]

Presently, China has about 200-300 nuclear warheads.[75] She could have deployed over 100 missiles, and there is evidence that at least some of the IRBMs can be moved cross-country.[76] Others are presumably transported by rail. This mobility makes it virtually impossible for adversaries to carry out an effective first strike and have reasonable assurance that such an attack would destroy China's ability to retaliate.

In the past decade, China had a high priority program to develop an intercontinental ballistic missile (ICBM). However, in the 1970s that program was deemphasized apparently in order to develop and deploy the present IRBM system. The technical challenges posed in developing an ICBM are enormous, and China's scientific and technological manpower pool is probably too small to have pressed ahead with IRBM and ICBM development simultaneously. At the end of the 1960s, U.S. analysts were predicting that China would first test an ICBM about 1972-73. This was based on the fact that a large launching pad and gantry had been built at the missile test range in Inner Mongolia. However, this was later torn down and a differently designed facility was gradually built in the last few years. Testing could begin again soon and by the end of the 1970s, China could possibly have an operational ICBM to deter distant enemies. The problem with a small ICBM force is that it is difficult to conceal from satellite photography, thus rendering China vulnerable to a first strike attack from the U.S. or Europe. Peking is believed to be countering that possibility by emphasizing the development of a submarine-launched ballistic missile (SLBM). According to U.S. intelligence officials in 1975, a SLBM system is expected to be operational by about 1980—possibly predating the deployment of the more vulnerable ICBM.[77]

Meanwhile, the strides made in rocket technology are gradually being applied to enhance China's strategic intelligence-gathering capability. The low orbits of three earth satellites launched in the last half of 1975 indicated to U.S. intelligence analysts that Peking is developing a spy satellite.[78] At present, only the U.S. and Soviet Union have such intelligence gathering systems.

Whether China will develop other nuclear weapons remains to be seen. Once the deterrent missile force is established, China's greatest military weakness will be the absence of tactical nuclear weapons to support the ground forces. It is probable that research and development efforts are now devoted to tactical weapons most likely in the form of small bombs which could be carried by fighter-bomber aricraft,[79] as well as ballistic missiles. The least expensive and most accurate delivery system is still the manned bomber. The Air Force has a few old Tu-4 propeller-driven medium bombers and about 100 Tu-16 medium jet bombers. Neither of those aircraft could penetrate the air defense system of the USSR, but they might be useful against the new nuclear threat posed by India. There is no evidence regarding which service controls nuclear warheads—the air force or the Second Artillery—but simplification of control would argue in favor of the Second Artillery's having responsibility for all nuclear weapons including bombs.

Recent History of National Organizations

The Central Military Commission

The chronicle of the CMC over the past decade provides a high-level perspective on the PLA during and after the GPCR. Due to its power, the CMC is a highly political organization; its leadership is vulnerable to packing or dismissal. The CMC Standing Committee has been packed with political supporters twice since 1966, and dismissal of individual members is not unusual: of the ten men on the committee in 1966, only three are serving today.[80] Although leaders come and go, the functions of the CMC have changed very little over the past fifteen years.

The Great Proletarian Cultural Revolution began in November 1965, as its name suggests, as an ideological campaign. Appropriately, the military newspaper— *Liberation Army Daily*—led the PLA involvement in the GPCR. That newspaper along with the Shanghai *Wen-hui-pao* got the GPCR started by attacking as "rightist" certain writers who were members of the Peking Municipal Government. Although the *Liberation Army Daily* is an internal PLA newspaper without public circulation, its editorials were routinely broadcast and reprinted. By the spring and summer of 1966, it had immense political authority and was heeded as a vanguard of the GPCR.

Such usage of the military paper had little direct effect on the CMC. However, in February 1966, the GPCR *within* the PLA began and eventually claimed hundreds of political victims, including some members of the CMC. Like the GPCR as a whole, the campaign within the military grew from very small beginnings. In February 1966, Chiang Ch'ing (Madam Mao) received permission from Defense Minister Lin Piao to conduct a "PLA Forum on Literature and Art."[81] The forum was intended primarily to enlist the propaganda and cultural assets of the PLA (since the 1930s, the PLA has maintained its own playwrights, musicians, writers, actors, and propagandists to enlighten and entertain the troops) in the campaign against the writers, educators, and propagandists in the Party bureaucracy who had deviated from Mao's ideology. At the time of the forum, Madam Mao also obtained permission to conduct an investigation of PLA literature and arts, and was appointed "Advisor on Cultural Work for the PLA" for this purpose.[82] In late March, Chiang Ch'ing's highly critical report on the state of PLA literature and arts was submitted to the CMC by Lin Piao.[83] It was presumably approved, and measures were begun to reorient "culture" within the military, beginning the GPCR within the armed forces.

During the spring of 1966, Mao Tse-tung revealed dual intentions regarding the PLA. On the one hand, it was to serve as a national model of socialist purity. In Mao's words, the PLA was "to be turned into a great school for revolutionization."[84] On the other hand, the military was to be further purified. As Mao put it in May of that year:

> Those representatives of the bourgeoisie who have sneaked into the Party, the government, *the army* and various cultural circles are a bunch of counterrevolutionary revisionists. Once conditions are ripe, they will

seize power and turn the proletarian dictatorship into a bourgeois dictatorship.[85]

Dealing with the "bad handful of persons" in the PLA was not to be deferred simply because Mao Tse-tung intended to use the leadership and assets of the military to help spearhead the GPCR.

There was, however, a very important difference in the treatment accorded the PLA compared with the civilian Party and governmental systems. Following the creation of the Red Guards in the summer of 1966, the civilian leaders were subjected to mass movement tactics—they were public targets for criticism and rectification. The PLA also carried out criticism and "struggle," but the movement was restricted to administrative echelons (excluding troop units) and was managed *internally*. In other words, the PLA had its own separate GPCR, run rather like a traditional Communist rectification campaign. A special organization was created in the summer of 1966 to manage the program—the PLA Cultural Revolution Group (CRG). It was headed by Ho Lung, a vice-chairman of the CMC. He was assisted by a deputy director of the General Political Department—Liu Chih-chien. The PLA/CRG was responsible to the CMC, thus the military leadership was firmly in control and could look out for its own. During its first year, the GPCR presented little hazard to the PLA compared with the serious threat it posed to Party officials.

Indeed, the CMC appeared to be a beneficiary of Mao's campaign against the Party bureaucracy. In August 1966, the Eleventh Plenum of the Eighth Central Committee reorganized the Politburo and Party Secretariat. Some leaders of the CMC were thrust into high-ranking civilian leadership posts concurrent with their military positions. Lin Piao became the sole Party vice-chairman and thus the heir-apparent to Mao Tse-tung. Nieh Jung-chen, Yeh Chien-ying and Hsu Hsiang-ch'ien were all added to the Party Politburo; Yeh was concurrently appointed to the Party Secretariat. Mao was using the military leadership to supplant his enemies at the top of the Party bureaucracy.

The political situation suddenly grew threatening for the

CMC at the beginning of 1967 when a full-fledged crisis developed. The issue was the direct involvement of the PLA in the national mass movement. From the standpoint of the GPCR leadership, the need for military support was vital. The Party bureaucracy in the provinces have proven very resilient to Red Guard attacks. The use of callow, disorganized youths to criticize and rectify a Communist Party apparatus was unprecedented. It may have caused Lenin to turn over in his tomb; it certainly caused the Party leaders to resist with all the considerable forces at their disposal. Local public security organizations harassed and arrested Red Guards, and conservative, status-quo oriented workers were encouraged to form their own mass organizations which often attacked Red Guard groups. By the end of 1966, the GPCR had bogged down. It needed an infusion of real power, and the PLA was the only institution which had the strength to break the back of the Party resistance.

The military leadership was very reluctant to involve the PLA in the GPCR. There were at least three sound reasons for such opposition. First, the number of troop units needed to support the national campaign would be large, and thus military readiness would be degraded. Also, this was the period when the Vietnam War was rapidly expanding and there were fears that the U.S. and China could come to a military confrontation in Southeast Asia. Second, it is virtually certain that some top-level PLA leaders disapproved of Mao's tactics in the GPCR and would have been quite content to see the campaign die a natural death. Finally there was very little to be gained by immersing the military in local and provincial political affairs, while the hazards were considerable.

In the latter half of 1966, editorials in the national media emphasized that the PLA must dedicate itself to politics first, claiming that military preparedness would then naturally follow. On December 31, a directive issued by the Central Committee (i.e., the Politburo) and the State Council ordered the PLA to give political and military training to Red Guards.[86] Since virtually all general directives which apply to the PLA are sent out under the name of the CMC, it may be significant that the order was not also issued under CMC auspices; the military leadership may have balked in this case. On January 1, 1967, the *Liberation Army Daily* called on the PLA to "actively participate in and defend the GPCR," and further stated: "Chairman Mao teaches us to concern ourselves with the affairs of the state and to carry through the GPCR to the end."[87] On January 12, the PLA Cultural Revolution Group was reorganized in a manner which weakened the effective power of the CMC. The previous director, Ho Lung, was dismissed, and Hsu Hsiang-ch'ien of the CMC was appointed as its new head. However, Madam Mao was made "advisor" to the reorganized group. Most importantly, it was stipulated that the PLA/CRG would "carry on its work under the direct leadership of the CMC *and* the Central Committee Cultural Revolution Group."[88] The military no longer had exclusive control over the internal PLA Cultural Revolution.[89]

A major editorial appeared in the *Liberation Army Daily* two days after the PLA/CRG reorganization which promised a much strengthened campaign within the armed forces.[90] The scope of the internal military campaign remained the same, with troop units remaining off limits for revolutionary activities. However, the editorial called for more extreme measures in those sectors where the campaign was permitted. A reference was made to learning "from the revolutionary rebel groups in Shanghai" which almost certainly meant "power seizures" or takeovers from below which began in the leading organs of the PLA about the time of the editorial. In power seizures, mass organizations within the PLA were encouraged not only to criticize "bad" leaders but also to oust the offending officers and themselves take over leadership of the organizations.

The reorganization of January 12 and the military call for much stronger revolutionary measures within the top echelons of the PLA seem paradoxical. Why should the Maoist leadership have thrown the top levels of the armed forces into turmoil just when the PLA was being developed as an alternate political power base to the Party? The most probable answer was that continued resistance by military leaders to Mao's plans for the PLA forced him to "get tough." This hypothesis is somewhat borne out by the techniques adopted: first, the CMC's exclusive control of the PLA/CRG was diluted, making effective resistance by military leaders more difficult. It would be one thing for a veteran senior commander to bring his influence to bear within the General Political Department and CMC; it would be quite another matter to pressure Madam Mao and the Central Committee Cultural Revolution Group. Second, the introduction of power seizure tactics in top echelon PLA organizations could serve to break the authority of particularly obstinate and powerful military leaders who might have opposed a further expansion of the GPCR.

The major military purge victim of that December 1966-January 1967 period was Ho Lung of the CMC. Since August 1966, Ho had acted as the leader of the PLA Cultural Revolution Group and the PLA advisor to the Red Guards. It seems likely that Ho was the leader of the resistance which necessitated the PLA/CRG reorganization and the announcement of a toughened military GPCR. His four months' experience with the PLA Cultural Revolution and the Red Guards may have convinced him that the military was entering a quagmire; at least it was a striking coincidence that his dismissal came just at the time when the armed forces were about to be immersed in political actions to support the revolutionary rebels.

Military leadership resistance to involvement in the GPCR was broken in the week of January 14-21. On January 14, a Central Committee directive was issued ordering the regional PLA bureaucracy to take over the communications equipment and archives of the Party committees in the provinces.[91] Once again, the CMC did not cosign the directive. Yet seven days later on January 21, a joint Central Committee, State Council *and* CMC directive ordered that the PLA should actively support the "revolutionary left." Why the CMC gave in is still an open question. Possibly it was a combination of threats, cajolery and argumentation. The purge of Ho Lung clearly revealed that CMC vice-chairmen were not politically sacrosanct. Moreover, Mao Tse-tung and Lin Piao could make a strong argument that PLA involvement was in the best interests of the nation, since violence and general chaos in the cities had grown to alarming levels in January. The PLA was, in fact, badly needed to protect the economy from grave disruption. Finally it is probable that promises were made to elicit cooperation. It was reported that Mao Tse-tung personally presided at the CMC meeting which resulted in the PLA entering the GPCR.[92] Subsequent events revealed that Mao appeared to have promised the PLA leadership full authority in dealing with provincial and local GPCR activities.

Those first three weeks in January 1967 may have been the most dangerous period of the GPCR for Mao Tse-tung. After he had completely committed himself to the GPCR as a mass movement, his main political base—the PLA—began to waver. There was no turning back. Mao brought all the pressure he could muster to force a continued and expanded commitment of the military to his political offensive; had he failed it might well have been his greatest and final political disaster.

For a few weeks immediately following the commitment of military forces, confusion reigned within the CMC. Orders were issued only to be countermanded shortly thereafter.[93] For example, a CMC directive of February 8 prohibited GPCR activities in the entire air and naval forces. The order was reversed three days later allowing "mass movement" activities at the administrative levels, but not in tactical units. There must have been much wrangling within the CMC to produce such sudden shifts in the Party line.

In April, the situation worsened for the military leadership. The PLA Cultural Revolution Group became paralyzed due to conflicts between subordination to the CMC and subordination to the Cultural Revolution Group of the Central Committee. This was reflected in disagreements between the PLA/CRG leader Hsu Hsiang-ch'ien and its advisor, Madam Mao. What the issues were between Hsu and Chiang Ch'ing, we can only speculate. One may have been the continuation of a free hand for leaders of the regional forces in dealing with revolutionary groups. On April 6, 1967, a central directive greatly restricted the PLA's authority to arrest Red Guards or to disband organizations deemed counterrevolutionary. The CMC leadership certainly would have resisted such a reduction in authority. A second likely issue was the involvement of main-force army corps in the GPCR. Tying down China's defensive backbone in domestic affairs bordered on madness when the Vietnam War raged in the south and the USSR was increasing its troop strength on the northern frontiers. Yeh Chien-ying of the CMC has long been primarily responsible for military readiness. He received strong Red Guard criticism at the same time as Hsu Hsiang-ch'ien even though he was not a member of the PLA/CRG.

When the dust had settled, it was clear that the military viewpoint had lost heavily. Hsu Hsiang-ch'ien was declared "too old to work" and receded from the limelight.[94] Little was heard about military readiness or Yeh Chien-ying for some months. Hsiao Hua, the Director of the General Political Department, became the new Chairman of the PLA/CRG, and additional military leaders who were committed to the GPCR were added to the group.[95] Madam Mao's influence was greatly heightened by the reorganization.

A few days later, the Standing Committee of the CMC was packed by the addition of four leaders of the PLA Cultural Revolution.[96] This gave a majority vote to men who were committed to the campaign, while the veteran leaders were outnumbered for the first time in the history of the CMC.[97] There was no longer any effective means at the national level for military leaders to resist the steady immersion of the armed forces in the GPCR. The PLA had become a political tool—insofar as the Maoist leadership could thus render it.

Total subjugation of the national level PLA organs to the dictates of a political campaign may have been one cause of what happened next: with no channel through which to make themselves heard in Peking, the military in the provinces grew increasingly restive, culminating in the Wuhan Incident of July 1967. Although the kidnapping of Mao's envoys was short-lived and the leadership of the Wuhan Military Region was quickly changed, the repercussions began a new round of organizational changes in Peking.

The weeks following the Wuhan Incident were the nadir of the GPCR for the PLA. During this period, the army was ordered to arm selected Red Guard groups, while others simply raided military arsenals. The month of August 1967 was devoted to "dragging out the small handful of capitalist roaders" in the army. Street violence reached its highest level while the authority of the PLA was at its low point.

The military high command lost control of the Cultural Revolution within the PLA. Lin Piao himself issued an order that the PLA should "ask the leftist forces among the civilians to be its teachers in the army's education on the struggle between the two lines."[98] That order resulted in PLA cadres in the provinces being seized by Red Guard groups who often subjected them to kangaroo courts or physical brutality. The real significance of the "dragging out the small handful of capitalist roaders" in the army and of Lin's order was that the PLA/GPCR was changed from a closed to an open movement. The military was no longer immune from civilian attack.

Ironically, organizational changes made in August 1967 which were intended to weaken the political power of the high command eventually worked to its favor. About the middle of August, the PLA/CRG was again reorganized and the General Political Department was ordered to suspend operations. The director of both organizations, Hsiao Hua, was dismissed. Since the GPD Headquarters had ceased to function, the CMC was forced to create a special organization to carry out some of the indispensible functions of the GPD. Originally called the PLA "Support the Left Group" of the CMC, the organization soon became known by its enduring title—the "Political Work Group."[99] It reported to the CMC Administrative Committee.[100] Together these two organizations regained control of the PLA Cultural Revolution in the autumn of 1967. Although the inside story of the military's resurgence has yet to be told, there is enough data to provide a meaningful framework.

At the end of August, the "drag out the small handful in the army" campaign was suddenly brought to a close. On August 25, a central directive prohibited mass organizations from plundering military arsenals.[101] On September 5, a much broader directive again closed the PLA to the civilian mass movement and restored the weakened public security powers of PLA forces in order to reestablish a modicum of order in the provinces.[102] On the same date Madam Mao, as the premier spokesman for the leftist forces in the GPCR, explained the order to her followers. The speech stressed moderation and restraint of the mass movement and the inviolability of the PLA. At one point Chiang Ch'ing did let slip a lame defense of the August excesses:

> You [the revolutionary rebels] said that you were unable to drag out the small handful in the army and you needed our help in doing this. In some places this has been done.[103]

However, the "dragging out" was clearly over as Madam Mao emphasized in the rest of her speech.

The August policy had been inherently untenable. The long-term strategy was to purify the PLA while using it as an alternate base of political power, temporarily replacing the old Party apparatus. In August, this alternate base was being intentionally undermined and there was nothing to take its place except the newly armed mass organizations. Had the policy long continued, anarchy would have ensued.

It was Mao Tse-tung who finally realized this and had the power to call a halt to the self-destructive actions. He began an "inspection trip" in late July which continued in stages until about early September, visiting several of the more strife-torn provinces such as Hunan, Anhui, and Chekiang. Probably in late August, Mao issued an order which showed considerable awareness of the danger to the PLA as a political power base:

> If there are problems within the PLA, they can be solved province by province. The handful of persons taking the capitalist road within the Party should not be lumped together with the group of people taking the capitalist road within the military. We should mention only the handful in the Party and strive to make the military a success.[104]

In another quote from the same period, Mao further ordered:

The army's prestige must be resolutely safeguarded. There can be no doubt whatever about that. Publication of editorials on the need to support the army and cherish the people is the center of our work at the present time. It was unavoidable that the army should have made mistakes in tackling for the first time the large scale fighting tasks of supporting the left, supporting industry and agriculture, and carrying out military control and military training. The chief danger at the moment is that some people want to beat down the PLA.[105]

Mao was apparently thinking of the Central Committee Cultural Revolution Group when he referred to "the chief danger" to the PLA, for in early September that body was purged of those members who had been most outspoken against the PLA.[106] Mao did much to save the PLA and himself from the destructive policy of July-August 1967.

The military leadership quickly moved to consolidate its gains. Sometime in the late summer or early autumn of 1967, the PLA Cultural Revolution Group was abolished.[107] Following its January and April reorganizations, the PLA/CRG had vitiated internal military control of the GPCR within the armed forces. The disbanding of that body returned the control to the CMC and its subordinates, the Administrative Committee and the Political Work Group. It was likely the PLA leadership who successfully sought the destruction of the PLA/CRG; air force commander Wu Fa-hsien, its last director, became chairman of the Administrative Committee of the CMC in August.[108] The other military leaders of the defunct organ also suffered no untoward consequences—they simply shifted their activities back into purely military channels and away from the Central Committee CRG. The PLA thereby recaptured its own internal GPCR.

In terms of the separation of functions, the Administrative Committee supervised the PLA/GPCR. The Political Work Group was responsible for the PLA role and performance in the national GPCR, dealing with such matters as relations between the military and mass organizations, and PLA execution of domestic political responsibilities. By 1968, it had expanded its powers to include investigation and evaluation of high ranking military cadres vis-à-vis their performance in the GPCR.[109] Through the remainder of the Cultural Revolution, the CMC jealously guarded its exclusive authority to deal with political affairs within the PLA. Even Premier Chou En-lai, who had immense prestige and executive power in the GPCR, deferred to Wu Fa-hsien whenever military problems were brought up at meetings with provincial representatives.[110]

With the PLA intervention in the GPCR beginning on January 21, 1967, the Central Committee CRG had little hope of competing effectively with the CMC for influence in the provinces: the PLA had its minions there while the Central CRG had only the Red Guards. If the leaders of the GPCR were to exercise effective nationwide power, their only chance was to capture political control of the PLA in Peking and thereby wield influence over the provinces through the army-Party system. As one of the leaders of the Central CRG put it: "In seizing power, you must seize military power; failure to seize military power amounts to no power."[111] The last hope for such a triumph disappeared along with the PLA/CRG in the autumn of 1967.

The Lin Piao Affair

From the latter part of 1967 until 1971, the CMC was essentially stable except for the purge of acting chief of staff Yang Ch'eng-wu, discussed below in the recent history of the General Staff. Suddenly in September 1971, Lin Piao and several CMC leaders disappeared. Lin and his wife Yeh Ch'un are known to be dead. The fate of several others remains uncertain, but the following top-level military leaders were dismissed at the time of the Lin Piao affair: Chief of the General Staff, Huang Yung-sheng; Air Force Commander Wu Fa-hsien; Navy Political Commissar Li Tso-p'eng; and General Rear Services Department Director Chiu Hui-tso. This constituted a purge of all but one member of the CMC Administrative Committee and the removal of all but four members of the Standing Committee (i.e., Mao and Vice Chairmen Nieh Jung-chen, Yeh Chien-ying, and Hsu Hsiang-ch'ien.[112] In the provinces, many more leaders whose military careers were linked with Lin Piao have since been dismissed. This extraordinary turn of events is best explained first by examining the events themselves, and second, the possible causes.[113]

The string of events which led to Lin Piao's sudden demise must be traced back at least as far as 1969 and the Ninth Party Congress, convened to legitimize the new leadership which had emerged from the GPCR. In the new constitution, Lin Piao was named heir apparent to Mao Tse-tung. However, Lin had made a great many enemies both within and without the PLA, due to his radicalism in the GPCR. Prior to the congress, he may have been seeking some means of ensuring political support. Possibly such domestic considerations had something to do with the Ch'en Pao Island clash which preceded the congress by a month.

On March 2, 1969, Chinese forces ambushed and virtually destroyed a Soviet Patrol which had crossed the ice-covered Ussuri River to Ch'en Pao Island, an uninhabited, marshy isle, clearly on the Chinese side of the main channel, although the Russians had often before trod its soil without serious incident. On March 2 the Chinese clearly had set a trap. It is highly unlikely that any local commander would undertake such action on his own responsibility; the border defense units are in direct communication with Peking precisely because of the international repercussions of any misstep. Thus, the order to ambush the Soviet forces probably came from the high command and with forethought. The intention might have been to provoke a war scare, thereby rallying support behind Defense Minister Lin Piao, while at the same time continuing the special authority accorded to the PLA (and Lin) during the GPCR.[114] If such a plan did exist, it worked, at least initially. The Ninth Party Congress was to be a "congress of unity" and the war scare contributed to that end.

The USSR nearly spoiled it all by overreacting: they heavily shelled the Chinese banks of the Ussuri, and several other border clashes followed in the ensuing weeks—a few as far away as Sinkiang. China did not fare well in any of those encounters. More Soviet divisions were rushed to the border area, and speculation on the possibilities of a Sino-Soviet war reached its apex. China began an extensive bomb-shelter building campaign which continued for more than four years (1969-73), cost immense sums of money, and drained labor away from productive tasks. The crisis atmosphere gradually subsided after Chou En-lai and Alexei Kosygin used the occasion of Ho Chi Minh's funeral to arrange negotiations. After some delays, border talks were started in October 1969. No resolution of issues was reached, but tensions have been much less acute over the past few years.[115]

In the months following the Ninth Party Congress, Mao Tse-tung and others began to be perturbed at high-handed behavior on the part of military leaders in the provinces, who had already squeezed out most of the revolutionary rebel representatives from the new provincial governments. Moreover, in 1969-70, it was dilatory in assisting Party rebuilding. Many veteran civilian cadres who had been suspended in the GPCR found it virtually impossible to rehabilitate themselves; they remained stuck in PLA-run "May 7th Cadre Schools." Military organizations such as people's armed departments and military subdistricts and districts often continued to be the locus of real political power while the new revolutionary committee governments languished.

In 1969, Mao Tse-tung began a rectification campaign directed at the PLA in the provinces, but it seemed to have little impact on Party rebuilding. During 1970-71, the province-level Party committees were finally reestablished. However, about 60 percent of all the Party secretaries were military men, and the PLA garnered fully 70 percent of the First Secretary appointments. There was a real danger that the civilian Party apparatus was becoming an adjunct of the PLA. Adding insult to injury, the military control committees which had been established in the GPCR to serve as interim governments and protect the economy were continued even after the Party committees had been rebuilt.[116]

By 1970, Mao Tse-tung apparently had second thoughts about his earlier decision to appoint Lin Piao as his political successor. The military bureaucracy under Lin's leadership was proving almost as unresponsive to Mao's wishes as had the old pre-GPCR Party appartus led by Liu Shao-ch'i and

Teng Hsiao-p'ing. In March, Mao began taking concrete steps to weaken Lin Piao's power. He removed the position of chief of state from the new draft constitution of the Chinese People's Republic. It had been generally assumed that Lin would become president of the Republic as a natural stepping stone in consolidating his power during the period of political transition. The elimination of this office directly threatened Lin, especially when coupled with a new media campaign emphasizing "collective leadership." Mao clearly had come to favor a coalition to succeed him after his demise.

Although Lin was obviously stung by Mao's actions, he was still far from politically impotent. As the Second Plenum of the Ninth Party Congress approached in the summer of 1970, Lin and his backers in the PLA formed a coalition with the other major political segment disgruntled by the outcome of the GPCR—the radicals led by the Chairman of the Central Cultural Revolution Group, Ch'en Po-ta. When the Second Plenum convened in August, they launched a "surprise attack" (as Mao later called it). First, they asked that the position of chief of state be restored to the pending constitution. In order to gain support for the idea, they proposed that Mao Tse-tung should hold the position until his death. Secondly, they criticized the down-playing of the "cult of Mao" which both Lin and Ch'en had used to their political advantage during the GPCR. Lin's CMC followers who were also Politburo members actively supported those motions.[117] Mao Tse-tung effectively broke the attack by announcing to the Plenum that he would not accept the office of the presidency even if the Plenum decided to ignore his wishes and reestablish the position.

Following the Second Plenum, Mao focused his attention first on Ch'en Po-ta. He was more easily politically eliminated than Lin. Lin had the backing of the CMC (and thus the PLA), whereas Ch'en had no powerful organizational base. The latter part of 1970 and early 1971 saw strong media attacks against ultraleftist extremism, "sham Marxist theoreticians, and phonies and charlatans" within the Party. By early spring of 1971, Ch'en Po-ta was thoroughly discredited. Self-criticisms were circulated at a Central Committee work conference in April 1971, written by several of Lin's military associates who had supported Ch'en Po-ta and Lin Piao at the Second Plenum eight months earlier.[118] Mao may have been seeking dual results from obtaining the self-criticisms. First, he might have hoped that some of Lin's supporters would veer away once they saw that the political heat was on. As events proved, none of the Administrative Committee of the CMC deserted Lin, although others at lower levels may have done so. Second, Mao probably intended to weaken the political stature of Lin's central military elite by humiliating them before their peers.

It appears that the Lin clique was in fact weakened by the work conference. Mao was able to reorganize the CMC Standing Committee, packing the membership so that Lin no longer could dominate its proceedings.[119] The CMC expansion in turn allowed Mao to reorganize the Peking Military Region, removing two of Lin's supporters, Commander Ch'eng Wei-shan and Political Commissar Li Hsueh-feng.

Having broken Lin's monopoly over the CMC and secured military control of the capital for himself, Mao next turned to the military in the provinces. In August and early September 1971, he traversed the Nanking and Canton Military Regions seeking support for a showdown which he believed was drawing near. Meanwhile, the Chinese official documents allege that Lin Piao, aware of his increasing isolation, was plotting to assassinate Mao and take power in a coup. In one version, the allegations state that Lin's daughter learned of the assassination plan and told Chou En-lai. Lin in turn learned that his plot and coconspirators, such as Air Force Commander Wu Fa-hsien, had been discovered. He then hastily ordered an air force Trident jet liner, boarded it with his wife, son, and a few other unidentified close followers and took off for the USSR. The Trident crashed in Outer Mongolia killing the nine persons on board, all of whom were so badly burned as to be unidentifiable.

Whether the coup plot allegations are basically true or not remains moot: it is clear that Lin Piao and his wife and son are dead and it is probable that they were aboard the Trident which crashed. (However, the USSR claimed, on the basis of autopsies, that none of those aboard were over the age of fifty.) Following Lin's death, his CMC followers were all dismissed, and the air force was almost completely grounded for the better part of a month. For more than a year following the incident, Lin's supporters in the provinces were ferreted out and dismissed or suspended.

All surviving PLA leaders who had been purged in the GPCR during the height of Lin's power have returned to favor. Finally, the military began disengagement from leadership of local and provincial governments. The separation of the PLA from civilian adminstrative duties, while never intended to be complete, was largely accomplished by 1975.

The Issues Behind the Lin Piao Affair

The above summary of events already provides the most important single reason for Lin's demise—civil/military competition for political power. Lin was Mao's designated heir; he exercised considerable control in the provinces through the military apparatus. Thus, Lin viewed efforts to rebuild the civilian Party leadership as a clear threat to his consolidation of power. Some of the military leaders outside Peking supported Lin in his view, e.g., Han Hsien-ch'u, then commander of the Fuchow Military Region. As radio Fuchow put it: "The three supports and two militaries[120] will remain the basic duty of our army throughout the whole historical period of socialism. It is a political task entrusted to us by the supreme commander, Chairman Mao."[121]

On this issue, the opposition to Lin was led by Mao and Chou En-lai. Perhaps Lin was able to strike a deal which allowed for Party rebuilding while using military men to fill the top positions. This would help explain the fact that 70 percent of the Party secretaries in the rebuilt provincial committees were PLA men. Mao Tse-tung countered this by stressing collective leadership as opposed to one man rule; Party committees were called upon to meet frequently and make decisions as a body, thus preventing the First Party Secretary, usually a PLA leader, from dominating the decision-making process. The struggle for control of the provincial leadership was continuing when Lin Piao suddenly departed the scene and, to some extent, it continued through 1974, although following Lin's demise the military steadily lost ground in terms of political power.

The foreign policy arena provided the other major issues where Lin Piao was clearly losing out before September 1971. Lin had been a primary spokesman for both national economic self-sufficiency and supporting antiimperialist wars abroad.[122] The trouble was, neither self-sufficiency nor "people's wars" were working to China's benefit. The economy of China in the 1960s grew at a slower pace than did that of Western Europe, Japan, the USSR, and even Taiwan. China was not catching up with the developed nations; it was falling further behind. People's wars of national liberation often proved dangerous or unproductive. In Indonesia, Thailand, Burma, and Malaysia, efforts to begin or heighten insurgencies proved fruitless or costly. Lin was saddled with an outmoded policy and that point was driven home in 1971 when China and the U.S. took steps which led to the Nixon visit in 1972. As primary spokesman for people's wars, Lin naturally disapproved of the Nixon visit and any hint of détente with the leader of capitalist imperialism. Moreover, improved relations with the U.S. might well lead to a reduced military budget, particularly in the areas of ICBM and advanced fighter-aircraft development. This proved to be the case following Lin's demise. Any significant reduction in resource allocation to the PLA implied a concomitant reduction in military influence and authority domestically.[123]

Finally there was the Sino-Soviet confrontation. If Lin Piao was indeed responsible for the March 2, 1969 ambush of the Soviet patrol, and if Lin then attempted to use the confrontation for his own political benefit, the tactic ultimately failed. True, Lin obtained the necessary support at the Ninth Party Congress, but the war scare continued for years thereafter at great economic cost. It took Chou En-lai's efforts to negotiate the crisis through.

Chou En-lai could be found leading the opposition to Lin on each of the policy issues. He favored a détente with the U.S. both to counter-balance the greatly heightened Soviet threat and to break China's isolated "self-sufficiency." Peking needed more international trade, and it was difficult to do much business; most of the industrialized countries ostracized China as a revolutionary threat. Chou thus benefitted greatly from Lin's demise and was a major cause of it. Mao Tse-tung's position is less clear-cut. Certainly he favored reconstructing a strong domestic Party, but he had also favored the people's war strategy. Moreover, following the Sino-Soviet split and the near total international isolation of China, Mao had made a virtue of the imposed self-sufficiency. Perhaps China's international and economic problems in the latter half of the 1960s made Mao amenable to a change of mind.

In the four years since the Lin Piao affair, the CMC has had a very low profile. Yeh Chien-ying has been the de facto and recently formalized leader of the PLA, but he remained in Chou En-lai's shadow, and after Chou's death and the dismissal of Teng Hsiao-p'ing, Yeh dropped out of sight for almost four months. The political heyday of the military leadership is definitely over, at least for the time being. The PLA is being told firmly that it must strictly obey the Party. Moreover, it should learn from the masses. This diet of crow and humble pie is in many ways deserved. It was not Lin Piao alone who, having tasted political power, thirsted for more. Many of the military men filling civilian posts in the provinces rode roughshod over the legitimate interests of others.

The PLA was invited into the civilian sectors in 1967, but it came reluctantly—especially at local and provincial levels where PLA disengagement has been painstakingly slow. At the national level, the civilian responsibilities of military leaders declined sharply after the Lin Piao affair. This is best seen by comparing the military leadership shares of the Politburo and Central Committees of the Ninth and Tenth Party Congresses of 1969 and 1973, respectively.[124]

Military Leadership Shares (in percentages)

	Politburo	Central Committee	Alternate Central Committee
Ninth Congress	55	47	45
Tenth Congress	28.5	32	30

Note that the drop, while sharp, came nowhere near elimi-
nating PLA leaders from the Party policy-making organizations. It has never been Peking's intention to expel the PLA
from civilian affairs, but rather to insert top-ranking civilians into responsible military positions.

In January 1975, the Fourth National People's Congress
promulgated a new state constitution. The chairman of the
Party was declared the commander-in-chief of the armed
forces. (The presidency was abolished.) The commander-in-
chief of the armed forces, rather than the defense minister, is
of course the chairman of the CMC. Following Mao's death
in September 1976, Hua Kuo-feng became party chairman
and thus automatically chairs the CMC.

The Fourth People's Congress also broke precedent by
appointing civilians as chief of staff and director of the
General Political Department—respectively Teng Hsiao-
p'ing and Chang Ch'un-ch'iao. Those two men were added
to the CMC. However, early in 1976, a left-wing political
offensive dismissed Teng from all his posts. Then in the
autumn, Chang was purged along with the other Politburo
"radicals," i.e., Madam Mao, Wang Hung-wen, and Yao
Wen-yuan.

The CMC Standing Committee, as presently constituted,
probably consists of Hua Kuo-feng, Yeh Chien-ying, Ch'en
Hsi-lien, Li Teh-sheng, Hsu Hsiang-ch'ien, Nieh Jung-
chen, and Chang Ta-chih. Two other possible members are
the deputy chief of staff, Chang Tsai-chen, and the Rear
Services Department chief, Chang Tsung-hsun. Their immediate and most important task is to heal the deep scars left
in the PLA by the Lin Piao affair and the GPCR. However,
the CMC is still politically powerful. It may have played an
important role in supporting Hua Kuo-feng's rapid ascend-
ency and the purge of the Politburo radicals. The CMC
probably was pleased to assist in the expulsion of the

civilians Wang Hung-wen and Chang Ch'un-ch'iao from its ranks. It remains to be seen whether or not the military leadership has any bills due against Hua Kuo-feng, and if so, what form of repayment will be sought. One likely demand might be no further appointment of civilians to top military positions.

The General Staff Department

The PLA chief of staff is in an unenviable position, since the weight of the work load is exceeded only by the political vulnerability of the office holder. Over the past decade, there have been four chiefs of staff and all have been purged—Lo Jui-ch'ing was dismissed in early 1966, Yang Ch'eng-wu fell in March 1968, and Huang Yung-sheng has not been heard of since the Lin Piao affair. The office was left vacant for over three years until a top-ranking civilian, Teng Hsiao-p'ing, was appointed at the beginning of 1975, and served for only one year prior to his removal. In at least three of the four cases (i.e., Yang, Huang, and Teng), the political downfalls came as direct results of internal power politics. Policy issues were emphasized in Lo Jui-ch'ing's dismissal, but here too, power politics was a major factor. At this writing, Peking has yet to identify a new chief of staff.

Lo Jui-ch'ing

Lo came in as chief of staff at the same time that Lin Piao became defense minister 1959. If Lo was not his handpicked candidate for the post, Lin must at least have approved of the choice. Lo's background certainly did not qualify him for the position over potential rivals. His career since 1949 had been devoted to internal security, first as commander of the old PLA Security Forces and later as minister of public security. He could hardly have been expert in military force building, training, readiness, and militia work—all of which are major responsibilities of the General Staff Department. However, Lo was well qualified for one major task facing Lin Piao in 1959—reestablishing political control over the PLA officer corps.[125]

Lo served as chief of staff from 1959 to 1966. His dismissal came in March and was formalized by a work meeting of the Central Committee the following month. Three reasons have been given for Lo's dismissal—two by the Chinese media and one by Western scholars. The Chinese claim that Lo Jui-ch'ing represented the "bourgeois military line" as distinct from Mao Tse-tung's concepts, that Lo disobeyed orders, and attempted to take power away from Lin Piao. Donald Zagoria and Uri Ra'anan view the Lo case from a foreign policy perspective and conclude that Lo was removed in a policy dispute involving China's strategy vis-à-vis the rapidly growing Vietnam War and related Sino-Soviet issues. Each of these explanations deserves separate treatment.

Was Lo Jui-ch'ing a representative of the "bourgeois military line"? The charges state that Lo opposed devoting resources to the development of the militia and the regional forces of the PLA. The implication was that he instead favored emphasizing the army corps, and spending the money saved from militia and regional forces to modernize the major ground-force units. A second and less important charge is that he conceived of and carried out "great competitions" among military units in 1964, although in the past few years, responsibility for this program has been placed on Lin Piao. These diverted efforts away from regular training exercises and tended to develop an elitist mentality much abhorred by Mao Tse-tung. Both charges are almost certainly true, but on balance, this writer finds the "bourgeois" categorization of Lo Jui-ch'ing to be specious and unconvincing.

There are three reasons why that shoe did not fit Lo: first, his background had nothing whatsoever to do with professional military units and he had no personal experience with modern combat conditons. His public security background would be far more apt to endow him with a keen political sense than it would provide him with the outlook of a former armored or artillery leader. Secondly, while he was not a great believer in the militia as a key to China's defense, he attempted only to avoid using main force units to expand the militia program. As to the regional forces, he proposed that they be converted into a part-time army, living at home during peak agricultural seasons and soldiering the rest of the year. This view is quite the opposite of a bourgeois military viewpoint and much closer to Mao's concept of having the army at one with the people.[126] Third, he proposed as late as 1965 that the regular troop units should have additional "production quotas"—i.e., they should grow more of their own food and produce more from their sideline industries. Mao himself implemented that same policy beginning in 1969-70 in order to make the PLA more self-sufficient.

Lo did ineffectually oppose the Lin Piao-led "cult of Mao" in the armed forces. He is quoted as having said: "A red head is no harder than an iron tank."[127] Yet he favored concentrating on political indoctrination in the militia where discipline and morale were low in the early 1960s. As chief of staff, Lo had to concern himself with military readiness, and he felt that the best way to do this was to modernize the army corps. However, modernization does not run counter to Maoism. Most evidence indicates that Lo favored an army which was closely tied to both the people and to production.

The second official charge against Lo was that he disobeyed orders and attempted to usurp power from Lin Piao. The evidence for this charge is convincing. Lo was seeking authority to administer the day-to-day affairs of the ground forces. This power was held by Lin, and Lo tried a variety of techniques to obtain the authority for himself. First he counseled Lin that as a sick man (Lin was wounded badly in 1937 and frequently disappeared for long periods of convalescence as late as 1970-71), he should rest more and delegate authority to others. This failing, Lo simply did things on his own authority in the absence of Lin Piao. However, the chief of staff is one of three key executive positions under the CMC, and having an atmosphere of competition, distrust, and antagonism between the CMC leader and his military operations executive officer would not do. There is no doubt that Lin wanted to be well rid of Lo Jui-ch'ing by 1965.[128]

The Vietnam War gave Lin Piao something more than a mere pretext to oust Lo: a serious policy dispute over military-diplomatic strategy in which Lo and Lin were the primary spokesmen for the opposing views. Following the ouster of Nikita Khrushchev in 1964, the USSR put out feelers to see if the Sino-Soviet conflict might not be cooled down. One of the Russian proposals was for a "united front" of socialist nations on the Vietnam War. Lo Jui-ch'ing favored accepting this offer in return for Soviet promises of a nuclear shield against possible U.S. attacks. If this condition could be obtained, Lo then favored taking a very hawkish attitude toward the Vietnam conflict and intervening in the war if North Vietnam were seriously threatened. His thinking was that the same as that of his American counterparts— it's better to meet the enemy on foreign soil than to fight later in your own backyard. He favored a "forward defense," as opposed to Mao's "protracted war" strategy in which the fighting doesn't begin until China itself has been invaded. Lo's position was supported by many top leaders and thus was not easily dismissed. His case was further strengthened because Mao himself had accepted the forward defense strategy in the Korean War.

Lin Piao countered Lo's arguments in September 1965 with the now famous speech, "Long Live the Victory of the People's War." This statement stressed that anticolonial and antiimperialist wars can be fought to a successful conclusion without outside assistance. It castigated Soviet "revisionism" as an impossible ally in such wars because Moscow itself was encouraging American imperialism. Following the presentation of the speech, the debate swung in favor of Mao and Lin.

Just prior to Lin's speech. Lo may have tried to stage a Chinese version of the Gulf of Tonkin Incident. On his own authority, he issued orders to the Fuchow Military Region Command directing that on the sea the PLA could take the initiative and carry the battle to the Chinese Nationalist ships which were occasionally raiding the coastline. According to one account, it was that order which led to small-scale naval clashes in August and November 1965,[129] which failed to have the necessary diplomatic effect. There were no threatening U.S. counter-moves that might have lent weight to Lo's contention that China needed the Soviet nuclear umbrella. However, Lo's temerity in issuing such an order under his own authority might well have been the final straw: he had made a speech a few days after Lin's in which he publicly capitulated to the Mao-Lin strategy.[130] Yet it appears that he was trying by means of his order to the Fukien Front to secretly provoke an incident which would revive hopes for his policy. The discovery of this would have been ample cause for his dismissal. He disappeared from public view in November 1965, and was criticized by the Central Committee in March 1966. Lo then jumped out of an upper story window in a futile suicide attempt—he succeeded only in breaking his leg. In April, he was formally removed from office. The conventional wisdom had it that Lo perished during the GPCR, but as it turned out, he was merely in political limbo—he reappeared in 1975. As yet, no official announcement has been made regarding his current position, but judging from protocol lists, he may be serving as a deputy chief of staff.

Yang Ch'eng-wu

Following Lo Jui-ch'ing's dismissal, Yang Ch'eng-wu was appointed acting chief of General Staff. Yang has a long and distinguished background as a unit leader, military region commander, head of the old Air Defense Command, and possibly some leadership role in the Korean War. His career well suited him for the job of chief of staff. However, he proved unable to survive the treacherous politics of the GPCR and fell from power in March 1968. It was not Yang's performance of his military functions that got him into trouble, but rather, it was the special GPCR responsibilities assigned him in the CMC which caused his downfall. Yang represented PLA interests against those of the Central Committee Cultural Revolution Group which sought to create a new order in China. It was mainly the PLA that stood in their way. However, in the GPCR, nothing was ever as simple as that—Yang was also involved in an internal PLA power struggle.

As mentioned above, when the General Political Department was suspended in July 1967, the CMC Administrative

Committee was assigned to run the PLA Cultural Revolution. Yang was the number two man on the committee under Wu Fa-hsien. In that capacity, he was charged with overseeing the PLA/GPCR in North China and later was given an additional duty of politically evaluating PLA officers.[131] He almost immediately encountered problems with the PLA Political Work Group led by Hsieh Fu-chih, which was responsible for evaluating the PLA as an instrument in the national GPCR, and was theoretically subordinate to the Administrative Committee. In fact, it operated autonomously. The potential for conflict was obvious since both organizations were independently evaluating PLA leaders and their GPCR performance. It was impossible to maintain the distinction between performance in the internal PLA/GPCR and the national movement as a whole. The situation was exacerbated because Hsieh was much closer in his attitudes to the Central Cultural Revolution Group than was Yang. At one point, Yang made a blatant effort to "pack" the Political Work Group, but was thwarted by Chiang Ch'ing.[132]

Yang Ch'eng-wu was one of the most effective opponents of Madam Mao and the Central CRG. He was careful to maintain a facade of unity with the radicals, but his actions sought to undermine their power. For example, at the end of the disastrous "drag out the small handful in the army" campaign of July-August 1967, Mao Tse-tung personally dispatched Yang to Peitaiho where Lin Piao was again convalescing. Mao instructed Yang to reach a decision with Lin as to what should be done within the ultraleftists with the Central CRG who had spearheaded the attacks on the army;[133] they were purged soon thereafter.[134] In October, Mao sent Yang to investigate problems in Shansi Province.[135] The chairman of the Shansi Revolutionary Committee was Liu Ko-p'ing, a civilian radical who reportedly had been hand picked for the post by Chiang Ch'ing. He was having trouble with the armed forces which were reluctant to support his brand of leadership. Yang apparently did nothing to help Liu, and in the aftermath of his visit, the military increasingly defied the provincial government.

On internal PLA matters, Yang also supported the conservatives. This led to increasing conflict with Hsieh Fu-chih, finally resulting in Yang's dismissal. In September 1967, Hsieh was ordered to investigate and solve factional problems between the 38th Corps on the one hand, and the 63rd Corps and the Peking Military Region on the other.[136] The 38th Corps had supported the radical Red Guard groups in Hopeh Province and Hsieh gave that unit his full support. Yang joined the investigation at some point prior to January 1968 and supported the 63rd Corps, the Peking Military Region, and the conservative mass organizations. The ensuing temporary deadlock was broken in February 1968 when the last of Madam Mao's ultraleft subordinates on the Central CRG, Ch'i Pen-yu, was purged. Yang claimed that some elements of the Red Guards supported by Hsieh and the 38th Corps were tools of the discredited ultraleftists, and obtained an order disbanding certain local Red Guard headquarters in Hopeh.[137] What happened next is still unclear, but it appears that Yang decided that was the moment to take the offensive against both Hsieh Fu-chih and the Central CRG. He worked out his strategy with Fu Ch'ung-pi who was then the commander of the Peking Garrison and had broad police powers within the capital. Fu dispatched a small PLA force to the headquarters of the Central CRG to make arrests of Ch'i Pen-yu's associates and to search certain files. The intention was probably two-fold: First, information linking the ultraleft with the radical Red Guards in Hopeh could have been used to discredit Hsieh Fu-chih. Second, Yang might well have hoped to unearth information which would severely damage the authority of the Central CRG itself. Whatever the exact intent, Yang had overreached himself. The national leadership saw this as a case where the PLA had overstepped the bounds of its authority, and Yang and Fu Ch'ung-pi were purged in late March 1968.

These struggles among Yang, Hsieh and the Central CRG were important beause a major policy issue was involved. Yang's approach to the removal and rehabilitation of cadres differed from that of both the Central CRG and Hsieh Fu-chih. In the speeches of March 24, 1968 which announced Yang's dismissal, the most consistent charge was that he had been attempting large scale "rightist reversals of verdicts," i.e., restoring to office numbers of civilian and military cadres who had been removed during the power seizures and purges of 1967. Chou En-lai described Yang's policy as follows:

> Their slogan of "preserving the old cadres" in reality did not mean the majority of cadres who were good or relatively good as stated by Chairman Mao. Their idea was to preserve the group taking the capitalist road.[138]

The remainder of Chou's speech was largely a defense of the Central CRG and its importance to the success of the GPCR. Yang had posed a serious threat and had many sympathizers in his efforts to rehabilitate a larger percentage of the politically fallen. His timing had also been good. The dismissal of the last of Chiang Ch'ing's ultraleft subordinates in February 1968 had further weakened the Central CRG. Even the leftist Shanghai newspaper, *Wen-Hui Pao,* called for a "rectification" of Red Guard organizations.[139]

Had Yang been more subtle in his "verdict reversals" and avoided an open clash with Hsieh, he might have had some measure of success. As a result of Yang's rashness, the PLA suffered a temporary setback. The GPCR leadership was alarmed at seeing numbers of their deposed enemies back in seats of power. To resist such restorations, the mass organizations were once again wound up via another newspaper and radio campaign. The levels of violence in the provinces again rose and poster attacks on military leaders became commonplace for the first time since August 1967. In areas where revolutionary committees had been established, defiance of the new governments became increasingly frequent. By late April, the policy pendulum had swung far enough that there were editorials approving "armed struggle"[140] and "proletarian factionalism."[141] The threat to the PLA, however, was slight compared to that of the summer of 1967. By May-June, the radical resurgence had spent itself without notable gains.

It was ironic that a little over a year after Yang's dismissal, Mao Tse-tung himself argued in favor of rehabilitating more dismissed and suspended cadres. With Yang's policies back in favor, it was not surprising that he too was rehabilitated in 1974. Yang is merely one of many PLA leaders who were sacked during the GPCR and have recovered politically in the post-Lin Piao period; he and Lo Jui-ch'ing are the highest ranking of the restored generals. It is this author's opinion that he probably would have made his reemergence sooner except for the staunch opposition of Madam Mao and the remaining radicals in the Peking leadership. Yang currently is the ranking deputy chief of the General Staff and may be the de facto chief of staff since Teng Hsiao-p'ing's dismissal. (Another likely candidate for this position is Chang Tsai-chen.)

Huang Yung-sheng

Formerly the commander of the Canton Military Region, Huang Yung-sheng was promoted to become Yang's replacement. He was an experienced unit commander and a longtime associate of Lin Piao. If Lin's purpose was to select a chief of staff who would be a loyal supporter, he made the right choice in Huang. Throughout the policy struggles between Lin on the one side, and Mao and Chou on the other, Huang seems to have steadfastly supported Lin Piao. In August 1971, Mao even mentioned the possibility of Huang attempting a military coup or mutiny. Huang disappeared immediately after the dramatic plane crash in Outer Mongolia in September 1971 and it is not known whether he is alive or dead.

Teng Hsiao-p'ing

In early 1975, over three years after Huang's disappearance, Teng Hsiao-p'ing was named the new chief of staff. Teng served as a political commissar in the 1930s and 1940s. After 1949 he became increasingly involved in civil administration; in 1954 he was appointed secretary general of the Central Committee, i.e., the first secretary of the Party, a post he held until his dismissal during the GPCR. As such, he served on the elite CMC Control Group, and thereby played a role in major military policy making decisions.[142]   His name was closely linked to that of President Liu Shao-ch'i as the leaders of anti-Maoist domestic policies. Unlike Liu, Teng was rehabilitated in 1973 and again held a Politburo seat along with a vice-premiership. Despite his broad experience, there were many high ranking officers with much better knowledge of internal PLA operations, military technology, training, and readiness. The only apparent reason for his appointment as chief of the General Staff Department was to help ensure civilian control over the military apparatus.

Just after the January 1976 death of Chou En-lai, Teng fell into an eclipse and was stripped of all his positions in the early spring of 1976. The issues involved seemed primarily to be domestic economic and social policies. Teng had too little concern with revolutionary objectives, and his cynically pragmatic approach to problems further offended the ideologues. The limited information on Teng's dismissal has thus far not identified military or national security issues as factors; however, there is much regarding the causes of that power struggle which is yet unknown. Meanwhile, the PLA is once again without a chief of the General Staff. Whether it will be deemed necessary to appoint another civilian remains to be seen, but whoever is chosen had best not plan on a long tenure in office followed by an honorable retirement.

The General Political Department

The General Political Department (GPD) is seen as concerned above all with political and ideological control of the PLA. The GPD leadership supposedly has a quite different view of PLA priorities from that held by professional military commanders. Frequently these diverging philosophies are referred to as competition between "red and expert." Western military analysts especially tend to view the political system as a hindrance to the "real" job of the PLA, i.e., maximizing military capabilities. The role of the GPD during the Cultural Revolution raises serious doubts about this stereotype. The first PLA victim of the GPCR was Liang Pi-yeh, a deputy director of the GPD who was dismissed

about February 1966. Lin Piao described why Liang was
ousted:

> During the winter of last year [1966] when I raised the
> point of giving prominence to politics . . . Liang Pi-yeh
> had a few things to say. He indicated that an emphasis
> on politics meant falling behind in military prepara-
> tions. This is in error. Military preparations and poli-
> tics are not to be brought up together like that.[143]

Thus the first voice raised to defend military preparedness
against the inroads of political activities came from the GPD
while the "professional" commanders were silent. This is
not to deny any "red versus expert" conflict within the
PLA—the division of military man-hours between training
on the one hand and political/civil work on the other is a
continuous issue. However, the GPD is not automatically
the leader of the "red" viewpoint.

Liang's dismissal did not harm the position of his boss
Hsiao Hua. Hsiao had become the GPD director in 1959
when Lin Piao was appointed minister of defense. Hsiao had
been a subordinate of Lin's for many years prior to 1949 and
it is generally assumed that he was hand-picked by Lin Piao
for the job.

For more than a year, the GPD led the Cultural Revolution within the PLA. In May 1966, Mao referred to "capitalist roaders" within the Party, government, and *army* who
must be dealt with. In the same month, Lin Piao specified
that the political targets were men in the top echelons.[144] By
June, the GPD had launched the PLA's own movement in
the national level organizations such as the air and naval
forces headquarters. Debates, criticisms, wall posters, and a
full airing of grievances were permitted. In terms of the
initial 1966 ground rules for a strictly limited PLA/GPCR,
the GPD seems to have finally accepted the campaign.

When the PLA Cultural Revolution Group was formed
(no later than August 1966), it was quite natural that the
GPD had a leading role in the new organization—its functions fell within the general realm of political work. The
first chairman of the group was Ho Lung, a vice-chairman

of the CMC, but much of the actual work was done by Liu
Chih-chien, a deputy director of the GPD. Liu was concurrently appointed to the Central CRG. When the GPCR was
rapidly expanded in early January 1967 and pressures were
mounting for PLA intervention, the GPD once again played
a leading role in resisting additional military involvement.
As described above, the PLA/CRG was reorganized on January 12. Ho Lung and Liu Chih-chien was dismissed and
GPD Director Hsiao Hua came under heavy Red Guard
attack. His home was ransacked, and soldiers subordinate to
Yang Yung (the Peking Military Region Commander)
passed out handbills in the streets criticizing Hsiao. A
special PLA meeting was called by Chou En-lai to resolve
the crisis.[145] Hsiao may have capitulated on the question of
military involvement because he was appointed to serve on
the new PLA/CRG along with Madam Mao. Yang Yung
was dismissed for his breach of military discipline.

Hsiao Hua again had his troubles in May 1967 when
Madam Mao's own PLA Culture and Art Troop gave a
performance in Peking which degenerated into a near riot.
The connection is obscure, but Hsiao was blamed.[146] He
weathered that crisis but was unable to hold his position
during the "drag out the small handful in the army"
campaign in August 1967. Several reasons have been given
for his dismissal but none seem totally satisfactory. One
possibility is that Hsiao resisted the campaign against the
military. The GPD leadership on the PLA/CRG had
dragged its heels each time the Cultural Revolution was
expanded. The anti-PLA campaign was the most drastic and
dangerous expansion of all. It is significant that the entire
GPD headquarters was ordered to suspend operations at the
time of Hsiao's dismissal. The political leadership within
the PLA may well have been too conservative for the tenor of
the times.

Lin Piao also charged that Hsiao Hua had run "an
independent kingdom" in the GPD: "In the past [PLA]
cadres were under the control of Hsiao Hua who neither
sought instructions nor reported to higher levels."[147] Chou
En-lai was quoted on the same occasion as having said: "Let
us not restore the practice of the GPD which took charge of

everything."[148] Chiang Ch'ing accused Hsiao Hua of "working behind closed doors"—presumably that meant running the PLA/CRG without seeking guidance from Chiang Ch'ing.[149]

Whatever the matrix of reasons, the head of the PLA political system was lopped off from its body and transferred into the CMC. As Chou En-lai explained at the time:

> The General Political Department will *temporarily* cease operations and undergo rectification, and Hsiao Hua will cease all public activities.[150]

Although "temporary," the suspension of the GPD lasted over two years, but it was not entirely moribund during that period. In March 1968, the GPD was taking in new personnel.[151]

In late 1969, a new director was finally appointed—Li Teh-sheng. Li was an odd choice since he had been a commander rather than a political commissar throughout his career. He began the GPCR as commander of the 12th Corps which was moved to Anhui Province in the spring of 1967. Following the Wuhan Incident in July, several provincial military districts were taken over and administered by army corps. Li became the commander of the Anhui Military District and later was appointed chairman of the provincial revolutionary committee. His appointment to the GPD was a further surprise considering the fact that scores of higher ranking, more senior officers were passed over in favor of Li.[152]

Another aspect of Li's appointment was unusual—he had no known connection with the "Lin Piao clique." His career experiences were in units other than the 4th Field Army (Lin's old unit). During the midst of the GPCR, practically all high ranking PLA positions in Peking went to Lin Piao's followers. Li's appointment in 1969 might be interpreted as the opening wedge at restoring some political balance within the high command. Mao was later to declare that one tactic he used in his power struggle with Lin Piao was to "mix in sand"—i.e., dilute Lin's hold on the national military establishment. Li Teh-sheng may have been the first officer promoted for that purpose. Also, charges were brought against Lin Piao (with good reason) that he overemphasized putting "politics in command." The appointment of a veteran troop commander as the leader of the political commissariat system might have been an effort to reduce the undue stress on politics. This is all the more likely since Li Teh-sheng's appointment came during the height of the Sino-Soviet border tensions and the massive war preparations campaign.

It is not surprising that Li survived the Lin Piao incident. He was one of the military leaders used by Mao to pack the CMC in 1971 and he was made a member of the Politburo Standing Committee at the Tenth Party Congress in 1973, probably as a reward for his political services in 1971-72. In late December 1973, he was transferred from his GPD position and made commander of the Shenyang Military Region. This might be considered a demotion, especially since there were unofficial wall poster criticisms of Li in 1974. Li's transfer to Shenyang was made during a general reshuffle of military region commanders; the directorship of the GPD was the only other position affected. Perhaps since he had served his political purpose, the Peking leadership preferred to see him out of the capital; military men who assist civilian leaders during political crises are usually seen as potential threats thereafter. This was certainly true for Lin Piao; it might have been true for Li as well.[153]

Although Li Teh-sheng fared moderately well while GPD director, the department itself was weakened during his tenure. Prior to the GPCR, the GPD was highly active and the most visible of the three general departments. Since 1969, it has rarely been in the news, and Li did not make important public pronouncements as did Hsiao Hua in the halcyon days before the GPCR. The GPD seems to have been reduced to handling routine administrative matters while important PLA political work is monopolized by the CMC. [154] Following Li's reposting, the directorship remained vacant for over a year during which time the leaderless GPD seemed nearly ineffectual. Any judgment as to why the organization has been down-played must be speculative, although one possibility is that the commissariat and the PLA-Party system have been intentionally deemphasized. Instead, the stress is on the newly rebuilt civilian Party apparatus, and the media has repeatedly emphasized the necessity for its independence from unwonted military influence.

Chang Ch'un-ch'iao

Chang was appointed to replace Li Teh-sheng as GPD director in early 1975. He was a civilian Politburo member who rose to prominence during the GPCR as the "Maoist" first secretary of Shanghai. Chang's experience with the PLA Party system was limited—he served as political commissar of the Nanking Military Region and the Shanghai Garrison from 1967 through 1974.[155] His appointment, like that of Teng Hsiao-p'ing to the General Staff, was intended to strengthen civilian control within the PLA. Chang was dismissed in October 1976 along with the other "Shanghai radicals" and Chiang Ch'ing. At this writing, the GPD directorship is again vacant. The next appointment will probably be a military man and he will have to do considerable rebuilding. The GPD is now the weakest of the three general departments (staff, political, and rear services). It could quickly regain much of its lost prestige and power under strong leadership; however, if a future GPD director uses that position as a launching platform for political power in the national Party apparatus (as did Hsiao Hua during the GPCR), it will indicate that the PLA is once again straining at the bonds of civilian control.

The General Rear Services Department

Until the Lin Piao affair of 1971, the General Rear Services Department (GRSD) had been comparatively stable under its director, Ch'iu Hui-tso, one of Lin Piao's old associates appointed to the GRSD at the same time that Lin became defense minister. The PLA/GPCR did, however, cause severe personal hardships for Ch'iu. In the spring of 1967, "revolutionary rebels" of the GRSD subjected him to a month long period of criticism and struggle. Lin Piao later averred that the ordeal had "nearly killed" Ch'iu.[156] However, Lin's support eventually seems to have pulled him through. In July 1967, the PLA revolutionaries admitted that they had attacked mistaken targets within the GRSD and Ch'iu's star thereafter was ascendant.[157] He was named to the PLA/CRG in the summer of 1967, and when the organization was disbanded shortly thereafter, he became a leading figure on the Administrative Committee of the CMC and a deputy chief of the General Staff. In 1969 at the Ninth Party Congress, he was selected to the most powerful organization in China—the Politburo.

There was a fair amount of turnover among GRSD deputy directors during the GPCR. However, after undertaking biographic analysis of Ch'iu's subordinates, Richard Gillespie and John Sims concluded in their detailed study of the GRSD that Ch'iu may have used the GPCR to consolidate his staff and get rid of those whose loyalties proved lacking during the struggles in the spring of 1967.[158] The same authors attribute some of Ch'iu's rapid political rise to the increased national importance of the GRSD during the period of extensive military control in the civilian sectors. His close ties with Lin Piao also helped. However, it was the latter which brought Ch'iu down. Like Huang Yung-sheng of the General Staff Department, Ch'iu loyally supported Lin to the very end. He has not been heard of since September 1971.

The GRSD was without a head for almost three years. In 1975, a new director was finally selected—Chang Tsunghsun. Chang served for over a decade as a deputy chief of the General Staff. Along with most of his colleagues, he was dismissed during the GPCR. In 1972, Chang reemerged as a deputy commander of the Tsinan Military Region, but by 1974, he was probably the acting director of the GRSD. Chang is not on the Politburo, nor is it certain that he is a member of the CMC Standing Committee. With so little access to the centers of political power, he will be unable to serve as a strong advocate of PLA interests in national resource allocations—one reason perhaps why he was chosen for the job.

Military Production, Research and Development

Secrecy in these fields is so tight that even the uncensored Red Guard tabloids provided mere glimpses of recent developments. One significant policy dispute was aired during the denunciations of former chief of staff Lo Jui-ch'ing. He was in conflict with Nieh Jung-chen—the chairman of the National Defense Science and Technology Committee. The issue was the NDSTC itself: Lo regarded it as not sufficiently productive in terms of military modernization. In his words, the NDSTC had "achieved nothing in any respect from data to design."[159] His solution was to make that organization subordinate to the military machine building ministries, thereby devoting a much larger share of technological and scientific manpower to improving production and design; in brief, there would have been less research and more development. The struggle between Lo and Nieh apparently was decided in Nieh's favor only after Lo's dismissal in 1966. Lo's alleged negative assessment of the NDSTC was obviously exaggerated in light of China's nuclear and missile programs. However, it may be that the NDSTC has neglected the ground forces, leaving much of conventional arms development to the smaller technical forces of the GRSD and General Staff Department.

Another policy debate was made public in the summer of 1971—the so-called steel versus electronics debate.[160] In an apparent policy reversal, steel became the leading factor while electronics slipped from top priority. This would seem to echo the earlier Lo Jui-ch'ing line since ground forces arms production is tied to steel, while sophisticated research and development programs rely heavily on advanced electronics. The ground forces are now obtaining proportionately more equipment while progress in electronics seems to have lagged; ICBM development especially seems to have suffered. Through the use of multiple stage rockets, China is capable of building sufficiently powerful boosters, but seems unable to work out guidance system problems. So far there has been only one report of a reduced range(2000-2500 miles) ICBM test, and full range firings are necessary to prove the reliability and accuracy of guidance systems.[161]

During the GPCR itself, defense production declined. The 2nd-7th Machine Building Ministries and the NDSTC were thrown entirely open to "revolution." Factional fighting among rival revolutionary groups, power seizures, and counter-power seizures snarled PLA scientific and production work at the top. By 1968, most of the struggles had been settled, although the 6th (ship building) and 7th (missiles) Ministries continued to have severe problems as late as April-June. Early in the GPCR, Lin Piao appointed Su Yu, a vice-minister of defense, to oversee military production. In June 1968, Su described production within the 7th Ministry as being "at a standstill."[162] The CIA estimated the overall military procurement decline in 1967 at 12 percent; however, it recovered quickly and reached a new high during the 1969-70 war preparations campaign.[163] New plants were constructed in the provinces and skilled manpower was supplied by stripping it away from civilian factories. Unskilled labor came from communes. Neither the needs of the harvest nor any other impediments were allowed to override the expansion of military production.[164] By 1971, procurement levels were approximately 240 percent higher than in 1964.[165] Military procurement from 1968 to 1971 had risen about 30 percent faster than the overall industrial output; thus it grew at the expense of civilian needs such as agricultural mechanization.

The situation changed markedly after the Lin Piao affair. The CIA estimated that military procurement declined about 20 percent in 1972—most notable was the cutback in aircraft production.[166] A good part of the decline was probably due to the severely weakened political power of the PLA following Lin's death. Military leaders were no longer able to win the budgetary wars over resource allocations. They had been receiving far more than their fair share from 1969 to 1971, so the balance was redressed at first opportunity. There is, however, a possibility that the military budget did not decline proportionately with reduced procurement. Some of those "lost" funds may have been spent in PLA research and development projects.[167] In any case the 1973 procurement level was double that of 1964, so the PLA is still rapidly expanding its inventory.

Of equal importance with the decline in military procurement has been the changing pattern of PLA expenditures and force building generally. Peter Sargent and Jack Harris have pointed out that the recent decline in aircraft production and ICBM development has followed hard on the heels of a new international security policy. In the mid-1960s, the conventional wisdom in Peking postulated that the two superpowers were colluding in an attempt to divide the world into separate spheres of influence. Soviet-American détente, the test ban and nuclear nonproliferation treaties, and strategic arms limitation proposals were all viewed as means of perpetrating superpower hegemony. In order to cope with this situation, China had to prepare for the possibility of a war in which Peking would be fighting on two fronts against the Soviets and Americans. Intercontinental strategic weapons would be necessary to deter the U.S. from attacking China, thus the air and naval forces and the Second Artillery received first priority in force building.

Beginning in 1968, the conventional wisdom was challenged by those who argued that Soviet-American détente was specious. The two superpowers derive their strength from imperialism, and imperialistic countries are bound to compete with one another for raw materials, markets, and the glory of empire, and the U.S. and USSR would prove unable to cooperate against China. This position was strengthened by the announcement of the Nixon Doctrine, Vietnamization, and the 1969 Sino-Soviet border clashes. The new view prevailed in the 1972-74 period which saw the Nixon trip to China, the continued decline of American military presence in Asia, and the normalization of relations with Japan. Over the past several years, Moscow has been deemed the major threat. Therefore, the PLA force building concept has switched to an emphasis on medium and intermediate range ballistic missiles and the modernization of the ground forces—especially in terms of additional armor and artillery. ICBM development virtually ceased in the 1972-75 period, although that could be attributed to technological problems as well as allocation of resources. Likewise, the production of China's only strategic bomber, the Tu-16, ceased after 1971, presumably in favor of the

IRBM, the deployment of which began about the same time. The Tu-16 would be ineffective against the USSR; the IRBM serves as a genuine deterrent against Russian attack.[168] In 1975-76, Peking has been attempting to shore up its own air defense weakness by shopping the international market for advanced jet engines and fighter aircraft. As of mid-1976, China had purchased $160 million worth of Rolls Royce "Spey" jet engines from Britain and fifteen "Super Frelon" heavy helicopters from France. Discussions concerning the purchase of Mirage and/or Hawker-Hunter jet fighters have not as yet resulted in any sales.

Conclusion

Together the GPCR and the Lin Piao affair have wreaked havoc with the high command. In addition to the disruptions recounted above, practically all of the service arms were heavily purged during the GPCR and again experienced many dismissals after Lin's death. It is probably not coincidental that the navy, which has had the greatest leadership continuity over the past decade, is now faring comparatively well in terms of growth and modernization. The CMC has also protected the high priority status of military research and development, and to a lesser extent, weapons production. However, the position of defense minister has weakened and a number of important military posts remained vacant for three to four years following Lin's disappearance. In terms of resource allocation and modernization, the PLA has been on the defensive since 1971.

Why were so many top level positions allowed to remain vacant for so long? Why did Peking choose politically weak officers or powerful civilians to eventually fill those posts in 1974-75? These questions can be answered in a number of contradictory ways. Given the total absence of evidence, any suggestions must be speculative. It is this author's belief that the high command was, for more than three years, intentionally kept as weak as possible in order to firmly reestablish the axiom that the Party must control the gun. The CMC was first packed by Mao Tse-tung, including the addition of the civilian Party theorist Wang Hung-wen. Then in 1971, those of Lin's followers on the CMC who did not perish with him were removed; the CMC is presumably now under control. At this writing, both the chief of staff position and the directorship of the General Political Department are again vacant. Precedent was shattered in 1974 when civilians were appointed to fill those military positions. Top officials have always played a role in military policymaking, but this was the first time that civilians penetrated the executive organizations of the PLA.

The military must have presented a very serious threat to Mao and the civilian leadership after the GPCR. Mao had launched the Cultural Revolution in order to regain control over the Party bureaucracy only to find at the end of the campaign that he had traded one uncontrolled bureaucracy for another. PLA dominance was so extensive that a protracted process has been required to disentangle it from political leadership roles and restore a normal governmental balance. The appointment of civilian Party leaders to executive PLA positions did much to restore such a balance. One might expect the pendulum to swing back somewhat in the near future. The 1976 death of Mao and the purge of Teng Hsiao-p'ing and Chang Ch'un-ch'iao could enable the military leadership to regain control of its own high command.

4

The Army's Main Forces

The infantry is the pride of the PLA. Although the air force may have aging planes and the navy is primarily a coastal defense force, the thirty-seven or thirty-eight army corps are comparable with the world's best soldiery. A high morale is the combined result of ideological commitment, pride of unit, nationalism, and readiness. In small unit tactics and individual fighting ability, the Chinese soldier has proven himself against United Nations forces in Korea (prior to PLA modernization and while woefully short of supplies and fire power) and against the Indian army in the one-sided 1962 border war. Equipment shortcomings render the Chinese somewhat weaker than the U.S. or the USSR on a division-to-division comparison; however, it is a basic tenet of both the U. S. and Soviet Union to avoid a conventional war on the Chinese mainland. That is a direct compliment to the infantry, as well as a realistic appraisal of China's geography.

Organization

In the mid-1960s, there were two or three types of army corps, divided according to the amount of vehicles, armor, and artillery in each. This distinction probably still holds true in the mid-1970s. The type A units are relatively modernized; the type B units rely heavily on pack animals and manpower and have less artillery and armor.[1] A third type C corps is a light infantry organization with about two-thirds the manpower of types A and B, no medium artillery, and no armor. Such units are best suited to mountain and jungle warfare, and most of the half-dozen or so type C corps are located accordingly.[2] It may be that additional type C corps would be activated in time of war to combine and coordinate the operations of the regional forces' light infantry divisions.

At full strength, A and B corps number 46,000-51,000 men of whom about 5600 are officers. While there are now far more type A than type B units, the latter are especially well suited to fighting in rugged terrain where vehicles and heavy equipment are more an impediment than a help. Nearly all of the corps in North China and Manchuria are type A. Chart VI is a simplified diagram of army corps organization applicable to both type A and type B units. Chart VII shows the standard separation of functions within the army corps, regardless of type. The Appendix at the end of the book, prepared by Harlan Jencks of the University of Washington, includes organizational charts for all infantry units from company through division levels. Also see Table 2 for a list of the equipment for a typical army corps.

Chart VI is self-explanatory, but Chart VII requires some explication. Within the Rear Services Department, there is a duplication which is not graphically portrayed. Most of the offices in the left hand column have a rear area component and a combat area component. The Military Service Office apparently handles personnel replacements and demobilizations—a function carried out by the political departments in smaller units. Most of the functional offices also exist at division level.

Military Regions

While not solely concerned with the infantry, the role of military regions should be discussed here because they have crucial command and support functions relative to the army corps. Should China be invaded, the regions would form "fronts" or "theaters" (see accompanying map) and the regional commanders would take full control of all forces in

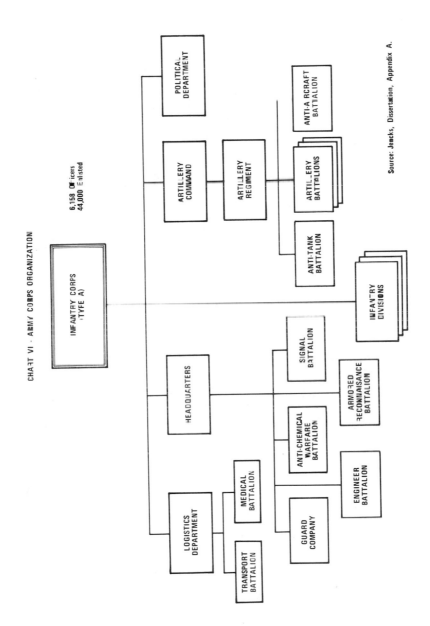

CHART VI - ARMY CORPS ORGANIZATION

INFANTRY CORPS (TYPE A)

6,158 Officers
44,000 Enlisted

POLITICAL DEPARTMENT

ARTILLERY COMMAND

ARTILLERY REGIMENT

ANTI-AIRCRAFT BATTALION

ARTILLERY BATTALIONS

ANTI-TANK BATTALION

INFANTRY DIVISIONS

HEADQUARTERS

SIGNAL BATTALION

ARMORED RECONNAISANCE BATTALION

ANTI-CHEMICAL WARFARE BATTALION

ENGINEER BATTALION

MEDICAL BATTALION

GUARD COMPANY

LOGISTICS DEPARTMENT

TRANSPORT BATTALION

Source: Jencks, Dissertation, Appendix A.

CHART VII · SEPARATION OF FUNCTIONS WITHIN ARMY CORPS

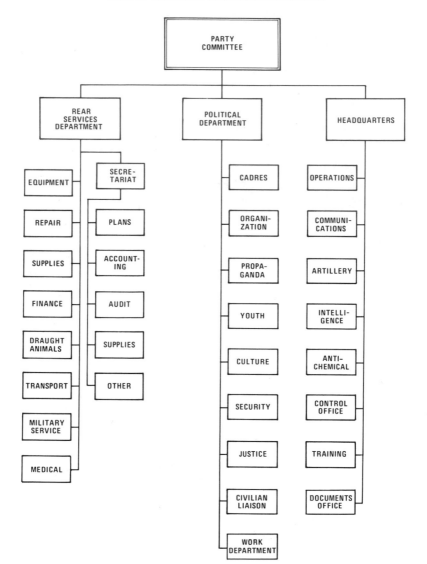

Table 2

Major Items of Equipment and Weapons, Type A Infantry Corps

Item	Corps total	Corps artillery command	Inf. div. (3)	Inf. regt. (9)	Inf. bn. (27)	Inf. co. (81)	Inf. plat. (243)	Inf. sqd. (729)	Tank regt. (3)
Pistol	10,000	*	*	*	*	*	*	*	*
Assault Rifle	17,000	*	*	*	*	*	*	*	*
Carbine	17,000	*	*	*	*	*	*	*	*
Light Machinegun	900	*	*	*	*	*	3	1	*
Heavy Machinegun (7.62mm)	550-750	**	**	63	21	3			**
Heavy Machinegun (12.7mm)	138		45	15					
Antitank Launcher (RPG)	729		243	81	27	9			
Mortar (60mm)	168		54	18	6	2			
Mortar (82mm)	243		81	27	9				
Mortar (120mm)	36		12	4					
Antiaircraft Gun (37mm)	72	18	18						
Recoilless Gun (57mm)	54		18	6	2				
Recoilless Gun (75mm)	54		18	6					
AT Gun (57mm)	324		108	21					
AT Gun (85mm)	12	12							
Field Gun (76.2mm)	36		12						
Howitzer (76.2mm)	48		16						
Field Gun (122mm)	48	48							
Howitzer (122mm)	48	48							
Howitzer (152mm)	12	12							
Flame Thrower	162		54						
Medium Tank	279		93						93
Tank (light and amphibious)	30								
Armored Personnel Carrier	0-200***								
Jeep	270								
Truck (¾ ton)	1,400								
Truck (2½ ton)	675								
Special Vehicles (Tractors, etc.)	310								
Draft Animals	50								

*Distribution of individual weapons and LMGs is not determinable with available data. Some individuals are not armed. Some support and HQ elements have LMGs for close-in defense.

**Numbers of 7.62mm HMGs vary depending on number of available APCs. Each APC mounts an LMG.

***APCs are probably held in special transportation units at corps, division, or regimental levels, and assigned on a task organization basis. Each APC carries one squad of infantry.

their regions—including tactical control of air and naval forces. There are air and naval departments within the regional headquarters (except for landlocked military regions such as Chengtu, Lanchow, and Sinkiang where naval forces are not present) which serve as liaison offices in peacetime, but could become operational departments during war. The air districts were recently reorganized, making them generally coterminous with the military regions, presumably to facilitate coordination between air and ground forces. Even in peacetime, the powers of the military regions are extensive—they have full operational control

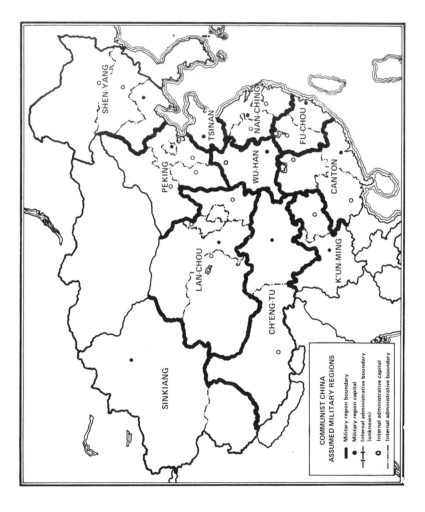

COMMUNIST CHINA
ASSUMED MILITARY REGIONS

Military region boundary
Military region capital
Internal administrative boundary
(unknown)
Internal administrative capital
Internal administrative boundary

over the regional forces, including the urban garrisons of all but the largest cities.[3]

The control of the army corps is a complex balance between the military region headquarters and the high command in Peking. Important operational orders to main force units originate or are approved in Peking.[4] Such orders are normally transmitted through the military region and then to the units; however, the high command has the capability of issuing direct orders to main force units as low as regimental level.[5] While the military regions cannot order about the army corps as they see fit, their powers are otherwise potent. They have *administrative* responsibility for all ground forces in their geographic jurisdictions. The regions (and to some extent, their subordinate military districts) are responsible for implementing all political and general directives to the army units and for handling military-civilian relations, training, and military justice. Perhaps their most important single peacetime role is looking after the logistical needs of the troop units. The Party committees of the regions make recommendations on promotions and transfers of main force division and corps leaders,[6] and have complete control over the leadership of the regional forces.[7] The regions are also in charge of recruitment and demobilization, and until 1974-75, had full control of the paramilitary production-construction corps. Finally, they are responsible for militia training and readiness, although the military districts do most of the work with the militia. The ground forces combat support arms—artillery, armor, and engineers—are represented in the military region headquarters, although they, like the army corps, may look to Peking for operational control in peacetime. For the approximate organization of a military region, see Chart VIII which is self-explanatory, except for the "Mobilization Department," which deals with war preparations, civil defense, and probably keeps track of demobilized servicemen, since the PLA has no formal reserve system. The "People's Armed Forces Department" is in charge of militia training.[8]

The military region system is clearly tailored for a defensive war. They are well prepared for deploying troops and mobilizing resources to protect their own territories, but are not organized to mount sizable military expeditions across China's borders. In the Korean War, for example, Peking created a special high level headquarters and used the adjoining Shenyang Military Region primarily as a staging area and logistics base rather than as an operational command center. The 1968-69 dissolution of the Inner Mongolia and Tibet Military Regions was a further indication of this

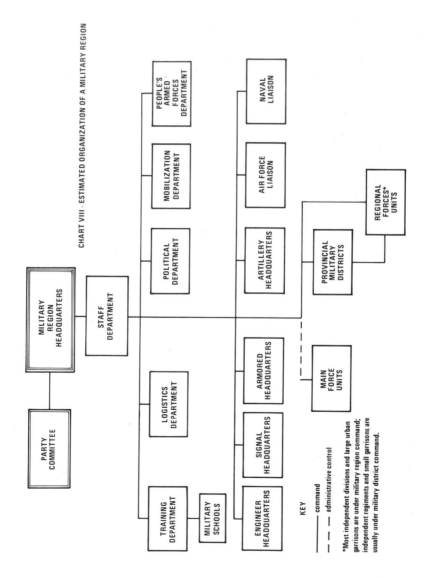

CHART VIII - ESTIMATED ORGANIZATION OF A MILITARY REGION

KEY

———— command

– – – administrative control

*Most independent divisions and large urban garrisons are under military region command; independent regiments and small garrisons are usually under military district command.

defensive thinking. Inner Mongolia has few natural barriers to slow a Soviet invasion force, and it is quite narrow on its north-south axis and very elongated to the west and north-east.Therefore, the region was subdivided among the Peking, Lanchow, and Shenyang headquarters, which are less apt to be cut in half and surrounded in the event of an invasion from the north. Tibet is too remote and the forces there too few to justify anything more than military district status, especially now that the threat of insurgency has been virtually eliminated. If China had aggressive designs against India, Tibet would not have been downgraded to a military district.

One military region serves as the strategic reserve area for the others: the Wuhan Headquarters was selected for this role, presumably because of its central location, large industrial base, and good rail communications with other areas. It contains at least half of the airborne units (the 15th Corps) several armored, artillery, and anti-aircraft artillery divisions, and two additional army corps which could be deployed toward any threatened area in case of need.

Training

The army corps train in a ten month cycle, preceded by two months in the spring which are devoted to the absorption and basic unit training of the annual draft of recruits. The cycle begins with individual training and progresses through small unit training to major divisional and corps exercises in late autumn and winter. At least one third of all training is at night.[9] Infantry forces practice close-in "hugging" tactics; the concept being to emplace PLA troops as near as possible to enemy positions, thus making it difficult for the adversary to use tactical nuclear weapons. It also serves to lessen any artillery advantage which the enemy might have. Once the fighting closes down to a few hundred yards, the PLA main forces have about as much firepower per unit as any army.

New recruits go through basic training in a "training division" attached to a military region headquarters. Most then go directly to their assigned unit for on-the-job training. A few go on for technical education, mostly at specialized branch schools. Military region schools also train company and field grade officers.[10]

Training was badly neglected during the GPCR, but proficiency has been fully recovered in the 1970s. Individual and small unit training are excellent. Combined arms training is probably less adequate and officers are more specialized than in Western armies—e.g., a typical infantry commander would know less about the employment of armor and artillery than his American counterpart. The ordinary foot soldier is also less technically proficient than Western infantrymen. The Chinese peasant soldier offsets that disadvantage with physical toughness, endurance, and a readiness to fight long and hard with minimal supplies and amenities.

Capabilities

For years the obvious weaknesses of the Chinese ground forces have been much reiterated; i.e., lack of firepower and mobility. Specifically, the PLA is described as short of artillery, armor, trucks, and personnel carriers. Much of the equipment is considered obsolescent. Critics point out that Chinese firepower does not begin to equal that of the U.S. or Soviet forces until the opposing troops are within a few hundred meters of each other. Furthermore, the capabilities of the ground forces actually deteriorated during the 1960s as compared with the previous decade. From 1960 to 1964, the economic aftereffects of the Great Leap Forward combined with the Sino-Soviet split to diminish the military inventories. During the latter half of the decade, the GPCR absorbed about one million men of the main forces in political and economic control roles. Military training also came to a virtual halt from 1966 to 1968.

By the mid-1970s, many of the weaknesses had been ameliorated. China now produces all types of conventional ground force weapons. Artillery production has gone up markedly in recent years and China now has as many guns as the USSR and three times as many as the United States.[11]

Of course, because the ground forces are so large, there are still fewer guns per unit than in the Russian or American armies. The artillery pieces are indigenously produced versions of World War II Russian designs. However, such guns are not outmoded—they have longer ranges than do equivalent U.S. weapons, although their fire control systems are less sophisticated. Chinese artillery pieces are towed rather than self-propelled, but that is probably a plus factor rather than a weakness: towed guns are more easily maintained, and if necessary can be moved by muscle. Guns which rely on their own engines and tracks are virtually useless in case of mechanical failure. One continuing weakness is antitank weaponry. The foot soldiers still rely on the conventionally styled RPG-7 rocket launcher, whereas the most modern armies have portable antitank guided missiles which have greater range, accuracy, and striking power than the old bazooka-type weapons. However, the RPG-7 is still quite capable of knocking out a modern tank.

As for armor, China is producing three types of tanks, an armored personnel carrier, and a light reconnaissance vehicle. The tanks are all copies of Soviet designs: the T-59 medium (the main battle tank, carrying a 100 mm gun), the T-62 light (not to be confused with the Russian T-62 medium), and the T-60 amphibious (i.e., a modification of the Russian PT-76 with a more powerful engine and a larger gun). All three types are now one generation out of date, but by no means obsolete. In total numbers, China has 10,000 tanks, which is about the same as the U.S. Army but only one fourth of the Soviet total.[12] Over the past several years, China has proven capable of producing almost 1000 tanks annually, although the average is probably closer to 600-800.

Thus many of the long-standing weaknesses of the ground forces have been at least partially overcome. Firepower has improved greatly over the past decade. Mobility is still lagging—the immense size of the ground forces partially makes up for the lack of strategic mobility, but the units are still at a disadvantage tactically. On balance, the strengths of the ground forces far outweigh their weaknesses. For fifteen years following the establishment of the People's Republic of China, the PLA ground forces were certainly the most important deterrent to would-be attackers. Although nuclear weapons are now a significant deterrent, had China lacked a powerful army, the U.S. or the USSR might well have taken military measures against China in the 1960s or early 1970s.[13]

Recent History

The old field armies were highly active in China's provincial administration from 1949 to 1953. However, with the establishment of the constitutional government in 1954, the political control apparatus was put in the hands of the civilian leadership. The field armies were abolished and their subordinate army corps were returned to their barracks, where they remained until the GPCR created a political crisis of such magnitude that they were reluctantly and gradually reimmersed in the business of running China's provinces. The story of the political reemergence of the main forces and the post-GPCR efforts to again disentangle them from the civilian sector constitutes the central theme of this recent history section.

Involvement in the Cultural Revolution

When the army was first ordered to intervene in the GPCR (January 1967) the regional forces bore the responsibilities (as described in Chapter 2). Some political cadres from army corps were dispatched to carry out liaison with mass organizations, but with few exceptions, the main forces played a token role from January to March 1967. Two developments in the GPCR brought a much deeper involvement: first, it became necessary to establish military control over all political and economic organizations, including relatively small factories and many schools. This was partly the result of Party paralysis which occurred in the aftermath of the January-February mass organization "power seizures" of government and Party offices. In addition, many cities bordered on anarchy, requiring a strong military presence to maintain essential services and to prevent the urban economy from grinding to a halt. The one-million-strong regional forces were insufficient, and the army corps (and some land-based naval and air force units) were called in to assist. Another major cause of main force involvement was the poor political performance of the regional forces (described in Chapter 2).

There were at least two important advantages in using army corps for GPCR roles. First, they had few ties to the old Party bureaucracy in the provinces and thus were much less apt to be opposed to the "revolutionary left" than were the regional forces. Secondly, the army corps were operationally controlled from Peking and so not entirely subject to the orders of military districts and regions, some of which had already proven hostile to the mass movement.[14] Offsetting these advantages was one very important disadvantage—the use of army corps seriously degraded China's defenses at a time when the Vietnam War was worsening and Soviet forces had already begun their buildup along the northern border. Therefore, initially, less than half of the army corps were assigned GPCR duties and several of those detached only one of their divisions for the purpose. Also, during the spring of 1967, main force officers were not given important provincial political posts. The corps have always been China's defensive bulwark, and tying their leaders to provincial jobs would be contrary to common sense as well as contrary to Mao's strategic principles. Yet political needs were soon to overwhelm all other scruples and the army corps were to be committed largely to political tasks.

The magnitude of the political crisis in the late winter and spring of 1967 can be seen by a glance at the accompanying map and Table 3. Nearly all of the relocations depicted occurred between late March and June of 1967;[15] more troops were moved in that brief period than at any time since the Korean War. A minimum of eleven corps either moved their headquarters or dispatched subordinate divisions to outside provinces. Other corps which did not relocate were also involved as "central support the left" units. Given the limited authority of military regions over main force units, it can be safely assumed that all unit moves were ordered by Peking, including relocations within a single province or military region.

On what basis were individual corps chosen for this role?

The field army origins of the units provided no correlation.[16] What is apparent from the map is the selection of units from areas of lowest external threat, e.g., the North Korean border. No units were moved from the Fukien Front nor from the Sino-Soviet border; Kiangsi, for example, was virtually devoid of troops in early 1967. When forces were required there, reserve divisions from one corps in Shantung and one in Kwangtung were dispatched. The much closer and larger Fukien Front forces remained undisturbed and played little role in the GPCR. The Foochow Military Region and its independent and garrison units in Fukien Province were quite active, but the strategic forces opposite Taiwan were left alone. Peking's political control over its main forces and its military regions was strong enough for it to select its corps on the basis of military expediency.

In one respect the table and map are misleading, since they suggest huge military units moving into concentrated areas. This was not the method adopted. When a unit arrived, it was broken into its subunits, often merely of company or platoon size, in order to cover the greatest possible territory and maintain "extensive liaison with the masses." For example, a company assigned to "support the left" was cited for its efforts in sideline production "despite the fact that the company relocated fourteen times in 1968."[17] A provincial radio station, reviewing the exploits of one of the more illustrious corps during the course of the GPCR, stated in 1969 that the 47th Corps had had men in "fifteen provinces and cities as far north as Shantung."[18] The Corps had initially been stationed on the Hunan-Kwangtung border in south China. Its headquarters was relocated once in 1967 and subordinate divisions were sent to Canton and Kwangsi. That small subunits and/or liaison cadres ranged as far as 600 miles in other directions is striking testimony to the high degree of decentralization imposed upon units in order to meet the extensive needs for military presence.

Following the dramatic breach of discipline by regional forces in the July 1967 Wuhan Incident, the GPCR involvement of the main forces was further heightened. Additional units were used bringing the total up to about twenty-two of the thirty-six army corps then in existence. The earlier ban

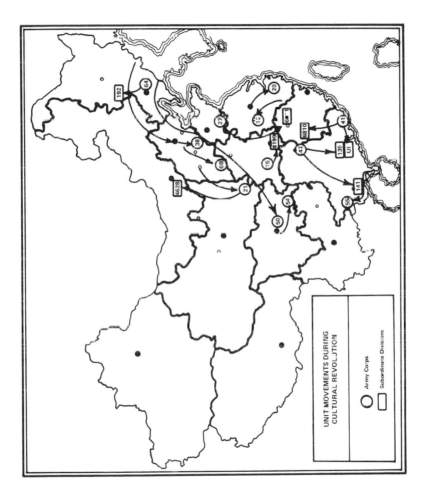

Table 3

Annex to Map Showing Approximate
Relocation of PLA Main Force Units, 1967

The 1965 locations of corps as listed in the *PLA Unit History* were accepted as correct unless otherwise stipulated. A survey of Red Guard, official and foreign journalistic reporting and Chinese radio broadcasts was carried out seeking indications of unit relocations during the Cultural Revolution. Evidence sufficient for inclusion in these notes consisted of direct mention of a unit move in Red Guard press, or known military leaders appearing in new locations while still identified in their unit roles. Corroboration was sought in semi-official Chinese Nationalist sources such as those of the Institute of International Relations (*Issues and Studies* and *Chinese Communist Affairs, Facts and Features*). The latter materials were useful because the Chinese Nationalist Government often quickly released " officially collected " documents and information. Such references were not, however, accepted as decisive. Some of the unit movements reported in Taiwan publications did not take place, or more often, lacked corroborative evidence. On the other hand, no genuine unit movements were discovered which had not been reported in Chinese Nationalist publications. Finally, there was my own previous knowledge of the subject. From 1965–70 I was employed by the U.S. Departments of Defence and State analyzing the role of the PLA in the Cultural Revolution.

12th Corps: (Unit 6408) Transferred to Anhui from Chekiang/Anhui border area, *Facts and Features*, Vol. II, No. 3, 27 November 1968, p. 17; *Issues and Studies*, Vol. II, No. 2, November 1970, p. 79. *PLA Unit History* placed the 12th Corps headquarters in Wuhan in 1964. It possibly moved to Anhui from there. Madam Mao made reference to its " return " to Anhui, see *SCMP*, No. 4069, 29 November 1967, p. 6. The 34th Division mentioned therein is subordinate to the 12th Corps. See also *SCMP*, No. 4099, 15 January 1968, p. 16.

15th Corps: A subordinate paratroop division No. 8199 moved from Hsiao Kan, just outside Wuhan, into the municipal area during the kidnapping incident there in July 1967. *SCMP* No. 4048, 26 October 1967, p. 13. See also, Thomas Robinson, " The Wuhan Incident," *The China Quarterly*, No. 47, July–September 1971, pp. 424–8. Robinson also cites Unit No. 8190 as moved into the city at that time as part of the airborne troops. Possibly No. 8190 was also part of the 15th, which may be the parent unit for the PLA airborne forces.

20th Corps: (Unit 6409) Moved from Nanking into Chekiang Province in May (?) 1967. *Facts and Features*, Vol. II, No. 3, 27 November 1968, p. 16; FBIS, 15 August 1967, pp. ccc 18–19.

21st Corps: (Unit 8133) Moved from Shansi to Shensi with one subordinate division No. 4628 going on to Hu-ho-hao-t'e, Inner Mongolia (refer-

Table 3 cont'd.

enced by Inner Mongolia Radio, 29 August 1967). Probably arrived in April with the dismissal of Ulanfu. *Facts and Features*, Vol. I, No. 24, 18 September 1968, p. 7; *Issues and Studies*, Vol. IV, No. 7, April 1968, p. 21. This corps did not move at a later date to Yunnan as reported elsewhere in Chinese Nationalist publications.

27th Corps: Dispatched the 6011 Division from Shantung to Kiangsi, possibly in May 1967. FBIS, 15 August, p. ccc 15, and 16 August, p. ddd 32. *SCMP*, No. 4081, 15 December 1967, p. 11.

38th Corps: (Unit 4800) Transferred from the Korean border area of Kirin to Peking and later to Paoting, Hopeh. Dates are uncertain, but the initial move to Peking was no later than March 1967. *SCMP*, No. 4227, 27 July 1968, p. 8; No. 4115, 9 February 1968, p. 19; *Issues and Studies*, Vol. VI, No. 12, September 1970, p. 25.

41st Corps: Sent the 6810 Division to Kiangsi, May (?) 1967 and in August dispatched a second division from the corps headquarters area in eastern Kwangtung to Canton City. The latter was reported by travellers to Hong Kong and others who had read posters welcoming the 41st to Canton; in *Sing-yao-yat Pao*, Hong Kong, 15 August 1967. For the move to Kiangsi, see the 27th Corps above.

42nd Corps: One division acted as a garrison unit in Canton City during the late spring and early summer of 1967. It was displaced in August by divisions of the 47th and 41st Corps. No information as to location after that date. *SCMP*, No. 4264, 24 September 1968, p. 7.

47th Corps: (Unit 6900) Moved from Kwangtung to Hunan in August 1967. Its 139th Division joined a division of the 41st Corps in occupying Canton, August 1967. The 141st Division of the 47th was sent to Kwangsi in June (?). The 140th Division remained in Hunan at the new Corps headquarters location – Changsha. Jürgen Domes did a neat piece of detective work in identifying all three divisions and their locations in "Generals and Red Guards," Part Two, *Asia Quarterly*, Brussels, No. 2, 1971. p. 129. See also, *Facts and Features*, Vol. I, No. 24, 18 September 1968, p. 7; *Issues and Studies*, Vol. VII, No. 2, November 1970, p. 84; also No. 6, March 1971, p. 99. Relevant Red Guard materials are in *SCMP*, No. 4264, 24 September 1968, p. 7; 4097, 11 January, 1968, p. 9; 4101, 22 January 1968, p. 10; 4070, 30 November 1967, p. 11; 4175, 10 May 1968, p. 6; and 4237, 13 August 1968, p. 15.

50th Corps: Moved from the North Korean border area to Chengtu, Szechuan, May 1967. *SCMP*, No. 4181, 20 May 1968, pp. 1–9.

54th Corps: Transferred headquarters from Chengtu to Chungking, Szechuan upon arrival of the 50th Corps, *ibid.*

55th Corps: (Unit 6955) Dispatched from Kwangtung to Kwangsi, June (?) 1967. Elements of the 55th were also mentioned in south-west Kwangtung, October 1967. *SCMP*, No. 4104, 22 January 1968, p. 10; 4119, 15 February 1968, p. 8; and 4202, 20 June 1968, p. 8. One regiment

Table 3 cont'd.

was dispatched to guard rail lines in the Canton area; *SCMP*, No. 4080, 14 December, 1967, p. 8. The presence of the 55th units in south-west Kwangtung makes that location the likely headquarters of the Corps prior to Cultural Revolution re-deployments.

64th Corps: Dispatched its 192nd Division from Liaoning to Changchun, Kirin Province by August 1967. *Facts and Features*, Vol. II, No. 3, 27 November 1968, p. 13.

69th Corps: Moved from Paoting, Hopeh to Shansi, March 1967. *Facts and Features*, Vol. I, No. 26, 16 October 1968, pp. 21–3. *Communist China Yearbook*, 1968 (Hong Kong: Union Research Institute), p. 208.

Other Army Corps Active During the Cultural Revolution

1st Corps: The major " central support the left " unit in Honan.

13th and 14th Corps in Yunnan: Factional struggles between these main force units in the winter of 1967–8.

18th Corps in Tibet: Its 52nd Division was seemingly delegated to support the left in Lhasa.

39th Corps: Administered the Anshan Iron and Steel Works in Liaoning Province, from August 1967.

63rd Corps: Hopeh-Shansi border area; was placed in charge of major coal fields there.

66th Corps: Provided troops in Tientsin, spring 1967.

67th Corps: Took over the Tsingtao Garrison, Shantung Province, August 1967.

Other Corps, *e.g.*, the 16th, 24th, 26th, 30th, 31st, 46th, 48th, 60th and 68th remained largely outside the political affairs of the Cultural Revolution, even though some were in strife-torn provinces.

against assigning responsible political positions to leaders of main force units was also forgotten. Mao Tse-tung had lost faith in the political reliability of the regional forces—especially the military district commands with their very close ties to the old Party apparatus. Even before the Wuhan Incident, Mao had expressed his concern:

> Towards the end of May, I wrote a few words to Comrade Lin Piao and Premier Chou En-lai pointing out that the antagonism between the Kiangsi Military District and the masses deserved study. I did not draw a conclusion. I referred to Kiangsi, Hunan, Hupeh and Honan.[19]

Beginning in early August, three of the four military districts referred to by Mao were reorganized (i.e., taken over) by main force units.[20] Four other provinces reorganized by main force units were Anhui, Chekiang, and Kirin military districts, and the Sinkiang Military Region.[21] Districts which possibly received such treatment but for which the evidence is inconclusive are Shensi, Kiangsu, Ninghsia, and Liaoning. The units and military leaders involved in this unprecedented development are listed in Tables 4 and 5.

Several cities and garrisons were taken over as well. For example, Chang Feng and Chao Shao-kang, the commander and political commissar of the 39th Corps were ordered in August 1967 to assume control of Anshan, Liaoning Province—the largest steel-producing center in China.[22] Elsewhere, Fang Ming, political commissar of air force Unit 7250, took over the Wuhan Garrison following the kidnapping incident. His unit was converted into the garrison force.[23] Virtually all those provinces not reorganized by main force units had army corps and/or air and naval officers added to revolutionary committees or the "preparatory groups" for revolutionary committees.

Those provinces which avoided the "reorganizations" of August 1967 may still have had their military district commands weakened. In Kwangtung, for example, the leaders of the military district survived the month of August politically intact; however, they may have been largely devoid of

Table 4

Military Districts Reorganized by Main Force Units

Province	Units	Unit Leaders and Provincial Positions Assumed	Source
Anhui	12th Corps (Unit 6408)	Li Teh-sheng, commander 12th Corps. Commander, Anhui Military District since August 1967. Became chairman, Anhui Revolutionary Committee when formed in April 1968. 12th Corps political commissar Chang Wen-i became political commissar of the military district in August 1967. Other 12th Corps leaders on the Revolutionary Committee are: Vice-chairmen Liao Ch'eng-mei and Sung P'ei-chang.	SCMP, No. 4099, 15 January 1968, p. 16 SCMP, No. 4069, 29 November 1967, p. 6
Chekiang	20th Corps (Unit 6409) 5th Air Army (Unit 7350)	Nan P'ing, political commissar of 20th Corps, became political commissar of Chekiang Military District, August 1967 and chairman of the Revolutionary Committee when formed in March 1968. Hsiung Ying-t'ang, commander of the 20th Corps, took command of the military district in August 1967, and was appointed a vice-chairman of the Revolutionary Committee in March 1968. Ch'en Li-yün, political commissar of the Fifth Air Army became a deputy political commissar of the district and later a vice-chairman of the Revolutionary Committee when formed.	SCMM, No. 622, 6 August 1968, p. 6 FBIS, 15 August 1967, pp. ccc 18–19 Issues and Studies, Vol. VII, No. 6, March 1971, pp. 34–5
Honan	1st Corps (Unit 8172) 15th Corps	Wang Hsin, political commissar of 15th Corps became 2nd political commissar, Honan Military District, August 1967. Made vice-chairman, Honan Revolutionary Committee when formed in January 1968. Yang Li-yung, political commissar, 1st Army Corps, made vice-chairman of Revolutionary Committee, January 1968, also political commissar of Kaifeng Military Sub-district, August 1967.	CB, No. 863, 1 October 1968, p. 31 SCMP, No. 4083, 19 December 1967, p. 4

Table 4—*continued.*

Province	Units	Unit Leaders and Provincial Positions Assumed	Source
Hunan	47th Corps (Unit 6900)	Li Yüan, commander 47th Corps became commander Hunan Military District, August 1967 and chairman, Hunan Revolutionary Committee, April 1968. Other leaders of the 47th Corps appointed to the Revolutionary Committee are Deputy-Commanders Cheng Po and Liu Shan-fu – both vice-chairmen, Deputy Political Commissars, Li Chen-chün and Chang Li-hsien. Also a "responsible person" of the 47th, Lin Chien-pin.	*SCMP*, No. 4080, 14 December 1967, p. 8
Kiangsi	Unit 6011 (A division of the 27th Corps) Unit 6810 (A division of the 41st Corps)	Ch'eng Shih-ch'ing, political commissar 27th Army Corps, which had dispatched the 6011 Unit from Shantung became political commissar of the Kiangsi Military District in August 1967 and chairman of the Kiangsi Revolutionary Committee when formed in January 1968. Yang Tung-liang, commander of Unit 5810 of the 41st Corps dispatched from Kwangtung, became commander, Kiangsi Military District in August 1967 and vice-chairman, Kiangsi Revolutionary Committee, January 1968. Yü Hou-te, political commissar of Unit 6810 was appointed vice-chairman of the Committee. Chen Ch'ang-feng, division-commander, Unit 6011 was also appointed to the Revolutionary Committee.	*SCMP*, No. 4388, 2 April 1969, p. 4 *SCMP*, No. 4081, 15 December 1967, p. 11 *Issues and Studies*, Vol. IV, No. 7, April 1958, p. 22
Kirin	192nd Division (Unit 7311?)	Ho Yu-fa, division-commander, took charge of Kirin Military District in August(?) 1967 and became vice-chairman of the Kirin Revolutionary Committee when it was formed in March 1968. Ho's division was probably transferred from Liaoning in August 1967.	*SCMP*, No. 4137, 13 March 1968, p. 15. *Facts and Features*, Vol. II, No. 3, 27 November 1968
Sinkiang	9th Air Army of the Lanchow Air District (Unit 7335)	Li Ch'uan-chün, commander of Unit 7335 was made vice-chairman of the Sinkiang Revolutionary Committee upon its formation in September 1968.	See n. 44

Table 5

Military Districts Possibly Reorganized by Main Force Units

Province	Units	Unit Leaders and Provincial Positions Assumed	Source
Kiangsu	27th Corps	No commander or political commissar noted for this district after October 1966. 27th Corps active in North Kiangsu.	*SCMP*, No. 4236, 12 August 1968, p. 10
Liaoning	Units unidentified	Former commander Ho Ch'ing-chi dropped from sight, late summer of 1967 when main force units were taking over military districts elsewhere. Chinese Nationalist sources identified Li Ya-t'ien as the new commander of the district and commander of an unidentified unit.	*Facts and Features*, Vol. II, No. 3, 27 November 1968
Ninghsia-Hui Autonomous Region	Unit 8037	Hsu Hung-hsueh, a " responsible person of Unit 8037 " was made a vice-chairman of the Revolutionary Committee there when it was formed in January 1968. No commander was noted for this district from late 1966–9.	FBIS, 23 August 1967, p. ddd 19. *Facts and Features*, Vol. II, No. 6, 8 January 1969, p. 30
Shensi	21st Corps (Unit 8133)	Hu Wei, commander of 21st Corps, made vice-chairman, Shensi Revolutionary Committee, May 1968. He had brought his unit from Shansi in March–April 1967. The former commander of the district was dismissed in late July 1967 ; the new commander was appointed only in December 1967 – Huang Ching-yao from the Heilungkiang District. Hu Wei was probably the key military man in the province during this hiatus.	FBIS, 15 August 1967, pp. ccc 18–19

authority during that period. When a Red Guard organization attempted to report a rather serious shooting incident of August 20 in Canton, the telephone at the district headquarters rang for more than an hour before it was answered. The tardy telephone answerer then informed the Red Guards that "the military district is closed on Sundays."[24] Perhaps the revolutionary rebels would have done better had they called the headquarters of the 139th Division, 47th Corps, which had entered the city a few weeks earlier. These examples suffice to show the Wuhan Incident's impact upon main force units—many of the officers were thrust into political jobs and the units themselves were tied down with provincial and local responsibilities. As a result, military readiness was severely degraded. From August 1967 through September 1968, China was probably less able to defend herself than at any time since the national disasters which followed the Great Leap Forward.

Factional Troubles

Chapter 2 explored the post-Wuhan factionalism between main and regional forces. In addition, by 1968 factionalism was spreading among main force units. Perhaps the first such outbreak was in November-December 1967 between the 13th and 14th Corps in Yunnan Province.[25] About the same time in Chekiang Province, political friction developed between the 20th Corps and the 5th Air Army.[26] The 63rd and 69th Corps in Shansi argued whether or not to support the military district leaders in 1968.[27] In Hopeh, the 38th and 63rd Corps experienced conflict over support to rival Red Guard groups.[28] Such cases were not commonplace nor were they bloody. Whether any armed clashes occurred among military units is a moot point; if intra-PLA firing incidents did take place, they were not of sufficient magnitude to warrant mention in the Red Guard press. The primary mode of main forces factionalism was the same as that between regional and main forces—proxy battles among contending mass organizations.

Regardless of the amount of violence involved, factionalism among main force units posed a grave problem to Mao and the GPCR leadership. They had thrown the army corps into the campaign to assist the work and correct the behavior of the regional forces. When their corrective effort itself began to stray, there was no one left to turn to—the main forces are the ultimate base of political power. The spring of 1968 saw several efforts to patch up the internal PLA problems, e.g., Mao Thought Study Sessions, "joint liaison committees" in the military regions, and, when conflict among army corps was especially serious, top level meetings with Lin Piao.[29] Little headway was made in resolving the intra-PLA differences. As suggested in Chapter 2, such factionalism was an intractable problem so long as the GPCR remained a mass movement attempting to carry out a "revolution from below." The realization of this fact, combined with other domestic and foreign factors, caused the Peking leadership first to set a May 1968 deadline for formation of the remaining revolutionary committees. After that failed, Mao himself eventually called a halt to the GPCR as a mass movement in late July 1968.[30] In succeeding weeks, the military imposed the remaining revolutionary committees from above. With the struggle for power decided (at least temporarily), the primary motivating force behind the PLA factionalism was removed and the treatment of the political wounds could begin.

The Main Forces and Lin Piao

As the old wounds from the GPCR began gradually to heal, Lin's political use of the main forces (and the PLA generally) opened new sores which are still troubling China. The post-GPCR treatment of military factionalism was simply to bury the hatchet. This was done in several instances by separating the contending military units—relocating one or both, or at least reassigning their leaders.[31] A new policy of rotating units and officers had been announced in 1968 (see chapters 2 and 5). However, the unit transfers in the 1969-71 period were not as extensive as one might have expected, and many of the shifts that took place were clearly in response to the Sino-Soviet border crisis and a concomitant decline in the U.S. threat to southern China.[32] In 1976, nine years after the "periodic transfer" policy was introduced, most of the army corps were occupying the same locations they held during the GPCR. (See accompanying map.) The 1973 reshuffle of region commanders indicated that the transfer policy had not been dropped, so why have more units not been relocated?

One initial reason was probably that unit relocations did not fit well into Lin Piao's political plans. He wanted to use the PLA—including the main forces—as the primary base for his national political power. Thus, unlike most other military leaders, he was not reluctant to see the PLA become involved in the GPCR.

> The participation of armed forces units in local work has its merits and this may be promoted courageously. Without promoting this, we cannot hold our ground. . . . Many cadres are needed and the armed forces units must be used as crucibles to supply them.[33]

Lin clearly intended that the PLA should create a political control network in the provinces and that the unit officers should receive many of the jobs in any eventual rebuilding of the civilian policy. Periodic transfers would do great harm to the policy if not destroy it completely. A second and more current reason is that relocations are time consuming, costly, and degrade military readiness. The same general political objective is more easily served by transferring key officers.

How were the military officers to be chosen for responsible civilian jobs or promotions within the PLA? By assessing their politics; and Lin, as the nationally proclaimed expert in the application of the Thoughts of Mao, was naturally the best qualified man to make the important selections.

> Our army cadres are numerous and there are talented ones, but the trouble is that they have not been discovered. As regards whom we should and should not promote . . . how we should assign the cadres, and how fill the vacuum caused by the dismissals by the Central Committee [i.e. civilian political vacancies], we have

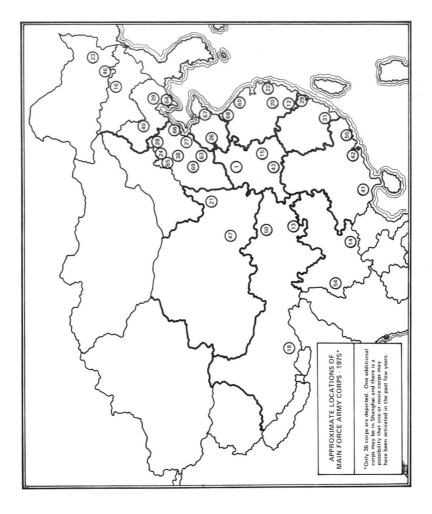

APPROXIMATE LOCATIONS OF
MAIN FORCE ARMY CORPS - 1975*

*Only 36 corps are depicted. One additional
corps may be in Shanghai and there is a
possibility that one or more corps may
have been activated in the past few years.

not yet found the ways of dealing with these questions and we should conduct a proper investigation. We should find out about the cadres' political attitudes and political performance. . . . The army . . . must examine the leadership groups. No matter what mountain stronghold a group belongs to, it cannot be used if it is opposed to Chairman Mao.[34]

With Lin (and subordinates acting in his name) deciding who measured up to leadership standards, it was little wonder that so few civilian Party cadres were reinstated while so many PLA officers (including thousands of unit leaders) became revolutionary committee chairmen and Party secretaries in the provinces and localities of China. Nor was it surprising that the military control committees (created during the martial law period of the GPCR) continued to exist in the provinces even after the civilian government and Party organizations were rebuilt.

The ultimate base of the PLA's political power in the post-GPCR period was still the "units engaged in local work," to use Lin's phraseology. These were the so-called "three supports and two militaries" units which had as their core the twenty-two army corps which had taken an active role in the GPCR.[35] Lin and his supporters made every effort to perpetuate the civilian role of military units, justifying it with the sacred name of Chairman Mao.[36]

In a Red Flag article written by a PLA unit, it was frankly asserted:

Whether we are dealing with politics, economy, culture, education, or other works, we [the PLA] must maintain the initiative and avoid being moved by others.[37]

The "others" presumably included the Party. Lin's writ for the domestic role of the military was broad indeed.

Following Lin Piao's death in September 1971, Mao and Chou En-lai were confronted with the problem of how to disentangle the PLA from the elaborate political-military web created by Lin (initially with Mao's blessings) over the previous five years. They did not act precipitously. It was only in 1973 that the term "three supports and two militaries" was dropped from the official lexicon. One report from that same year stated that a central directive personally approved by Mao ordered all officers from the "three supports and two militaries" units to resign from their local civilian Party and government positions.[38] In 1974, the military control committees also disappeared. Thus the main forces have been largely disengaged from local political responsibilities. However, the unit leaders had grown accustomed to a good deal of autonomy and independent political power, and it was probably this situation which led Mao Tse-tung to infer in 1972 that the troop units were acting independently of the military regions:

> The region Party committees must take charge of unified leadership. Would it not be odd if things already decided by the regional Party committees were to be discussed again by the Party committees of the troops?[39]

Later, Mao said that the PLA under Lin Piao's leadership had failed to heed orders, treating civilians improperly and "behaving like warlords."[40] Mao's own statements go far to explain why he moved cautiously after the Lin Piao affair. Even with the main force units now largely out of the civilian administration, it may still take more time to bring them under a tight leash and restore political discipline.

5

Military Life

A Civic Action Army?

The official Chinese media projects an image of the soldiery selflessly serving the people whenever not actively engaged in military training; millions of words have been devoted to the subject of soldiers assisting sowing, harvesting, capital construction, and industrial production. This represents a long-standing revolutionary ideal of Mao Tsetung. In 1949, following the successful conclusion of the civil war, he stated that the PLA should be converted into a work force and great training school for cadres.[1] Although the military has served as a training ground for Party officials, it has never been a significant work force in support of the civilian economy. According to calculations by Bernhard Grossman, the military contribution to civilian agriculture has never exceeded five hundredths of one percent (0.05%).[2] Moreover, there has been no serious attempt to use the PLA as a labor force. By far the highest level of PLA work days in the civilian sector was in 1960, when the nation was suffering severely from economic failures of the Great Leap Forward combined with drought. The PLA devoted over 40 million man-days to civilian work—mostly disaster relief. However, impressive as that figure may sound, it amounted to only 4.6 percent of the total available man-hours.[3] Under Lin Piao's leadership the PLA's contribution as a work force declined steadily, despite the fact that Lin had a highly political approach to the PLA as opposed to the "bourgeois military line" which argues that soldiers should spend their time soldiering.[4] Since Lin's demise, the situation seems little changed: PLA personnel do token farm work in the civilian sector and contribute somewhat more to various capital construction programs. Medical and veterinary troops use their expertise to teach veterinary skills, train some of the paramedical "barefoot doctors," and assist communes in the care of domestic animals.[5] Even though the Cultural Revolution absorbed billions of PLA man-days in the civilian sector, in that instance the military was serving as a surrogate political control mechanism, rather than as a productive work force.

Instead of directly supporting the civilian economy, the PLA has attempted to become as self-sufficient as possible, running its own farms on its own lands and establishing many small-scale industrial plants, machine shops, and the like to support its technical and maintenance needs. In general, units are assigned on a rotating basis to training and soldiering, agricultural production, and construction/industrial production.[6] It is not uncommon for a peasant youth to be inducted into the PLA only to spend a year or so of his three years of active duty slopping hogs on a PLA farm. Company-size units within the Canton Military Region average thirty pigs each. Naturally, the main force infantry corps spend less time in such pursuits than do the regional forces, but all participate to some degree.

While these production efforts by no means meet all the needs of the PLA, they make it, man for man, one of the least expensive standing armies in the world. But this does not explain why Peking chooses to stress military self-sufficiency rather than supporting the civilian economy directly as a work force. After all, isn't the PLA supposed to be at one with the people? How much better it would be if the peasant soldiers of the PLA were working shoulder to shoulder with their civilian counterparts. It would not only strengthen the prestige and proletarian spirit of the PLA, but it would also greatly assist militia building and perhaps even achieve Mao Tse-tung's ideal of making "every man a soldier." Therefore, why not have the PLA enlarge the

economy as a whole rather than attempt to meet as many of
its own needs as possible?

This writer has yet to find a totally satisfactory answer to
the question but can offer a few suggestions. First, if the PLA
worked within the civilian agricultural economy, it would
mean a greater tax burden on the peasant. While it would be
nice having a PLA comrade assisting in the agricultural
chores, the peasant would have to feed his helper, and this
might be sorely resented. Second, by the nature of their
activities, military reservations absorb vast tracts of land, at
least some of which is arable. Why let this go to waste? The
planting of PLA lands also helps explain why more soldiers
are not sent out to the communes during peak labor-
intensive weeks of sowing and harvesting—the army crops
are labor intensive at the same times, thus absorbing most of
the spare military manpower. Third, in case of invasion or
nuclear attack, the civilian agricultural economy would be
adversely affected by mass evacuations to safe areas. Under
such circumstances, rather than depending on local communes, the soldiers would be better off with an independent
food supply. The same point also applies to the small-scale
PLA industrial enterprises. Fourth, regular use of troops in
communes would be inefficient if they had to return to their
barracks every night—too much time would be spent in
travelling. Yet if they stayed for longer periods, military
readiness would suffer and logistics would become exceed-
ingly complicated. Finally, as the PLA becomes more modernized, the soldiers become slaves to their machinery and
the amount of surplus manpower declines accordingly, even
when the units are not involved in active training. Despite
all the foregoing, China has managed to sucessfully project
an image abroad of PLA soldiers taking up hoes and shovels
every time they put their rifles down. The symbol is more
important than the reality.

The Men and Their Officers

Due to their effort to become as self-sufficient as possible,
the PLA is much less afflicted with "make work" problems
than are most Western armies. Rather than digging ditches

only to fill them in again, the soldiers engage in productive labor. True, much of the work is routine, tedious, and tiring, but it is for a good cause and the results are tangible. Presumably both boredom and bellyaching are ameliorated by such meaningful work.

The needs of the soldiers seem to be adequately met. The pay for new recruits is meagre—only 6 JMP per month, about 3 U.S. dollars, while squad leaders get about 10 JMP. However, food, clothing, lodging, medical care, on-base entertainment, and travel allowances are provided. In rare cases, a family-support allowance is given if the recruit's absence from home causes an economic hardship on the family. As a general rule, youths who provide the main household income are not inducted, and if a father or brother dies while a young man is serving in the PLA, he is usually discharged to prevent family hardship resulting from the loss of a male wage earner. Of course, older enlisted men—equivalent to noncommissioned officers—earn more and receive support allowances for their wives and children. The officers are far from being overpaid, although with their allowances and fringe benefits, they live well by Chinese standards. There are about twenty-four ranks—pay gradients from new recruit to the top PLA leaders. The equivalent of a full general receives about 350 JMP a month ($175). A battalion commander might receive 80 JMP, and the lower-ranking junior officers are paid about 60 JMP monthly. Officer salaries used to be higher, but were "voluntarily" cut by one-third following the GPCR.

Uniforms

The 1965 abolition of badges of rank has made it somewhat difficult to visually distinguish the officers from the enlisted men. The latter wear canvas shoes and have uniforms which are often ill-fitting and look unpressed, and their tunics have only two pockets. Officers (platoon leaders and above) wear leather shoes and their tunics have four pockets—two side and two vest pockets. Field grade and high-ranking officers often have much finer cloth and tailoring than do their subordinates. The service branches have distinctive colors in their dress uniforms: the army wears olive green while the air force also has olive green tunics, but with blue trousers.

In 1974, the naval forces adopted new white dress uniforms with blue trousers. The enlisted men wear jumpers with traditional sailor caps and a horizontally striped jersey under the jumper. The omnipresent quadrilateral red PLA insignia are worn on the shoulders rather than on the tabs of the collar, as in the other branches. The total effect of the naval enlisted men's uniform resembles a Gilbert and Sullivan operetta sailor. The officers wear a white tunic with the red PLA tabs in the usual collar position, and their hats are peaked caps with a red star; the latter is found on all PLA headgear. Overall, the naval uniforms are now similar to the pre-1965 style. This indicates a gradual return of clear distinctions between officers and enlisted men and it may be leading to the eventual reestablishment of badges of rank.

The Officer Corps

To become an officer, one must first serve in the ranks. The most promising young soldiers are sent to training schools run by the military regions in conjunction with the provincial Party committees.[7] Schooling includes military science, language study, and ideology. Prior to the GPCR, similar academies accepted middle school graduates who became officers upon completing a one or two year program. However, with the present national policy against elitism, such direct entry into the officer corps has been abolished.

Promotions in the PLA have been rather slow. The situation is not bad in the ranks where there is a considerable turnover of men, but within the officer corps, advancement is a very gradual process—the result of a widespread neglect of the 1955 Military Service Law which fixed maximum ages for officer retirement on an inclined scale according to rank.[8] Field grade and general officers often remain on active duty well beyond the stipulated retirement ages.

Slowness of promotion is also exacerbated by the generally methodical ascent of the career ladder. For example, if an officer has the ambition to become a leader in the PLA administrative system in the provinces, he must first distinguish himself in a unit, then serve in a menial staff position at military subdistrict or district level. Following this, he is apt to be transferred back to a unit. If the officer is lucky, he might later be promoted to a responsible position at the subdistrict level, perhaps even as a deputy commander or deputy political commissar. He must then wait along with the other deputies until a vacancy at the top occurs, which is filled primarily on the basis of seniority. The process is repeated at military district and regional levels.[9] Prior to the GPCR, it was very unusual for anyone to be selected to a major post in Peking without having first served in a leadership post at military region level. It is not surprising that only a hundred or so aged leaders have made it to the upper rungs of the military ladder of success.

The Young Turks

There is evidence that the field grades and lower-ranking generals feel frustration and resentment at their limited opportunities for advancement. This manifested itself most clearly during the GPCR in a trend which might be described as a "young Turk" movement. Some initial background information is necessary to explain this development.

During the latter part of January 1967, the PLA/GPCR got out of hand; power seizures were occurring within units which were needed for national defense and political/economic control functions. Althought the evidence is scant, many of those takeovers seem to have been led by second echelon officers eager for a chance to prove their leadership abilities and ideological fervor. On January 28, the CMC ordered a halt to such activities in troop units.[10] Another CMC directive issued the same day "postponed" the internal PLA Cultural Revolution in seven military regions: the Sinkiang, Nanking, Foochow, Canton, Tsinan, Kunming, and Wuhan Regions. The action was explained as necessary to maintain China's defensive posture.[11] The regions proscribed were all border or coastal areas except Wuhan which is the "strategic reserve" region. Whatever the reasons might have been for attempting to circumscribe the geographic bounds of the PLA/GPCR, the effort failed.

Within two weeks of the order, PLA activists "seized" the Canton Military Region Headquarters.[12] A similar seizure was planned for Wuhan, but was squelched at the last moment by the leader of the PLA Cultural Revolution Group, Hsu Hsiang-ch'ien.[13] Also in February, a deputy political commissar of the Sinkiang Military Region, Tso Ch'i, launched public attacks on his Commander, Wang En-mao.[14] Clearly the geographic restrictions proclaimed on January 28 were ineffectual. The PLA/GPCR had gathered too much momentum to be confined to stipulated areas, and whether Peking liked it or not, all of the (then) thirteen military region commands were involved.

In the months that followed, there were four well documented challenges of top military region leaders by second echelon subordinates, and it seems probable that other similar, less publicized cases took place at lower echelons (e.g., the military districts and subdistricts).[15] There were common themes among those struggles: most of the initial challenges were internal PLA Cultural Revolution issues, and they were fought out in the Party committee meetings of the military regions. After this approach proved fruitless, the challengers aligned themselves with one or more mass organizations seeking to discredit the regional military leadership. In all cases cited, the most obvious motive behind the attacks was ambition—the removal of the regional leaders would have made room at the top for these "young Turks." Such political ploys were uniformly unsuccessful, and in all cases cited except Tibet, the challengers were purged.[16] The end of the GPCR wrote finis to any further overt attacks by subordinates against their superiors.

The ending of the GPCR did not result in a strict return to the seniority system. Instead the "three way alliance" (Party-military-mass organizations) of the GPCR was given a new interpretation beginning about 1970. The young, middle aged, and elderly were all to be "allied" in leadership organizations—including those of the PLA. In recent years there have been numerous cases of politically outstanding young men who vaulted over one or more intermediate

grades to become leaders within their units. They are popularly known in China as "the children's corps." For example, a regiment in the Nanking Military Region was praised
for "boldly selecting an excellent group of young cadres to
join the regiment's headquarters and placing them as deputy
regimental commanders, deputy political commissars, and
in positions within the military justice and political organizations."[17] One regiment commander was only twenty-five
years old. Mao called for the appointment of military region
commanders in their thirties, but that wish was not ful-
filled.[18] Perhaps the most dramatic case was the selection of
the young civilian Party theorist-writer, Wang Hung-wen,
to serve on the Standing Committee of the CMC. The
thinking behind this policy is probably partly grounded in
Mao's oft repeated remark that he wished to groom revolutionary successors, and partly it reflects a desire to alleviate
the frustration and anger of talented officers who had
previously been on career treadmills. In the discussion of
central organizations (chapter 3), most of the promotions
and appointments mentioned during and after the GPCR
similarly ignored the seniority system in favor of selecting
politically reliable leaders. There is an obvious price exacted
by such policies—those men who have seniority and who
have been passed over in favor of officers very much junior to
themselves must now be the ones who feel frustration and
resentment.

The Promotion System and Military Factions

There is yet another reason why officer promotion has
tended to be slow—traditionally there has been little lateral
mobility within the military chain of command; when a
man entered a unit, he usually was promoted within that
particular chain of command. In other words, a company
commander would ordinarily be promoted to the battalion
headquarters which controlled his company, and so on up
the line. It is possible for an officer to request a transfer, but
he is actively discouraged from doing so. At army corps level,
opportunities widen. A corps commander might become a
district commander. Later still, he could be promoted to a

responsible position at military region level. Relatively few troop commanders are assigned to the PLA administrative network below the level of military district. Missions assigned to subdistricts and people's armed departments (e.g., militia work and conscription) are not well suited to the talents and training of unit commanders, so those posts usually go to political officers. Thus the political commissariat system offers somewhat more career opportunities through lateral transfer than does the command chain.

Why have commanders usually been promoted up a single line of command? The explanation lies in the promotion system itself. When an officer vacancy occurs, the PLA Party committee at two echelons up decides who should fill the position. The selection is usually based on candidates suggested by the Party committees (or branches) of the unit having the vacancy and its immediate superior. For example, if the position of company commander were vacant, the regimental Party committee would fill the post, usually selecting a man suggested by the Party branch of the company and the Party committee of the battalion.[19] In larger units the principle is the same, but there is a distinction between promotions in main forces and regional force units.

In the main forces at division level and above, candidates for vacancies are suggested by the units involved, the military region then makes its recommendation, and the final decision is made by the CMC.[20] In the regional forces, the military region headquarters selects its own regimental and divisional leadership, and then presumably reports its decisions to the CMC.[21] This promotion system has been in effect since the late 1920s, so it is not surprising that officers are apt to spend their entire careers within the same regiment or division. In 1970, Edgar Snow interviewed a regimental commander and one of his comrades from the same unit who had recently been demobilized to become vice-chairmen of a revolutionary committee. The two men had entered the PLA together in 1933, had been assigned to the same squad and had served together ever since.[22]

The PLA promotion system has three advantages. First, it develops a high esprit de corps. The men, and especially their officers, feel that they are part of the recent history of their unit. Second, it provides for a good deal of stability. The officers come to know thoroughly their jobs and each other; a routine is well established. Third, experience is cumulative. In a U.S. infantry unit, last year's training is of little use since both officers and enlisted men are rotated frequently. In a Chinese unit, last year's training is still beneficial to virtually all but the new recruits.

There are also disadvantages to the system. Stability and well-established routine can verge on stagnation, so that there is little incentive to adopt new practices and procedures. The situation is worsened because many of the commanders have had little opportunity to become familiar with operations of sister units. It would be quite feasible for an infantry officer to rise to the rank of division or corps commander with scant knowledge of how best to apply artillery and armor in combined arms operations. This disadvantage presumably is ameliorated through intermediate level officer training courses.

There remains a disadvantage which is more important and intractable than the above-mentioned problems. The Chinese refer to it as "mountaintopism," i.e., the development of vertical cliques which compete with each other for high-level positions. The higher the echelon, the more important this nascent factionalism becomes, because top-level leaders have a long string of subordinates with whom they have served and the power to promote and transfer these trusted associates. Thus, the top men in the CMC, general staff, political, and rear service departments have their own mental or real "black books" of men they know and trust and would like to promote to responsible positions. As a result, high-level appointments tend to precipitate political struggles and are a potential source of disunity in the PLA.

Until recently, the national leadership apparently felt that the advantages of the career promotion system outweighed the disadvantages. However, during the GPCR, "mountain strongholds" and clique-like behavior were denounced several times in PLA political crises.[23] In 1968, a new policy of rotating both officers and military units was initiated.[24] However, as discussed in the previous chapter, it has only been partially implemented. Although during and after the

GPCR several army corps were relocated and a number of troop commanders were transferred, most units have remained in place and many senior officers are still leading units with which they have been associated for years. In December 1973, the military region commanders were thoroughly reshuffled, indicating that the rotational policy remains in force, but it is making only gradual headway against the entrenched traditions and interests of the PLA officer corps.

In some Western and most Chinese Nationalist studies of the PLA, the importance of vertical cliques is overemphasized. Such analyses present the "field army theory" (or modified versions thereof) which hypothesizes five or six cliques of PLA leaders derived from shared experience in the old field armies (abolished in 1954) and the 1930s precursors of such units. The cliques are seen as each controlling a certain number of main force army corps in a delicate balance of power. Each clique is viewed as dominating the particular region in which its units are stationed.

Because of China's recent history, the field army thesis seemed reasonable. At the end of the civil war, each field army occupied a region of China where they had successfully campaigned against the Nationalist forces. The field armies operated during the civil war in a decentralized fashion with the PLA headquarters coordinating their efforts, but not controlling their operations. From 1949 to 1954, the provincial governmental system was largely martial—the key leaders in each region were the commanders and political commissars of the field armies and their subordinate units. In 1954, the provincial system was placed under civilian rule, and the field armies were abolished. However, the army corps successors of the old field armies remained in the same localities and many of the key officers were demobilized to become provincial and regional political leaders. Thus it was plausible to view the PLA as split into several large cliques, each with its national leaders on the CMC and political dominance over a region.

In this writer's opinion, the "balance of power" interpretation of the PLA is no longer tenable. It ignores the elaborate organizational system described in this book with its strong central control and constraints on the authority of military leaders in the provinces. The theory also falsely presupposes that the military region headquarters have full operational control over all units in their jurisdictions. The 1973 geographic reassignments of military region commanders made a mockery of the concept that each military region is a quasi-independent political-military bailiwick. Moreover, the extensive relocation of army corps during and after the GPCR (described in the previous chapter) flatly contradicts the theory. Corps with different field army backgrounds were relocated into areas supposedly controlled by other cliques. Those corps movements revealed far greater central control than the theory allows, and units selected for relocation seem to have been chosen on a purely military basis. The forces in strategic areas were kept intact, often with little or no involvement in the national GPCR, while the army corps chosen for political roles were relocated from the areas of lowest external threat. The field army history of the units was apparently irrelevant.[25]

While the field army theory as a whole should be discarded, some of its parts are salvageable. In particular, military leaders have tended to favor their former subordinates as proteges. The problem was frankly discussed by Lin Piao after the dismissal of the acting chief of the General Staff, Yang Ch'eng-wu:

> Yang Ch'eng-wu's chief mistake was that he advocated the mountain stronghold mentality, individualism and factionalism . . . Yang believed only in himself and his tiny group of men with whom he has close ties. . . . He used only that group of men and took the attitude of eliminating others.[26]

Lin's remarks were laden with unintended ironic humor. During the GPCR, Lin had appointed many of his own former subordinates to high positions in Peking; indeed, the large majority of choice PLA appointments in the capital went to men associated with Lin's old 4th Field Army.

While the career/promotion system of the PLA has created cliques based around large units, the Chinese military is by no means unique in that regard. The U.S. Army is at the opposite pole from the PLA in terms of career development. An officer never spends more than a few years with any unit. Yet, U.S. military leaders also favor their old subordinates in promotions. General George Marshall kept a small notebook in which he had entered the names of men whom he felt to be outstanding in some regard. Dwight D. Eisenhower was one of the names in his book. More recently, an "airborne club" has dominated the leadership of the U.S. Army. These generals began their rise to prominence when two airborne divisions were created early in World War II and dominated the army chief of staff position from the 1950s into the 1970s. The names include Maxwell Taylor, James Gavin, Matthew Ridgway, and William Westmoreland. Their Second World War junior officer subordinates have fared remarkable well. For example, of General Taylor's known protégés, one rose to four star general rank, two became lieutenant generals, and one a major general.[27] Clearly favoritism, personal relationships, and shared experiences are important in Western military circles as well as in China's.

In the PLA, the personal relations factor in officer promotions has been at least partially legitimized through a recognized system of sponsor/guarantor and protégé relations. For example, Yang Ch'eng-wu was for many years a subordinate to CMC vice-chairman Nieh Jung-chen. Yang served Nieh as a unit commander and later as an administrator in North China. There is evidence that Nieh sponsored Yang's appointment as acting chief of General Staff in 1966 and served as the guarantor of his reliability and good behavior. When Yang was dismissed in March 1968, Chou En-lai reported that Nieh "felt quite uneasy after the question of Yang Ch'eng-wu was brought up."[28] Chou went on to report that Nieh wrote a letter to Mao, Lin Piao, and Chou himself in which he shouldered some of the blame related to the dismissal of Yang. Nieh next began a self-criticism which underwent a review for over a month, although he was eventually exonerated.

Recognized systems of guarantor/protégé relations are rather unusual in the West, but have a long tradition in

China. In imperial times, before an official was promoted to a responsible post, one or more other higher-ranking officials had to sponsor the appointment. If the protégé proved incompetent or misbehaved, the blame and punishment would be shared by the offender and his sponsors. Of course, the reverse was also true—when a sponsor fell from grace, his protégés could also expect dismissal. There seem to be remarkable similarities in the system today.

Apart from the promotion system, there is another potential area of factionalism within the PLA, in the relationship between commanders and political commissars. Western military men regard the idea of a commissariat with undisguised loathing, but, as it works in China, the system does not appear to engender much conflict.[29] The separation of functions is well defined, and the political commissar removes many bothersome chores from the commander, e.g., personnel problems, relations with the local civilian population, entertainment for the troops, and the continuous stream of political campaigns and meetings. The commander is thus enabled to concentrate on military affairs. Should conflicts occur, they are referred to the unit's Party committee for resolution. Still, the possibility always exists that there could be a severe personality clash or widely diverging military philosophies between a commander and political commissar. In such unusual cases, the potential for harm to the effective leadership of the unit would be great due to the nearly coequal powers of the adversaries.

On the whole, it seems that the problem of factionalism within the PLA is not out of hand. If the policy of periodic transfers becomes thoroughly implemented, it will gradually weaken the existing cliques built around large units. By recognizing and using personal relationships on a sponsor/ protégé basis, the PLA regularized behavior which otherwise might tend to divide PLA leadership. In any case, a strong whiff of favoritism, factions, and politics is inevitable at the top levels of any military system. Due to the ravages of time, the old field army leadership cliques are fading. The internal structure and dynamics of present-day factions in the PLA are poorly understood. William Whitson has theorized that new cliques may have formed around interservice rivalries and military generational differences.[30] Whatever their hidden complexities, there is no doubt that the PLA has its share of internal cleavages.

Controlling Military Elitism

Recently there have been measures taken to foster a spirit of humility among military officers. In Shensi, leading officers of the District Headquarters, main forces and regional units implemented a rotational *hsia-fang* (sending down). Beginning in 1973, officers were selected to spend one year on rural communes where they devoted two-thirds of their time to labor, and one-third to political and ideological work. The first group of officers had finished their year in the communes and a second group was being dispatched in 1974.[31] This is one of the more extreme forms of "proletarianizing" officers to be tried in PLA history. Before the GPCR, it was common practice for field grade and high ranking officers to spend a few weeks in the ranks as common soldiers on an aperiodic basis. Apparently this was deemed insufficient in the political atmosphere following the Lin Piao affair, although the practice was revived in 1975-76. As early as 1968, a deputy chief of the general staff announced to a red guard meeting that military cadres would soon be sent to do labor in rural and frontier areas,[32] but nothing came of that remark until the Shensi Military District announcement of 1974.

A program of sending officers to communes does have one significant political advantage over the previous system of having officers spend time in the ranks. In the latter case, officers are still soldiers and the "sending down" does nothing to weaken the special status of being in the PLA. When officers are sent to communes, it breaks down the military-civilian barrier and temporarily makes the officers "common people." Apparently PLA elitism became so serious following the GPCR that this extreme measure was tried as part of the general program to trim the horns of the military. In the opinion of this writer, dispatching PLA leaders to communes will not become a generalized national policy. If the program is widely implemented in the future, it will indicate that the problems of civilian control over the PLA have again become very serious.

A more recent and widely publicized campaign against PLA elitism inveighs against officers demanding special privileges while on active duty and expecting favored treatment upon retirement or discharge. In Kwangtung, a young regimental commander resisted pressure from relatives to get one teenage relation into the PLA and another returned home to the city from a rural commune where she had been assigned (thereby revealing the considerable political clout wielded by unit cadres, even in this post-Lin Piao period). In another account, an air force political commissar showed his proletarian colors by not demanding a private berth when traveling by train.[33] In 1975-76, numerous provincial broadcasts made models of retiring PLA officers who willingly accepted rural job assignments in communes.[34] The latter probably reflects increasing competition for responsible jobs as well as the desire to combat PLA elitism.

On the whole, such attempts to proletarianize the military leadership seem mere palliatives. The very fact that there has been one campaign after another over the years, trying a series of different techniques, indicates the lack of real success. The PLA as a whole is a privileged group and the officers of the PLA are now and always will be a special elite.

6

Air and Naval Forces

The Air Force

For many years the People's Liberation Army Air Force
(PLAAF) has been the world's third largest—after those of
the U.S. and USSR—with 4000 aircraft in its inventory.
About 70-75 percent are jet fighters; the remainder is made
up of about 500 fighter/bombers, 300-400 transports, and
about 300 helicopters. In case of a mobilization, a few
hundred transports now under civilian control could be
added to the PLAAF. In addition to the flying units, there are
ground-based air defense and early warning systems, and
airborne infantry units. Total personnel is estimated at
about 300,000; however, the PLAAF is now not nearly as
strong as its size would indicate. In the mid-1950s, it was a
formidable air defense system equipped with the latest
model Soviet supplied fighter—the MiG-17. Since the Sino-
Soviet rift, most of the inventory has become increasingly
obsolescent.

The PLAAF has seen no major military action since the
Taiwan Straits of the late 1950s, so it has been able to devote a
portion of its resources to support civilian needs. For the
better part of two decades, China has produced copies of the
Soviet Mi-4 "Hound" helicopter and the An-2 utility bi-
plane. Both of these have been used for disaster relief,
deliveries of supplies to remote areas, and other civilian
emergency measures. China is quick to publicize any case in

which the PLAAF has been of assistance to the populace, but the other air forces of the world may render as much or more assistance to civilian sectors.

Organization

Except in the case of an air defense alert, control over the flying units of the PLAAF is highly centralized. The national headquarters exercises tight operational control via its own communications system which is divided into two parts. First, there is a command network under the Operations Department which is designed for the flow of orders downward. Second, there is an early warning and alert network which begins at the local radar stations and funnels upwards to the air defense sectors and air district headquarters. In the latter network, operational authority is very decentralized, but sharply limited in scope to ground control/intercept functions. When unidentified aircraft near China's airspace, fighter interceptors can be sent aloft quickly without having to relay orders through many echelons. In an emergency situation, possibly the air defense sector could order a "scramble" from local airbases without going through the air district headquarters. However, higher authority would undoubtedly be required before firing upon intruding aircraft. The early warning, ground control/interception and air base radars are manned by specialized troops organized into twenty-two independent radar regiments.[1]

There are several administrative departments within the PLAAF headquarters. Positively identified are General Staff, Political, Rear Services, Operations, Communications, Training, Air Force Academies, Engineering, Civil Aviation, Organization, Cadre Management, Meteorology, and Military Justice Departments.[2] There is a subheadquarters for antiaircraft artillery (AAA) forces which may be an operational command. It is divided into at least two departments—radar and missile forces. The twenty divisions and twenty-eight regiments of antiaircraft troops are the main responsibility of this headquarters, thus there is no specialized department for them. Still another subheadquarters within the PLAAF controls the airborne forces.

Only a few of the subdepartment organizations have been identified. The Rear Services Department has an Aviation Technology Bureau and a Science Institute. The Air Force Academies Department is in charge of the Peking Aviation Institute, twelve aviation academics, and thirteen technical aviation schools. The Engineering Department presumably controls the five aviation engineering schools; likewise the Communications Department probably is in charge of the aviation communications school. The Political Department almost certainly controls the PLAAF political cadres school.[3] Flying schools would naturally fall under the purview of the Training Department. There are undoubtedly other headquarters elements which have not been identified. These are likely to include a finance department; since the naval forces have their own paymaster, the PLAAF presumably has one as well.

Below the national level, the PLAAF is now divided into ten air districts.[4] These are coterminous with the eleven military regions except in the far northwest, i.e., there is no separate Sinkiang headquarters; that territory is part of the Lanchow Air District. While the districts are responsible for air defense, the military regions would control tactical air units in combat. Beneath the districts are subdistricts or "sectors." This seems to be the lowest geographic echelon in the PLAAF since the next step is the "air armies." As a general rule, there is one air army for each air district.[5] These are troop units, but do not themselves possess any tactical capability, rather they are relatively small headquarters units. The air armies look after the administrative needs of the flying units beneath them. One of their major functions is logistics. The air armies probably have little operational control over the flying units.[6] Both the air districts and armies administer the air bases and support the flying units. While differences in their roles are not clear, districts are probably primarily concerned with air defense, air armies with administrative support. The air defense sectors might have some administrative role as well, but their primary duty is early warning, ground control/interception of enemy aircraft and coordination of antiaircraft fire.

The air division is the largest tactical unit. Apparently the number of divisions in each army or district can vary somewhat depending upon mission, locale, external threat, and the number of air bases and independent regiments in the area. Divisions occupy the large air bases while the smaller fields support one regiment or wing. Tactical organization is normally triangular; three regiments comprise a division, three "wings" make up a regiment, and three squadrons comprise a wing. Each squadron has about twelve planes, with considerable variation according to type of aircraft and mission (e.g., bomber squadrons often have only six to eight aircraft). There are independent regiments made up of special mission or badly outmoded aircraft. Chinese Nationalist analysts have also identified one independent squadron,[7] almost certainly made up of the few old Tu-4 propeller-driven bombers which are used as drop planes in atomic tests.

The PLAAF controls two different types of ground forces—antiaircraft artillery (AAA) and airborne infantry units. The AAA units are equipped with a wide array of weapons including surface-to-air missiles (similar to those use by North Vietnam), radar guided antiaircraft cannon, and heavy machine guns. The airborne forces are organized into at least four divisions, three of which comprise the 15th Corps.[8] These are under PLAAF control during peacetime, but would necessarily come under ground force control after being parachuted and/or airlifted into a battle zone. However, the PLAAF has very few transport planes. Only a few regiments can be airlifted or air-dropped at any one time. Since China is not producing medium or large transports, the airlift capability will not grow significantly in the near future.[9] A medium helicopter is being produced.[10] However, it has been given low priority, and despite some recent purchases from France and the Soviet Union, the helicopter fleet is not large.[11] The PLA nevertheless has begun some training in air-mobile operations similar to those used by U.S. forces in Vietnam.

Capabilities

The military capabilities of the PLAAF have grown

markedly in absolute terms over the last decade. However, it is not catching up with the world's more advanced air forces because of the old designs of the airplanes. China cannot afford to build aircraft beginning from a blank sheet of paper; her technical manpower and resources are too precious to spend thousands of man-hours and millions of dollars on a research idea which may well reach a dead end. Instead, the PLAAF develops aircraft from existing designs through a process of steady but unspectacular improvement, well chronicled in Richard M. Bueschel's *Communist Chinese Air Power*. For example, engine output on MiG 19s has been improved, and the old Tu-4 copies of the World War II American B-29 bomber have been fitted with turboprop engines.

Over the past decade, China has been producing large numbers of combat aircraft. A fair portion of the military budget during the 1960s went into developing serial production of the MiG-19 and-21 jet fighters and the Tu-16 medium jet bomber. China established those production lines under the very adverse conditions of a worldwide embargo on strategic goods. The aircraft are close copies of the Russian models, but they are truly "made in China" without relying on foreign components. However, they are also obsolescent by contemporary standards. Worse still, there has been a major setback in the program to upgrade the interceptor force: the Chinese-produced MiG-21 was a failure. About eight years were required to set up the plant in Chengtu, Szechwan, and begin serial production. After all that effort, only about fifty MiG-21s were added to the PLAAF inventory, then production suddenly stopped after only two years of operations (1971-72).[12] It is not certain what the problem was, but the MiG-21 uses a high output single engine which demands very sophisticated metallurgy, perhaps beyond China's present capabilities. The indigenously produced MiG-21s were nearly all out of operation in 1974-75. That production failure was probably the major reason why China contracted with Rolls Royce for the purchase of, and licensing rights to, the Spey jet engine. By 1977-78, the assembly line should be moving again with an improved version of the MiG-21. Production of the Tu-16 bomber also ceased about the same time as the MiG-21, after less than 100 had been produced. However, the reason for stopping production of the bomber was strategic rather than technical—with about 100 total Tu-16s in the inventory, the PLAAF had little use for additional obsolescent medium bombers. All available resources were shifted to missile production and development.

The most spectacular advance made thus far is the F-9, a twin-engine multi-purpose jet fighter with a Chinese designed airframe. Resembling an enlarged MiG-19, this aircraft is intended to serve primarily as a fighter-bomber. Estimates on the performance and range of the plane vary markedly, but all agree that it outperforms the MiG-19 and it is probably capable of supersonic speeds in level flight.[13] One thing is a certainty—it is not an all-new aircraft—but this does not detract from China's success in designing and producing a high performance airframe of its own. The F-9 has been in serial production since 1969; in 1975, the PLAAF had about 400 of the aircraft. U.S. intelligence analysts believe that production has been hampered somewhat by technical difficulties.[14] Another new aircraft of Chinese design has been dubbed the Sian-A by U.S. intelligence agencies. It too has had its problems, having been in prototype testing for seven years. The Sian-A may be capable of Mach 2 speeds when it enters serial production—about 1977.[15]

The ground-based air defense system was strengthened considerably during the Vietnam War years. An elaborate radar network was constructed in South and Southwest China. It proved successful at directing interceptors or AAA fire at reconnaissance drones and strayed U.S. military aircraft. The air defense system was effective enough by the late 1960s that the Chinese Nationalist U-2 reconnaissance aircraft ceased operations over China. Beginning about 1969, the radar system along the northern borders was improved, and it now includes a ballistic missile early warning system. Many squadrons of interceptors formerly stationed in South China were relocated to northern airfields.

Despite undeniable improvement, the PLAAF has severe

deficiencies which render it relatively weaker in the 1970s than in the 1950s. There are more MiG-17s in the inventory than any other type of plane, and that aircraft is badly outmoded. It is not capable of supersonic flight and the design is twenty-four years old. The MiG-19s and the few available MiG-21s are much better aircraft, but they date from the mid-1950s and would fare poorly in aerial battles with more recently designed planes. Even the F-9 is probably years behind the latest European, Soviet, and American fighter-bombers. In the bomber fleet the story is much the same. The most numerous is the Il-28, a light jet bomber designed in 1947. The indigenously produced Tu-16 medium bomber has a much greater range and load capacity, but the design is still over twenty years old.

A second serious weakness is the interception ability of the fighter aircraft. They are equipped with relatively primitive avionics. Most navigation is visual, and until recently, only the naval air force flew over water where visual navigation aids are few or nonexistent. Chinese pilots receive night flight training, but routine flights are cancelled when the cloud cover is low. The PLAAF possesses only a few old MiG-17 all-weather interceptors, although the USSR claimed that one or more all-weather MiG-21s were stolen by China while transiting that country en route to Vietnam.[16] This is not to say that the air force relies solely on visual contact with the enemy—its interceptors are equipped with air-to-air guided missiles.[17] If an enemy air attack came in daylight with reasonable visibility, the PLAAF would put up a strong defense (given the age of its aircraft). However, if the enemy should be dastardly enough to attack at night or in foul weather, China would have to rely mainly on its ground-based defenses, supplemented by its small force of MiG-17 all-weather interceptors.

The ground-based air defense system also has serious weaknesses. The core of the system is the radar-guided surface-to-air missile (SAM). The latest models of the Soviet designed weapons (SAM-6) proved very effective in the 1973 Middle East war. However, China's SAM dates from the 1950s (SAM-2) and American pilots flying against similar missiles in North Vietnam found them capable of being outmaneuvered or neutralized by electronic countermeasures. Should China find herself at war with the USSR or the U.S., air superiority would quickly be lost to the enemy. It would require all the PLAAF's capabilities to control skies against the much smaller but more modern Chinese Nationalist or Indian Air Forces.

Recent History

The PLAAF got off to a quick start in the Great Proletarian Cultural Revolution. The national headquarters was in a turmoil as early as June 1966, and a "power seizure" was attempted the following year. The first few months of 1967 were especially chaotic with the radicals within the PLAAF attacking a number of leaders who were later declared to number among Mao Tse-tung's loyal followers. Those who instigated the sweeping attacks were later described as "fish eyes representing themselves as pearls."[18] The main target of the early 1967 attacks was Wu Fa-hsien, then commander of the PLAAF, but instead of being brought down, his star rose throughout the remainder of the GPCR. By August 1967, he was the chairman of the Administrative Committee of the CMC and wielded immense power within the PLA. This goes far to explain why there were not too many GPCR victims within the PLAAF—Wu was able to protect his own. Indeed, many of the air force purge victims were those who had led the attacks against Wu Fa-hsien.

As for the national GPCR (as distinct from the internal PLA campaign), the PLAAF was not as heavily committed as was the army. In late January 1967 an air force company made news when it sent four men to a nearby production brigade in order to support revolution and production—this at a time when hundreds of thousands of army men were already involved.[19] Later some of the air districts and armies did become involved, but the flying units supposedly had little to do with the GPCR in any of its modes. Peking did turn to the PLAAF in crises—it was primarily airborne units which smashed the Wuhan "mutiny" and an air force unit took over the Wuhan garrison in the aftermath of the incident.[20] In Sinkiang, the 9th Air Army (unit 7335) took over that military region following prolonged political trouble in the military region headquarters.[21] One advantage of PLAAF units in such situations was that they were under tight central control; another was that they could avoid many of the early mistakes made by army units.

PLAAF units were not used in the GPCR to any great extent until after the Wuhan Incident. It was easy for them to avoid backing mass organizations disapproved by Peking; whereas the army had become involved seven months earlier, when most of the political evaluations had not yet been made regarding the hundreds of major Red Guard groups. It is not surprising that one radical mass organization leader in Canton was quoted as having said: "The air force and navy are revolutionary but the army is conservative."[22] The "Johnny-come-lately" nature of the air force in GPCR politics led to some conflict between PLAAF and army units. On Hainan Island, the air and naval forces were involved in a factional dispute with the Hainan Military District.[23] In Chekiang Province, there were difficulties between the 20th Corps (unit 6409) and the 5th Air Army (unit 7350)[24] because of support to rival mass organizations. After the revolutionary committees were completed in 1968 and the mass organizations disbanded in all but name, nothing more was heard of intra-PLA conflicts except for general calls for unity.

The flying units were supposedly not to be involved in the GPCR, and they may not have been. Still, after Mao Tse-tung made it known that he desired periodic troop unit and officer rotation, the PLAAF was the first to be affected. In early 1969, most tactical units of the PLAAF were relocated—without changing the national deployment pattern. The infantry units which were relocated later in the same year were those which had encountered serious political troubles during the GPCR. There is a chance that this was also why the PLAAF was reshuffled, but on balance the more likely explanation is that it was easiest for the air force to carry out Mao's new instructions, so they took the lead in implementing them.[25]

One responsibility which was thrust on the air force in 1967—control of civil aviation—remained a military duty until the mid-1970s. The Civil Aviation Bureau was taken

over during the general imposition of military controls in
the first quarter of 1967. A new director was appointed in
1973, Ma Jen-hui, an air force officer, but in 1974, he was
reassigned to the General Rear Services Department. Thus, it
now appears that military control over civil aviation has
come to an end.

The air force fared relatively well under its 1965-71 commander, Wu Fa-hsien. The PLAAF seemed to have gotten
more than its fair share of the defense budget, and all of the
combat aircraft produced by China, except the MiG-19, were
begun under Wu's leadership. In North Vietnam, Chinese
AAA divisions proved their merit against U.S. bombing
raids, downing many medium and low altitude attackers.
The conventional air defense artillery from Hanoi north to
the Chinese border seems to have been mostly Chinese until
after the March 1968 bombing pause. True enough, the
PLAAF was not making great strides in overtaking the U.S.
and USSR, but at least it was not falling rapidly backwards
as had been the case from 1960 to 1965.

Wu Fa-hsien's implication in the Lin Piao plot brought
the palmy days for the PLAAF to an abrupt end. The air
force was highly suspect politically, was grounded totally for
about two weeks following the Lin Piao incident, and
remained largely grounded for over a month. It is now clear
that the PLAAF was the most heavily purged branch of the
PLA in 1972-73: in the national headquarters, twelve out of
thirty-one top positions were purged (as identified by Chinese Nationalist analysts). The Nanking, Shenyang, and
Canton Air Districts also lost important leaders. The dismissals extended down at least as far as air army level.[26] Military
priorities were also rearranged; aircraft procurement
dropped sharply, and the PLAAF has received a much
smaller proportion of the budget over the past few years.[27]

Finally, in June 1974, a new commander was named—Ma
Ning. He is a younger man than the Long March veterans;
born in 1912, he joined the Communist armed forces in 1938
and transferred to the air force in 1950—a few years after it
was formed. During the GPCR, he was a "responsible
person" with PLAAF unit 7311 in Manchuria. Ma was
involved in the national mass movement and became a

Standing Committee member of the Kirin Revolutionary Committee. Twenty-one months after the Lin Piao affair, he vaulted to the position of deputy commander, PLAAF, and became its commander a year later.

There are scores of officers in the PLAAF with more seniority, experience, and better professional qualifications than Ma. To outsiders the only apparent reasons for this choice are first because his career was not connected to Lin Piao, and second, his political loyalties were well tested during the GPCR. Ma's selection throws into a cocked hat the normal career development and expectations of senior officers. The position of air force political commissar has had more continuity in recent years. Wang Hui-ch'iu has held the post since 1969 and he was a deputy political commissar prior to that time. Both Ma and Wang are veterans of the old Second Field Army, and thus have no career connections with Lin Piao. While the PLAAF leadership is still far from strong, Wang may provide the much needed continuity and experience in the high command.

The Naval Forces

The People's Liberation Army Navy (PLAN) comprises the smallest branch of the Chinese military system. Although naval craft now total about 1500, there are only about 150 fighting ships (including submarines). Most of the remainder fall into the "fast attack craft" category. Total naval personnel, including the naval air force and all shore-based support elements, number around 200,000.[28]

Organization

Although the smallest of the three branches, the organization of the naval forces is quite complex (see Chart IX). In addition to the major General Staff, Political, and Rear Services Departments, there are some other first echelon organizations peculiar to the PLAN, e.g., the Naval Air Force Headquarters, Engineering, Weapons, and Oceanographic Departments, and a Business Office (or "Administration Office"), which handles control of classified documents along with conscription/demobilization work. The Rear Services Department is especially complex due to the

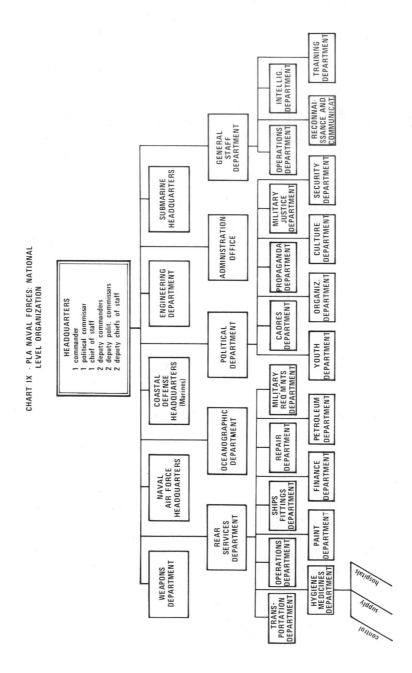

CHART IX - PLA NAVAL FORCES: NATIONAL LEVEL ORGANIZATION

technical and maintenance requirements of the PLAN. In addition to the usual transportation, petroleum, finance, medical, and equipment sections, the Naval Rear Services includes ship's fittings, repair, and paint departments along with its own operations unit to coordinate the multifarious logistics activities.

The naval forces per se are three tiered, rather like the foot soldiery. The equivalent to the main force units in the PLAN are the North, East, and South Sea Fleets. Roughly equivalent to the regional forces are the seaborne public security units, administered by the navy but operationally controlled at military region or province levels. Thirdly, the PLAN has its own militia made up primarily of fishing vessels.

The North Sea Fleet is headquartered at Tsingtao, Shantung Province, and is responsible for the Yellow Sea. The East Sea Fleet's Headquarters are at Shanghai, and it is responsible for the East China Sea from Kiangsu south through Fukien, including the Taiwan Straits. The smaller South Sea Fleet is headquartered at Changchiang, Kwangtung Province, and is responsible for the South China Sea area along the Kwangtung and Kwangsi coastline and south to the Chinese-claimed Paracel (Hsi-sha) and Spratley (Nansha) Islands. Fleets have operational control over vessels in their jurisdictions; however, in wartime, operational command of naval forces in coastal defense functions may be transferred to military regions.[29] Fleets also supervise the work of naval bases and coastal defense installations. According to Chinese Nationalist analysts, the forces afloat are subdivided into divisions, regiments, and squadrons.[30]

Another component of the PLAN is the Naval Air Force. It has about 30,000 personnel and 500 aircraft—jet interceptors and bombers. The Il-28 light bombers attached to the Naval Air Force are all equipped to carry torpedoes. Some of the longer-range Tu-16 medium bombers are under naval control; these are used for reconnaissance and anti-submarine warfare. Since China has no aircraft carriers or overseas bases, all naval planes are stationed on the mainland and Hainan Island. The three fleet headquarters have operational control over the Naval Air Force; however, the fighter aircraft are also on the national air defense network and have often been sent aloft to intercept intruders. The naval flyers are the cream of the crop; regularly facing more difficult navigational problems over water, they seem to be better instrument pilots than those of the PLAAF. Many, if not most, of the Chinese flyers who brought down American planes during the Vietnam War were Naval Air Force pilots. The U.S. soon learned to give an especially wide berth to the airspace surrounding Hainan Island—patrolled solely by navy pilots.

There is yet another component of the PLAN—the "marines" (*hai-lu-chun*, literally "sea-land troops"). Their nature is quite different from the American force of the same name. Chinese marines are coastal defense troops rather than a ship-borne assault force. Amphibious landing exercises are small, infrequent, and primarily aimed at improving defenses. Marines provide security for naval bases and man coastal defense artillery. The latter includes "cruise missiles"—subsonic radar guided surface-to-surface missiles of some 23-mile range. Marine personnel are estimated at about 30,000 men.

Capabilities

Even more than the air force, the PLAN is defensive in nature. Its warships do not range far outside of Chinese territorial waters; its submarines have never been known to take extended voyages. The largest ships in the inventory are seven new missile firing destroyers and a half dozen frigates.[31] Moreover, the last new keel for the destroyers was laid in 1971, but another new class of guided missile frigate is expected to appear in a year or so. Several older vessels have been refitted with the Styx guided missile system. Submarine construction has been quite active and the underwater fleet now numbers about sixty vessels. Most of these are of World War II Soviet design, but fully one-third have been built in Chinese shipyards over the past decade. Two of the subs are more modern—one Soviet "G" class ballistic missile-firing submarine (for which the Chinese probably have no missile as yet), and a nuclear-powered vessel designed and built within China. The latter is a "hunter-killer" submarine which was launched in 1972. However, four years later, it was still not operational, perhaps because of propulsion problems.[32]

The strength of the PLAN lies in its large fleet of fast attack craft. Among these are about 75-100 Soviet-designed Osa and Komar guided missile patrol boats, many of which have been constructed in China. They are intended to present a dangerous obstacle to any adversary attempting to penetrate Chinese coastal waters. The Osa and Komar classes are small, fast boats which carry 4 and 2 radar guided missiles, respectively. China has recently designed and produced her own twin guided missile craft which supposedly is superior to the Russian designs in rough seas. The Styx cruise missiles are the same as those used in coastal defense installations and on the new Luta class destroyers. They carry a high-explosive warhead with enough power to cripple large fighting ships and aircraft carriers.[33] Guided missile patrol boats are highly cost-effective, since they are relatively inexpensive, easy to build, and provide a coastal defense system which theoretically can hold its own against a much more powerful naval force.

Against advanced navies, China's guided missile patrol boat system has one severe weakness. The Styx missile is vulnerable to electronic countermeasures, as was proved in the 1973 Middle East war. The Egyptian navy, supplied by the USSR, was equipped with Styx missiles, and they scored a very low percentage of hits against the Israeli navy which jammed the homing radars carried by the missiles.[34] China is not in a position to compete effectively in the electronic arms race, so presumably her missiles will remain vulnerable to enemy jamming. Partially offsetting this weakness is the large number of boats and missiles available; even if many firings were to be thrown off course by electronic countermeasures, a few missiles might still get through to their targets. Other weaknesses of the missile patrol boats include a short operating range and the possibility that they cannot be used effectively on very rough seas. Also, although the boats have low profiles which would be difficult for enemy ships to detect prior to their coming into firing range, the missile craft are almost defenseless against air attack. In addition to the Osa/Komar, China has 430 high-speed gunboats and 220 torpedo boats, including about 75 hydrofoil torpedo boats of their own design. All of the attack craft train in high speed mass formations, often at night and in foul weather. The tactical concept is to combine surprise with sheer weight of numbers in order to overwhelm the defenses of enemy ships and to avoid aerial detection.

The navy is virtually useless is terms of projecting China's power abroad. For example, following the abortive Indonesian Communist coup d'état in 1965, the large overseas Chinese population there was indiscriminately persecuted and thousands were killed. China could do nothing but protest: her navy did not have the wherewithal to pressure the Indonesian government, nor could China demand and carry out an evacuation by sea, since the PLAN has a very weak troop-lift capability. Its landing craft are few and old, troop transports are practically nonexistent, and her merchant marine, though growing rapidly, is still small for a country the size of China. Should it eventually be necessary to invade Taiwan, China will have to gain undisputed control of the air so that her vast junk fleet can be used to carry and supply the invasion force. The PLAN also receives only limited combined arms training and would have to undertake an intensive training program before it would be capable of launching a major amphibious invasion.

Recent History

Like the air force, the navy entered the national GPCR rather late in the game. Its first highly publicized role was in the Wuhan Incident of July 1967. In support of Peking's efforts to rescue the kidnap victims, the East Sea Fleet dispatched ships up the Yangtze River to the tri-city area. By the time they arrived, the incident was all over, but they had shown their support for the Maoist leadership against the "mutiny."[35] Shore-based naval personnel played a significant political role in the larger coastal cities—often in support of "radical" mass organizations. Ship crews and naval pilots were not involved.

The internal PLA Cultural Revolution caused considerable strife at naval headquarters in early 1967. One faction, apparently led by the navy political commissar, Su Chen-hua, subjected Deputy Commanders Li Tso-p'eng and Wang Hung-k'un and Political Department Director Chang Hsiu-ch'uan to heated criticism and struggle. However, the Su Chen-hua faction failed, resulting in his purge around May 1967. (Virtually all of the naval GPCR victims were rehabilitated by October 1974—including Su Chen-hua.) Li Tso-p'eng then jumped career lines to become the political commissar of the PLAAF. Oddly enough, the naval commander, Hsiao Ching-kuan, seemed able to avoid the fray, perhaps due to his advanced age. Hsiao's public activities have been infrequent in recent years and he may be semiretired.

It was Li Tso-p'eng who garnered the limelight from mid-1967 until the Lin Piao affair in 1971. He seemed to be fully in charge of naval affairs as well as serving as a member of the Administrative Committee of the CMC. Li was one of Lin Piao's old comrades-in-arms, and that connection stood him in good stead for five years. Chang Hsiu-ch'uan, then the head of the navy Political Department, was also active as a member of the PLA Cultural Revolution Group. However, it was Deputy Commander Wang Hung-k'uan who proved to have the greatest political durability. He was appointed political commissar of the PLAN some months after the Lin Piao incident. Hsiao Ching-kuan is still the commander, but it can be safely presumed that Wang has most of the power.

In the never-ending battle over resource allocations, the PLAN fared very well until after the Lin Piao affair. Since that time, submarine and attack craft production has continued apace with merchant ship building, and only capital warship production has tailed off. Chinese Nationalist analysts claimed that from 1970 to 1972, there was a 10 percent annual increase in naval ships.[36] While expansion has been much slower since that time, there is no doubt that the navy has recently fared much better than the air force.

Even the present rates of naval construction seem high to this writer. Where is the naval threat to China in the late 1970s? The U.S. Seventh Fleet no longer patrols the Taiwan Straits and the general policy of détente pursued since 1971-

72 makes it highly unlikely that the U.S. will launch a naval attack on China's coastline in the foreseeable future. The Japanese navy is an expanding and highly modern force, but the chances of Sino-Japanese naval warfare seem quite remote. The Soviet threat is much more immediate, but it is mainly from the air and ground. Of course, if the Russian Pacific Fleet were deployed to Chinese waters, it would present a formidable menace. However, China's present naval building program—attack craft and diesel-powered subs—would be of little use against the sophisticated arms of the Soviet fleet.

There are at least three possible explanations for the present naval force building pattern. First, the PLAN leadership has been comparatively strong both before and after Lin Piao's demise, and thus has been able to win budget battles regardless of current threat estimates. Second, the first nuclear sub may be the harbinger of a fleet of modern ballistic missile submarines which will serve as an additional "safe" nuclear deterrent, supplementing the more vulnerable land-based missiles. U.S. intelligence analysts are predicting that China will develop a submarine-launched ballistic missile, but it will not be operational until the early 1980s.[37] A third reason may be offensive rather than defensive—the submarine force is now large enough to blockade Taiwan, especially if aided by the new guided missile frigates and destroyers. China's fast attack craft could sweep the Nationalist fishing fleet and smaller craft from the seas. Peking might thereby attempt to force a political settlement of the Taiwan issue short of a risky full-scale invasion. Of course, such a scenario presumes the abrogation of the U.S.-Nationalist defense treaty and Taipei's rejection of peaceful reunification offers.

7

Paramilitary Forces:
The Militia and
Production-Construction Corps

In theory, the militia and production-construction corps (PCC) are not now part of the PLA—both their organizations and functions are supposedly controlled by the civilian Party committees at provincial and local levels. In actual fact, there is an ongoing struggle between the PLA and the Party over which organization will control the paramilitary forces, and how those forces should be used in China's society. Regardless of who eventually wins this struggle, both the militia and PCC will remain important components of China's defenses; they have served as the PLA's reserve system since the old military reserve was abolished almost twenty years ago. No general study of China's military system would be complete without a discussion of these organizations.

The Militia

Organization

The militia is a production and paramilitary force organized around occupational enterprises; it is a part-time volunteer service with its members working at their regular production and service jobs, although a few "militia cadres" at commune level do spend full time administering the local units.[1] Both men and women from about ages 16 to 50 are eligible. Entrance requirements have always been loose, accepting all but persons with "landlord" or "reactionary" class backgrounds and criminal elements.[2] It is doubtful if anyone knows precisely how many workers in communes, factories and offices, and students in schools nominally belong to the militia, but current estimates are in the range of 44-250 millions; fortunately the numbers are of little importance.

The "common militia," which comprise at least 75 percent of the total, receive virtually no military training and would function only as a labor and manpower pool in wartime. The "basic militia" numbers about 15-20 millions and receives some individual and small unit military training.[3] The age group in this category is more restricted—about 18-40—and women constitute a small minority. Within this group there is a still smaller elite—the "armed militia"—which numbers around 7-10 millions. These are the politically screened basic militiamen who carry arms on coastal and border defense patrols and assist in maintaining public security. The age limits are 18-25 years.[4] Were China to be invaded, the common militia would serve as a manpower pool, while the basic, and especially the armed, militia would assist the PLA logistically, providing rear area security, and serving as local defense forces.

Militia control and financing is highly decentralized (see Chart X). To this writer's knowledge, there is no national-level militia organization other than the Mobilization Department of the PLA General Staff. Its functions are probably to keep records, distribute arms, coordinate PLA training of militia and, as its name suggests, develop mobilization plans in case of war. At the next lower level, the military regions have mobilization departments and "people's armed departments" (PADs) as well. The division of responsibilities between the two organizations is largely speculative, but based on the activities of the PADs at lower levels, they appear to be the records-keeping and arms control office, while the mobilization department handles regional war

CHART X · THE MILITIA ADMINISTRATIVE AND SUPERVISORY SYSTEM

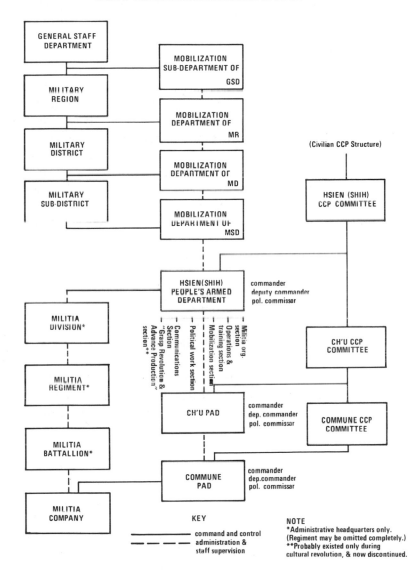

planning and the militia as a reserve system.

Direct control functions begin at the provincial level in the Party committees and military district headquarters. In the last few years, after about five years of subordination to the PLA during and after the GPCR, a national campaign has attempted to place the militia under civilian control. Beginning with the demise of Lin Piao, publicly discussed orders called upon the provincial and local Party committees to "assign special persons to take charge of militia work."[5] The aim was to preempt the provincial and country people's armed departments which had been under PLA dominance since the beginning of the GPCR. More recently urban (*shih*) "militia commands" have received much media coverage. These have three organizational levels—a general headquarters which is in charge of an entire city, militia departments, and subdepartments which correspond to urban districts and subdistricts.[6] City PADs have not been abolished, but they have lost some of their personnel to the militia commands, and moreover, they have been ordered to "coordinate and work together with" the militia command organs.[7] Clearly, these new Party "commands" are intended to place militia affairs securely in the hands of the civilian polity.[8]

Militia organizations per se begin only at the hsien or county level. In theory each county has a militia "division," each commune a militia "regiment," each production brigade a "battalion," and each production team a "company," but in fact the larger units exist only on paper and for wartime mobilization planning purposes. The company level seems to be the highest organization with meaningful activities during peacetime. Every commune has a people's armed department which is in charge of militia work within the collective organization. In urban areas, large enterprises also have armed departments and militia units of varying sizes, depending upon the number of personnel employed.

In 1961, the Ministry of National Defense ordered that each militia battalion was to have one basic or "backbone" company, but it is debatable whether or not that goal has yet been achieved. The order also stated that basic militia units were to be no larger than company size,[9] and that is still true today. Armed militia patrols are usually of platoon size and, to this writer's knowledge, paramilitary activities and armed training exercises are not carried out above the company level. Demobilized and retired armymen serve as cadres and provide routine drill and training for the basic and armed militia.

Relationship with the PLA

Paradoxically, in recent years the PLA has been ordered to intensify militia work even while Peking has been striving to effect strict Party control over militia organizations. The provincial military bureaucracy has been ordered to consider militia work as its first priority:

> The provincial military districts, subdistricts and PADs at various levels should direct their main energy to militia work. The locally stationed troops should consider doing a good job with militia work as their own glorious task. They should actively participate, helping the administrative districts do well with militia work.[10]

In Mao Tse-tung's mind, there was no contradiction between wresting control of the militia from the PLA and simultaneously ordering the military to intensify its militia work (although, in fact, such a contradiction has emerged). In 1972, Mao set forth a general directive on militia work which today remains the basic policy. He called for "three implementations"—organization, political indoctrination, and military training. The Party is to be totally responsible for organization, the PLA for military training; both Party and military can and should provide political indoctrination. Thus by means of role differentiation, Mao intended to have his cake and eat it too. However, it is one thing to order the Party to "organize" the militia; it is quite another for the Party to do so independent of PLA influence, in part because the PADs are the local organs with expertise in militia organization and they are PLA dominated. The PADs have been called upon to "play an advisory role" to the Party committees, but they probably often wield the real control.

In late 1975, several military districts issued general militia directives without reference to Party committees.[11] While the Party-army contest is far from over, the PLA seems generally to have primary control over the rural militia, and is making inroads upon the Party-dominated urban militia.

It is safe to say that PLA-militia ties will remain strong for the foreseeable future—not only does the militia need the PLA for training, the PLA needs the militia because it has no formal reserve system of its own. The armed and basic militia are now the reserves; military subdistricts and districts keep track of the names and locations of demobilized PLA veterans, but in case of war, the younger armed militiamen would probably supply the bulk of PLA replacements.

Capabilities

During the 1960s, few outsiders took the militia seriously. Khrushchev called it "a heap of human flesh."[12] The captured *Work Bulletins* of the CMC showed that the militia was a shambles in the early 1960s. There were many paper units, much corruption, and some cases of armed militia using their weapons for banditry. The situation is greatly improved in the 1970s. Much attention has been paid to improving the organization of the basic and armed militia. Over the past fifteen years, literally millions of demobilized and retired PLA veterans have been assigned jobs as local militia cadres.[13] Discipline and military training are better than ever before, although there is still ample room for improvement in both.

Militia arms are presently in a period of transition. Until recently, they have been equipped only with sidearms, rifles, and hand grenades, and even those basic weapons were in very short supply. In 1967, Mao Tse-tung made the offhand remark that the militia had three million guns.[14] Many of those were various caliber World War II Japanese, Chinese Nationalist, and American weapons. Mao has not let slip any arms figures of late, but it is known that production levels of the AK-47 and SKS rifles far exceeds PLA and export requirements. However, it is doubtful whether there are yet as many modern rifles as there are armed militiamen.

In the autumn of 1974, a central directive ordered that PLA ground forces equipment which had been replaced should be turned over to the urban, coastal defense, and border militia units.[15] About the same time, the Sinkiang Military Region announced the creation of specialized squads (i.e., antitank, sapper, and antiaircraft), in at least some of its armed militia.[16] Obviously, considerable attention has recently been devoted to upgrading the military capabilities of the militia.

Despite these efforts, the fighting ability of the militia remains low. Of course, it was never intended to be anything other than a local self-defense and security force, but the armed and basic militia's ability to perform even those functions seems to vary markedly from province to province. The coast opposite Taiwan and the northern border areas have the best militia, and many of the interior provinces lag far behind—both in terms of arms and training. Primary attention is still devoted to improving organizational and ideological aspects of the military; military training rates a poor third.[17] Live fire training exercises are rare, and so little ammunition is allocated that even armed militiamen fire only a handful of target practice rounds each year. Given their physical setting, the urban militia has even less opportunity for realistic training. A training slogan for 1972–73 was "small scale, within the locality, and scattered."[18] The slogan would seem equally applicable today. Yet, despite these shortcomings, if an invading army were to penetrate deeply into China, behind-the-lines harassment provided by regional and militia forces would become an increasingly critical problem. The enemy might eventually be forced into a complete withdrawal or reduction to a small perimeter holding operation.

Recent History

The domestic peacetime role of the militia has undergone a radical change in the past decade. The two quotations below sum up what amounts to a role reversal; the first is from 1966 and the second is dated 1974.

Since the militia is designed for dealing with the enemy,
it should not take part in the people's internal affairs.[19]

The active participation in class struggles in society by
the people's militia is an important experience.[20]

The militia has become a major domestic political instrument.

This change occurred quite suddenly in 1967 due to the
events of the GPCR. Just after the PLA was ordered to
"support the revolutionary left," the Peking leadership
opted for the "revolutionary committee" as the new government form for political rebuilding. The committees were
comprised of the so-called triple alliances—i.e., representatives of the military, Party, and revolutionary rebels. This
occasioned a problem for the PLA because revolutionary
committees were being established all over China from
factories and communes up to province level. The main
forces had not yet entered the GPCR, so the proposed myriad
of revolutionary committees posed a serious manpower
problem for the regional troops. In March, the militia was
enjoined to take the PLA's place in the triple alliances and
revolutionary committees below the county level.[21]

As it happened, the revolutionary committees were not
formed nearly as rapidly as Peking expected, partly due to
factionalism among the revolutionary rebels and partly
because Peking refused to recognize the legitimacy of many
of the committees which were formed. All too often the
revolutionary committees set up in the first months of 1967
were engineered behind the scenes by the very Party bureaucrats who were the target of the GPCR. Moreover, the
Cultural Revolution in the countryside was delayed (actually there was very little mass movement activity in the
communes at any stage of the GPCR). Finally, with the
involvement of the main forces in the ensuing months, the
military manpower available for political work was greatly
expanded. As a result of these factors, the militia did not play
its envisioned role in the political rebuilding process.

Still, the militia did play an important part in the GPCR,
but hardly in the manner desired by Peking. By late winter of

1967, little remained of the Party organizations in the provinces. The people's armed departments (the militia control organizations) came under the exclusive control of the PLA. These were convenient organs through which to administer local military control, and they soon were immersed in such functions, which was unfortunate for the GPCR leadership since the armed departments proved very conservative in their politics and used the rural militia to oppose the revolutionary left. Because civilian Party functionaries make up much of the armed departments' staff, such conservatism is understandable. There are about 2200 county armed departments, so it was clearly impossible for the national leadership to exercise effective control over them, yet their military control functions were indispensable.

The *Liberation Army Daily* frankly revealed the severity of the problem in an editorial of August 1967:

> We must see that the handful of powerholders in the Party and army who take the capitalist road are adopting sinister means of hoodwinking, deceiving, threatening, and inciting the people in order to prevent their doom. They vainly attempt to drag some cadres responsible for militia work and some militia men to the bourgeois reactionary line and turn them into tools for protecting themselves and enforcing the bourgeois reactionary line. They use militia to arrest, assault and detain the people and incite the militia men to go to the cities and suppress the proletarian revolutionaries. They even go to the extent of instigating the militiamen to sabotage production and communications and upset the social order.[22]

Such cases of using the militia against the revolutionary left were the rule rather than the exception in 1967. The Minister of Public Security at that time asserted that "80 percent of the people's armed departments supported the conservatives."[23]

Through most of 1967, the deportment of the armed departments grew worse rather than better. Probably the most spectacular means of resisting the GPCR began in the spring and summer. Some armed departments handed out weapons and instigated peasants and rural militia to flood into the cities where they attacked Red Guards. Such actions were justified with an old Mao quotation: "Surround the cities from the countryside." A central directive of July 13 ordered the cessation of such attacks and specifically blamed the armed departments for causing them.[24] In the weeks following the issuance of that directive, Peking remained preoccupied with this alarming use of the peasantry. In mid-August, the Minister of Public Security claimed that peasant "invasions" of the cities were still going on in Kiangsi and Hunan Provinces and in the tri-city complex of Wuhan. He also pinpointed the militia departments as the instigators of the attacks.[25]

In the months following the Wuhan Incident, the extensive use of main force units along with special "Mao Thought Study Sessions" for regional PLA officers, including tens of thousands from the armed departments, combined to virtually eliminate such overt "counterrevolutionary" activities. November 1967 saw the last reported major instance of militia departments instigating peasantry and militia to besiege a city.[26] The armed departments also became more cautious in their handling of revolutionary left mass organizations.

In early 1968, Peking became eager to complete the revolutionary committees. The PLA was allowed increasing authority to impose solutions upon factional differences in order to form "great alliances" among competing mass organizations, thereby clearing the way for the establishment of revolutionary committees. The armed departments again became bold enough to reveal an unreconstructed political cant. For example, in June, some months after the Kwangtung Provincial and Canton Municipal Revolutionary Committees were formed, Red Guard groups protested the right-wing stance of militia departments and their "packing" of factory revolutionary committees with militiamen.[27] In Kwangsi the departments were accused of providing arms to favored mass organizations, thereby fueling the highly destructive factional conflicts in that province.[28]

During the formation of local revolutionary committees

in the period from late 1967 to mid-1968, armed department leaders were often high-handed. In addition to packing basic level committees—such as those in factories and rural production brigades—with their own militiamen, the departments often rode roughshod over the interests of mass organizations. The following charge was leveled against armed departments in Kwangtung:

Some people of the militia departments monopolize everything without full consultation or any consultation at all with the masses, and without cadres properly making public appearances. "You need not care who the revolutionary committee members are. Those who go up on the platform at the inaugural meeting will be committee members." Such is the situation. Some people did not even know they had been named to the committees until inaugural day.[29]

A similar complaint came from Kwangsi, where armed departments and their militia forces were alleged to have set up local revolutionary committees immediately after the radical "April 22nd" Red Guard organization had been ejected from the areas.[30]

Due largely to such extensive political powers accorded the PLA, China's revolutionary committees were nearly all established by the end of 1968. There followed a period of political consolidation in which the military bureaucracy still retained extensive political powers. For example, one of the "model" armed departments frankly recounted its experience in managing an urban revolutionary committee over a period of several months.

We of the armed department reorganized the eight groups and one office dealing with agriculture, forestry, industry, communications, finance and trade, and culture and public health under the municipal revolutionary committee into four groups: namely the political work group, the general service group, the defense group and the production group. We reduced the staff from more than 200 men in the past to the more than 60 men at the present. We . . . organizationally insured the relations between the revolutionary committee and the masses and brought the revolutionary building of politics to the fore.[31]

Clearly the militia department maintained more political power than the revolutionary committee for many months following the establishment of the latter.

At these local levels, checks and balances on PLA authority seem to have been the least effective. Central approval was not exercised in appointments during political reconstruction and was probably only nominal at the special district/ military subdistrict level. References to central investigation teams were generally on provincial and subdistrict levels. Except for a certain accountability to the military district commands and the inherent GPCR hazards of attacks from mass organizations, the people's armed departments seemed able to run the "revolution" as they saw fit. Those local PLA administrative organs may have blunted the GPCR more than any other institution. Had the armed departments been free of Party influence and given firm backing to the revolutionary left, the GPCR would have had quite a different outcome. Unfortunately for the Maoist leadership, those organs of the PLA most identified with old Party apparatus were the most vital to administering the grass roots PLA role in the GPCR, and simultaneously were the least susceptible to central controls due to their large numbers and low administrative level.

Meanwhile, the urban militia suddenly acquired importance through the creation of new public security organizations. These had different titles in various cities, but the original Shanghai model was called the "mass dictatorship command." It was comprised mainly of basic and armed militia and its purpose was to relieve the PLA of much of its urban security functions. The old public security apparatus was deemed to be thoroughly antirevolutionary and was not allowed to rebuild itself through the formation of revolutionary committees. Instead, local security organs remained under military control until about 1973-74 while many of the actual police functions were performed by militia. Once again, the militia proved to be a mediocre domestic political instrument. Warrants and other regularized police procedures were notable by their absence. Large numbers of persons were arrested and held for extended periods or given long sentences without trial. Some of the arrests were arbitrary or capricious and there was no appeal.[32] Over the past few years, the police forces have been rebuilt and again placed under Party control—a development which did much to rectify the abuses of police and judicial powers, although it did not entirely eliminate them. Militia patrols still roam urban streets at night, sometimes dispensing "justice" in the form of on-the-spot beatings. Such vigilante actions have provoked popular criticism, and in 1975, one militia unit in Hangchow was reportedly ordered to turn in its arms.[33] So far, Peking has not directly confronted the problem of such abuses; instead, the urban militia is still ordered to serve as a watchdog, but its role is supposed to be primarily ideological.[34]

The very existence of a militia system presents China's leadership with a continuing policy issue. Should the militia be structured primarily as a military reserve, a militarized work force, or a political mass organization? The so-called Maoist radicals have favored an active, independent, political role for mass organizations generally and the militia in particular. Their concept is to use the militia to help counter elitism and bureaucratism within the Party establishment and bourgeois tendencies in the populace, and also to serve as a power base for the radicals. Many of the relatively new urban militia organizations were tailored for such missions. The moderates would structure the militia as part of the national defense and as a work force. The rural militia has long been organized along those lines.

The future role of the militia is one of the many imponderables of post-Mao China, but at present, the radical viewpoint seems to have lost much ground. When Hua Kuo-feng initially consolidated his national leadership in autumn 1976 and removed the key radicals (Chiang Ch'ing, Yao Wen-yuan, Wang Hung-wen, and Chang Ch'un-ch'iao) from the politburo, the urban militia were quick to abandon their radical patrons and voice their support of Hua. One might reasonably expect a larger military and productive role for the militia in 1977-79, with a de-emphasis of the internal security and ideological functions.

The Production-Construction Corps

Organization and Military Capabilities

The production-construction corps (PCC) are paramilitary work forces organized into units up to division level.[35] Unlike the militia, PCC work is full time—personnel are paid, fed, clothed, and housed by their units. High-ranking officers of the PCC are active duty PLA personnel;[36] low-level cadres are usually demobilized PLA veterans.[37] Over the past decade, the rank and file manpower has come mostly from urban youth who have been sent out of the cities following their middle school education. Urban underemployment and crowding have proven very difficult problems for the national leadership, especially since the population has been rising steadily at about 2 percent annually. Because the number of new urban jobs created by economic growth are fewer than the number of graduates each year, sending people out to the countryside, especially to less densely populated frontier provinces, provides a convenient relief valve. The PCC receive the elite of the "sent down" youth. According to figures from Inner Mongolia, fully 28 percent of those entering the PCC there were members of the Communist Youth Corps and 3.8 percent were full Party members. Of the young people assigned to communes in the same region, only 8 percent were in the Youth Corps and 0.7 percent had been admitted to the Party.[38] However, in the past many political undesirables were also sent to PCC to undergo "reform through labor," and some penal farms may still be under PCC administration.

Of course the purpose of these corps is not primarily to disguise unemployment or to provide penal discipline—their primary function is to undertake large scale, labor intensive projects assigned by Peking and regional authorities. Such projects include land reclamation, road building, defense construction, afforestation, mining, water conservancy, and the running of some industrial plants and state farms, especially in the outlying provinces. Finally, PCC are not merely work brigades but have a paramilitary role as well. As least some of the units are armed—one study asserts that there is one fully armed company in each regiment, and all personnel receive basic military training.[39] Pay scales seem to be similar to the PLA with new recruits receiving 18 JMP monthly and basic level cadres about 50 JMP. The uniforms are very similar to those of the ground forces except that the red star on the cap and red collar tabs are absent.

Recent History

The number of PCC increased dramatically during and after the GPCR. Previously they were only in Sinkiang, Heilungkiang and Tibet, but by the early 1970s, PCC had been formed in every military region. A large-scale population relocation away from urban areas was carried out from 1968 to 1970 which provided personnel for the new units. While total strength is not known, about 1.5-2 million were probably in PCC at their peak. In the 1973-75 period, the PCC in interior provinces were reduced in size, redesignated as "Agricultural Production Divisions" and placed under civilian control at the province level. The older, better established PCC in frontier areas probably have not changed character, and they may well still be under military control. The Sinkiang PCC is by far the largest, oldest, and most militarized. It has been divided into agriculture, industry, and mining sectors, and its personnel now probably number over one-half million. In terms of fighting effectiveness, PCC fall somewhere between the armed militia and the independent units.[40]

Additional tasks were assigned to the PCC during the last few years of Lin Piao's leadership, and it is likely that they built a substantial portion of the defense construction associated with the war preparations campaign of 1969-73. They also took over state farms in frontier areas which had previously been under civilian control. For example, in 1969, the rubber plantations of Hainan Island were subsumed into the PCC of the Canton Military Region. Civilian workers were subjected to tough discipline, long working hours, and frequent evening political meetings. Worst of all, the PCC leadership decided that the rubber production must be raised and ordered that the rubber trees be "bled" more frequently. The predictable result was that most trees were damaged, many died, and rubber production dropped sharply. The results of the disastrous PCC management practices became clear by the end of 1972, and the rubber plantations were returned to civilian control in 1973.[41]

The recent reduction in size and redesignation of PCC in the interior provinces seems sensible to this writer. They play a valuable role in frontier development where conditions are so difficult that only a militarized labor brigade can function effectively. In most cases, wages are not tied to productivity, so a PCC unit can spend years making a desert area bloom without concerning itself with financial solvency as a commune must. For example, the twenty-seven-year-old Sinkiang PCC has greatly expanded the arable land in that region, and now runs a system of farms and enterprises which more than pays for the cost of the corps.[42] However, in areas where agriculture is already developed, the PCC seem to offer few advantages over the commune system. The ultimate test of the PCC is whether or not they justify the cost to the state. As long as there are important roads and water conservancy projects to be built—especially in lightly populated areas—the PCC will have a role. However, in the early 1970s PCC personnel numbered almost one-half the size of the PLA. It would seem doubtful that land reclamation and labor intensive projects repay the cost of that many men to the state budget.

In the border regions, PCC can be expected to continue in their present enlarged form. Their contributions have made them too valuable to disband or seriously cut back. In the words of one specialist on China's minority peoples, Captain William Heaton,

> The PCC have done much in achieving the social, political and economic integration of the border regions into China, particularly in Sinkiang. The economic projects have not only helped the respective regions to

advance, but have more closely linked their economies with the center. The training of national minority personnel and the promotion of Han colonization have also contributed to this process. . . . The economic work has lessened the possibility of minority separatism; it has the secondary effect of securing the dominance of Han culture and language in the national minority areas.[43]

In addition to these integrative roles, the PCC also lightens the logistical and defense burdens of regular PLA forces, especially those stationed near China's northern borders.

8
China's Quest for Security

> Regarding the question of world war, there are only two possibilities: one is that war will lead to revolution, and the other is that revolution will prevent war.
>
> —*Mao Tse-tung*

The first seven chapters of this book are devoted to the military system. In this last chapter, the broader topic of China's quest for security is discussed in order to see the PLA in proper perspective—as one component of Peking's international security strategy.

Since the founding of the People's Republic in 1949, China's search for security has gone through three broad phases. The first was the close military alliance and political/economic cooperation with the USSR, which lasted from 1950 until about 1959-60. The second phase, dominant from about 1961 to 1971, was the "people's wars of national liberation" period which consisted of supporting anti-imperialist guerilla wars abroad in order to defend China's homeland. Its importance has been much reduced since China entered the third and most recent phase which emphasizes state-to-state relations, balance of power diplomacy, and cooperation with a broad spectrum of third world and industrialized nations. Each of these phases merits discussion, although the time frame of this study demands that primary attention be focused on the two most recent international strategies.

Under the Russian Umbrella

The Sino-Soviet alliance served China's security interests none too well. Almost from the start, the cost of the USSR's nuclear insurance was high. Nine months after the alliance was joined, China had to pull Russian chestnuts out of the fire in Korea. As a direct result of Soviet adventurism with Kim Il-sung, the Taiwan Straits were neutralized by President Truman and the communist leadership has, to this day, been unable to conclude its civil war with the Nationalists. A second important consequence of the Korean War was the U.S.-organized strategic embargo against China which kept her economically isolated from the West well into the 1960s.

In 1955, China made a determined effort to weaken its undeserved pariah image in international circles. At the Bandung Conference of Non-aligned States, China reaffirmed the "Five Principles of Peaceful Co-existence" which had been agreed upon between Peking and New Delhi the year before. These promised mutual respect for sovereignty, territorial integrity, noninterference in one another's domestic affairs, and peaceful coexistence between differing systems of government. That *démarche* did serve to open some of the newer Asian nations to contact and cooperation with China—Indonesia as well as India especially come to mind. However, the noncommunist industrialized nations remained hostile, so the embargo was still virtually intact.

During the Taiwan Straits Crisis of 1958-60, Peking learned that Russian security guarantees did not extend to playing brinksmanship with the U.S. for the sake of Chinese national objectives. The USSR also reneged on its pledge to provide nuclear and rocket technology to the PLA. In 1960, the Sino-Soviet split reached an advanced stage in which Khrushchev cut off all technical and economic assistance programs in China and withdrew Soviet manpower and materiel. Trade between the two nations dropped drastically, placing China in a severe economic squeeze made much worse by the collapse of its own ambitious domestic economic development program, the Great Leap Forward. The early 1960s found China isolated from both East and West. It was doubtful whether the military clauses of the Sino-Soviet treaty were still operative. China had also lost ground among the nonaligned nations due partly to the bloody suppression of the Tibetan rebellion (1959-61), and resultant strained relations with India. Clearly, it was time for new and hopefully more effective national security policies.

People's Wars of National Liberation

The combination of enforced isolation and weakness prompted China to make a virtue out of the necessity of self-sufficiency. Drawing from their own experience in protracted war against the Japanese, the Peking leadership launched an international strategy which they hoped would turn their weakness into strength and their enemy's strength into weakness. At that time, capitalist imperialism (led by the U.S.) was seen as the main threat which had to be countered since the Sino-Soviet rivalry had not yet assumed a military dimension. China had neither the economic nor military might to protect herself against the U.S. and its allies, much less to carry the fight to them. One of the major appeals of people's wars of national liberation (PWNL) is that the strategy is both defensive and offensive. As a defense it bogs the opponent down in wars away from China's soil. It can be an offensive strategy in an era of nuclear stalemate. The superpowers check each other, while, in theory, major regions of the world undergo revolutions leading to social-ist, or at least antiimperialist, societies.

The Concept and Its History

The original idea of using revolutions in nonindustrial-ized nations to attack and weaken the capitalist countries was first evolved by Rosa Luxemburg and Lenin.[1] Commu-nist ideologists were faced with an unpleasant truth—the European proletariat was becoming wealthy rather than sinking into a desperate poverty and thereby providing the base for the revolution as Marx had predicted. The proletar-iat was increasingly contented with its lot and turned to-ward peaceful trade unionism to handle remaining griev-ances. This made a mockery of communism's basic tenets, and had to be explained away. The "solution" was that European capitalists could afford to pay their workers more because of the extension of imperialism in the nineteenth century. The European and North American workers had become a "labor aristocracy" because the workers, resources, and markets of colonial and "semicolonial" countries were being ruthlessly exploited. It was, therefore, fruitless to foment revolution in the developed countries; instead the capitalist system would be destroyed by "bourgeois nationalist" revolutions occurring in Asia, Africa, and Latin America, which would destroy the mercantilist colonial system and put an end to Europe's ability to exploit others' raw materials and labor for its own benefit. The capitalist economic system would then be thrown into an unprecedented crisis which would touch off the revolution of the proletariat.

No later than 1946, Mao Tse-tung had added his own contribution to the concept. He argued that war in poor countries can result in "revolutionization leading to modernization"; hence, changing the political and social structures of poor nations became an end in itself as well as a tool for the destruction of imperialism. In addition, Mao identified three distinct groupings of nations—the socialist bloc at one end of the spectrum, the capitalist imperialist nations at the other, "separated by a vast [intermediate] zone which includes many capitalist, colonial and semi-colonial countries. . . . I believe it won't be long before these countries come to realize who is really oppressing them. . . . Only by victory in the [antiimperialist] struggle can a third world war be avoided."[2] Mao believed that if the revolution does not come to the developing nations, competition among the imperialist nations will lead to World War III.

By the 1960s, the "intermediate zone" separating communist states from the capitalist imperialist nations was seen as divided into two parts. The "first intermediate zone" consists of the poor, nonindustrialized nations, while the "second intermediate zone" consists of small and medium-sized industrialized countries which are also somewhat exploited or dominated by the great imperialist powers. The first zone is seen as having the revolutionary potential. Following an initial wave of successful revolutions in the poor nations, portions of the second intermediate zone were expected to oppose great power imperialism and "swing over" in support of the rising socialist tide, even without themselves having undergone violent revolutions.

The full-fledged Chinese model of PWNL was not set forth until September 1965 when Lin Piao delivered a major address on the topic.[3] Lin and Mao felt that the Chinese revolution provided the pattern on which other nonindustrialized countries would undergo their socialist revolutions, while the Russian model of 1917 would apply to industrialized, imperialist nations.

PWNL are basically nationalistic movements, each of which is carried out independently and with little or no outside assistance. Peking believes that revolution cannot be exported; indigenous conditions determine the success or failure of guerilla warfare by nationalistic partisans. So, too, the leadership must be native. However, China has proven willing to provide concrete assistance as well as moral support to many PWNL, usually in the form of money, small arms, and training of cadres. In order for a rebel movement to obtain Peking's approval, it must, theoretically, be antiimperialist, antifeudal, have a popular base, and be aimed against a national government which is subservient to imperialist influence.

Ideally PWNL should be led by communist parties based on the Chinese model of the 1930s and 1940s, but even a "bourgeois nationalist" movement can achieve the same favorable results, i.e., the establishment of a vigorous, independent, and antiimperialist government. For example, in Angola the Marxist revolutionary contingent—the Popular Movement for the Liberation of Angola—was supported to victory by the USSR. China claimed neutrality, but backed the ill-fated, noncommunist National Front for the Liberation of Angola, withdrawing that assistance only after it became politically embarrassing due to the U.S. and South African support of the same faction.

The insurgencies per se are to fit the classical guerilla warfare mold, including the formation of a popular base, establishing a remote operational area in difficult terrain, avoiding battles against superior forces, concentrating one's forces for surprise attacks on small units or weakly defended installations, and continuous political/propaganda work to extend the popular base while undermining confidence in the government. The insurgents should seek to form the broadest possible united front, cooperating with all antigovernment and antiimperialist movements. After the insurgency has grown to major proportions, the military tactics should change to "mobile warfare" in which large troop concentrations overwhelm government units one by one. Foreign intervention against the insurgents is not to be feared. Indeed, such intervention may further the cause of the revolution by demonstrating the "imperialist lackey" nature of the government and by weakening its will to carry on the protracted war after the foreigners have been worn down and departed.

The Strategy in Operation

So much for the theoretical aspects. How did the PWNL strategy work out in practice during the 1960s? The results certainly did not come up to China's expectations; moreover, Peking's actions were often disappointing to foreign revolutionaries. First of all, China did not support all PWNL— Peking's revolutionary ardor was directly proportional to the hostility which the target government demonstrated against China. If a nation was a member of a U.S. alliance, refused to recognize the P.R.C., or provided bases for U.S. forces, Peking was quick to support virtually any dissident movement, even those which had little popular base and less hope of success. If a government recognized Peking and did not militarily cooperate with the U.S. in East Asia, then China would not normally recognize any insurgency, even if it fitted completely the parameters of PWNL.[4]

China was behaving like any other state; national self interest took precedence over ideology. Favorable state-to-state relations counted for more than revolutionary potential. This became embarrassingly obvious in the formation of Bangladesh from East Pakistan in 1971. It was a classic liberation struggle in every sense, yet Peking supported Pakistan, refused recognition of the new state, and blocked its entrance into the U.N. China's friendship with Pakistan was more important than liberation and independence for the Bengalis.

Second, China's interest in PWNL declined as the distance from home grew. Only representatives of major Asian insurgenices were accorded official status in Peking. In Asia, PWNL were actively supported in Vietnam, Thailand, Laos, Burma, Malaysia, and the Philippines with primary emphasis on the first three nations. Activities in Latin America were virtually ignored. In Africa, tangible support was given to independence movements in the Portuguese colonies of Mozambique, Angola, and Portuguese Guinea (Guinea Bissau). However, the PWNL strategy played second fiddle in Africa because China's main interest was to curry favor with the newly independent black African states in order to maintain and extend its diplomatic status.[5]

In theory, China's PWNL strategy was intended to develop solidarity with nations threatened or oppressed by imperialism and neocolonialism. In fact, PWNL were primarily aimed against Asian nations cooperating with the U.S. against China, or where U.S. forces were active such as in Laos. The ideological aspect of fostering revolution for the eventual destruction of capitalism was less important than state-to-state relations and much less important than the security of China vis-à-vis the U.S. "containment" policy.

Divergence between the theory and the reality of China's PWNL strategy does not determine the success or failure of the concept. However, in the opinion of this writer, PWNL did more harm than good to China's national interests. Initial attempts to apply the concept in Africa were clumsy. On one of Chou En-lai's trips, he let slip a line to the effect that "Africa is ripe for revolution." That garnered more attention than all of his statements on coexistence and efforts to improve state-to-state relations. At best revolution was seen as irrelevant by the newly independent states and, at worst, was perceived as threatening by moderate African leaders. Only a few "radical nationalist" leaders already in power evinced sympathy for the PWNL concept, and three of the most important of those—Kwame Nkrumah of Ghana and Presidents Sukarno of Indonesia and Ben Bella of

Algeria—were all ousted under circumstances which caused serious embarrassment to Peking.[6]

The Indonesian case was particularly tragic since it led to the death of tens of thousands of innocent overseas Chinese. It began in October 1965, when the Indonesian Communist Party (PKI) attempted to assassinate rival military leaders. The PKI killed some generals and their families, but in the retaliation which followed, the PKI was destroyed along with thousands of overseas Chinese who were not Party members. President Sukarno, China's most important non-communist supporter in Asia, became a figurehead and was eventually removed. The PKI had been the world's third largest Communist party and was aligned with Peking in the Sino-Soviet dispute. There is no evidence that China ordered the assassination of the army leaders, but many members of the PKI were overseas Chinese, and Peking may well have known of the plot in advance. It would seem that the spirit of left-wing adventurism fostered by the PWNL concept was partly responsible for the disaster.

On the Southeast Asian mainland, Chinese support for the Malay communist insurgents did not prevent their ultimate failure, but did contribute to the serious racial tension between ethnic Malay and Chinese-Malaysian citizens. In Thailand, Peking pressed hard to develop a strong insurgency to counter the growing U.S. military presence there. Despite nearly ideal conditions of safe havens, remoteness from government administrative centers, grinding poverty, and the presence of foreign forces, the insurgencies in north and northeast Thailand never grew to proportions which threatened the government or pressured them into changing their support of the U.S. in Vietnam and Laos. Chinese assistance to the White Flag Communist Party in Burma, and to various insurgent ethnic minorities during the mid-1970s, achieved no tangible results.

In 1967, I was working as a "China watcher" in the Pentagon when confirmed reports told of an international meeting at the Headquarters of the Kunming Military Region. This was an elaborately prepared session which brought together representatives of insurgent movements and disaffected minority peoples from throughout Southeast

Asia. The purpose of the meeting was to launch wide-scale PWNL offensives wherever possible in Asia. Possibly one intent was to prove to the U.S. that its use of Asian allies to enforce containment of China was doomed to failure. Another purpose may have been to take some of the pressure off Vietnam by over-extending the U.S. in attempts to control new "brush-fire wars."

The reaction within U.S. intelligence and military circles was one of considerable consternation. Alarmists felt that the Southeast Asian nations might soon be immersed in warfare or even fall to communist control. Actually, Peking's efforts fell flat. As a result of increased activities, with money and arms supplied by China, some of the insurgents fell to squabbling among themselves. In Burma, the most important Maoist insurgent leader was killed by his own followers in the White Flag Party in 1968.[7] Most of the hill tribes in Southeast and South Asia used their Chinese-supplied arms indiscriminately—even against each other. In Thailand, increased insurgent activities provoked more intensive government counterinsurgency efforts which may have caused a decline in the number of guerillas active in northeast Thailand in 1968.[8] It may have been true that security for China lay not in one, but in many "Vietnams." However, the leadership's eagerness led them to ignore their own precepts; revolution cannot be exported and local conditions must be ripe, otherwise revolutionary efforts become counterproductive left-wing adventurism. In Asia in the 1960s, the anti-colonial call to arms had lost much of its earlier relevance, imperialist exploitation was not severe enough, and national governments were too well established for successful PWNL.

Both the U.S. and China saw Vietnam as the ultimate proving ground for the PWNL potential. In retrospect, it is apparent that if the communists couldn't win in South Vietnam, they couldn't win anywhere. The government in Saigon owed its very existence to Ho Chi-minh and his Vietminh forces which humbled France in 1954. The Saigon government was never able to establish its own authority throughout South Vietnam. Vietnamese nationalism was either embryonic or often focused on the Democratic Republic of Vietnam. The glue that held the South Vietnamese armed forces together was comprised of individual bravery, pride of unit, and some anticommunism. They were not fighting for a cause; at best they were fighting against a threat.

The size of the U.S. intervention caused the communist strategy to change sharply. Guerilla units played a lessening role while regular D.R.V. army units in South Vietnam carried an ever-increasing share of the fighting. Moreover the D.R.V. relied mainly on the USSR and China for supplies, as opposed to the self-sufficiency stressed by Lin Piao in his exposition of PWNL. But this is mere carping. China can and does claim that Vietnam was a successful example of PWNL; so too were Cambodia and Laos, thanks to D.R.V. assistance.

From the standpoint of Chinese security interests, the Vietnamese communists may have succeeded too well. Certainly it is desirable to have U.S. forces pulling out of mainland Southeast Asia, but too much of the new power there is devolving into Vietnamese rather than Chinese hands. All great powers seek to keep the states on their borders friendly, weak, or both (e.g., the U.S. and Mexico, the USSR and Finland). The Vietnamese army is now the second strongest in Asia. Hanoi has, over the past nine years, relied mainly on the USSR for equipment, and exercises the predominant foreign influence in Cambodia and Laos. China has two choices: it can either continue to give Vietnam a free rein in Southeast Asia or it can attempt to compete for political and economic influence. One testing ground will be the oil-rich offshore islands claimed by both nations. If China chooses to compete, Vietnam could potentially give China more trouble along its southern border than SEATO ever did. In 1975, it was already evident that Thailand's eagerness to mend its relations with Peking is partly due to a fear of Vietnam's quest for Southeast Asian hegemony.[9] If China seeks to blunt Vietnamese dominion in the area, Hanoi will undoubtedly move still closer to Moscow and could serve as a vehicle for Soviet penetration of the area.

The Decline of PWNL and China's New Diplomacy (1969-76)

As early as 1969, it began to dawn on the top U.S. policy makers that China's PWNL strategy was not the world threat which they had supposed. By this time the "Nixon Doctrine" had announced reduced U.S. military manpower commitments in Asia. President Nixon gave a "background-er" news conference in Guam at which he said there were three major reasons why the U.S. did not have to fear China. First, China's model for revolution had insufficient attraction to make its support for subversion dangerous to other governments. Second, China had too many domestic problems to undertake expansionist aggression abroad. Finally, China's nuclear power could easily be deterred in Asia and elsewhere by the U.S. retaliatory striking ability.[10] It was this reassessment of the Chinese "threat" which permitted Washington to explore the possibilities of détente with Peking.

Following the GPCR, China too was reassessing PWNL. There were three interrelated factors which caused the decline of that strategy in the 1970s: first, the international situation changed, and with it, the U.S. threat to China was reduced; second, domestic economic conditions called for an abandonment of self-sufficiency; and finally, the internal political battles preceding the Lin Piao affair ended in victory for Chou En-lai and defeat for the premier spokesman of the PWNL strategy. Each of these causes deserves separate treatment.

The major factor in the foreign policy reappraisal was the greatly heightened Sino-Soviet tension in the aftermath of the March 1969 border clashes. The Soviet military buildup along with the 1968 enunciation of the "Brezhnev Doctrine"[11] combined to raise the USSR to the rank of China's number one enemy. PWNL were counterproductive regarding the Russian military threat: Chinese support for such wars reduced world recognition of Peking and caused many nations to view China as an international renegade, and such feeling reduced the political disadvantages to the USSR of a preemptive nuclear strike on China. However, established foreign policies have a good deal of momentum, and it was not until 1971 that China began a campaign to achieve a new international image.

In Sino-American relations, the initial "ping-pong diplomacy" and Henry Kissinger's secret flight to Peking in mid-1971 are too well known to require repeating here. In Southeast Asia, Burmese President Ne Win was invited to Peking, and Chinese support to Burmese insurgents dropped off to little more than broadcast propaganda. In a major 1971 diplomatic triumph, the P.R.C. was admitted to the U.N. on the "Albanian Resolution" which expelled the Republic of China from the Security Council and General Assembly. Following the Nixon trip in February 1972, the flood gates opened. During that year alone, West Germany, Australia, New Zealand, Japan, Mexico, Guyana, Peru, Chile, and Argentina, among others, granted recognition to Peking.

Such respectability made it far more difficult for the USSR to justify an attack against China. It also provided Peking with the necessary channels to play the "balance of power" diplomacy game.

Of late, Peking has been especially interested in getting Tokyo to tilt in the direction of the P.R.C. Japan and China are natural trading partners, but the purpose goes beyond commerce. Over the past 100 years, the key to the balance of power in Europe had been Germany. Any nation which sought to exercise major influence over West Europe had either to woo Germany or destroy her. In the twentieth century, Japan has played the same role in Asia. China's attempts to weaken Japan in the 1950s and 60s by means of the Japanese Communist Party ended in total frustration. The JCP made no serious inroads and eventually aligned itself with the USSR. Since the 1972 Tanaka visit, Peking has been wooing Japan with trade deals, petroleum supplies, and visions of much greater commercial opportunities to come. In this struggle for Japan, China has the USSR at a disadvantage; Japan and Russia have a long-standing territorial dispute over the Kurile Islands. Of course, Japan remains primarily in the U.S. orbit, but the weakened American presence in Asia provided Peking with opportunities to influence Japan's foreign policy. The Chinese leadership fully realized its limitations in playing an Asian balance of power game. Peking is not yet ready to challenge the U.S.-Japan military alliance. Since the USSR has become the primary threat, it has urged that Washington and Tokyo maintain their defense axis lest Soviet power in the Pacific be expanded.

The domestic economic situation was the second major factor which caused the decline of the armed struggle tactic in China's foreign policy. From the last year prior to the Great Leap Forward (1957) through 1970, the GNP grew at just over 4 percent annually.[12] Even that modest figure is probably high in real terms, since the population grew by almost 200 million in the same period. Thus the per capita growth rate was just over 2 percent and some of the 4 percent GNP growth was "wasted" in government expenditures necessitated by the increased population.

During the same time period (1957-70), Japan's "economic miracle" took place with annual GNP increases often exceeding 10 percent. In Europe, the Common Market stimulated exhilarating growth rates for its member nations. China's burning desire for wealth and power was not being realized; instead of catching up with the industrialized nations, the gap was growing bigger in the 1960s. Some, if not most, of China's slow economic growth was due to the disruptions caused by the Great Leap Forward and the GPCR. However, another important factor was China's isolation and imposed economic self-sufficiency. So long as PWNL was the primary foreign policy strategy, it was difficult to break out of the isolation, since China could hardly trade and share technologies with the same governments it was attempting to overthrow. If the national leadership was convinced that China's foreign trade and contacts needed priority attention, then PWNL automatically would be relegated to a back seat. That brings us to the third major reason why the foreign policy changed.

The political aspect of the swing away from PWNL saw Chou En-lai, and probably Mao Tse-tung, arguing for change while Lin Piao, his military followers, and Ch'en Po-ta, with a group of ideologists, argued for a continuation of present policies. Ch'en was eliminated on domestic issues before the real showdown came in 1971. Naturally the sticking point was whether or not to seek détente with the

U.S. Prior to Henry Kissinger's visit in July, the maneuvering between the Chou and Lin factions remained behind the scenes. One hint was dropped in the July 5 joint editorial celebrating the Party's thirtieth anniversary. It spoke of "interference" from the "left" regarding "proletarian internationalism"—i.e., PWNL and solidarity with approved socialist countries.[13] When opposition from the left is mentioned, it often means that the Party line is swinging to the right. The Party line by definition is always correct; therefore changes in one direction are often masked behind attacks on "deviations" in the opposite direction.

It is possible that Kissinger's "secret" visit to Peking may have been a secret from Chou's opponents as well as Western newsmen. Apparently he dealt only with Chou En-lai and did not meet any of the PLA leadership. In any case, following the Kissinger trip, the issue of détente with the U.S. became public. In his August 1, 1971 Army Day speech, Chief of Staff Huang Yung-sheng concentrated on uncompromising struggle against American imperialism.[14] In the same month, *Red Flag* countered by attacking those opposed to consultations with the U.S. as motivated by subjectivism, dogmatism, and idealism—all symptoms of "ultraleftism."[15]

Lin Piao's death in September terminated the debate and clinched Chou En-Lai's victory. The foreign policy issue, however, does not seem to have been a basic cause of the Lin Piao affair. All of the primary source materials emphasize domestic political issues and the alleged coup attempt (discussed in chapter 3). Still, Lin's demise cut short what might have been a prolonged struggle over how best to achieve security in the international arena.

China's Present International Strategy

Peking's recent foreign policy is probably more complex than at any time in the history of the People's Republic. It is being carried out in at least three basic modes: (1) balance of power diplomacy, (2) "united front" tactics with a broad range of small- and medium-sized nations which now recognize Peking, and (3) PWNL. At present, the first and second modes are receiving much more emphasis than the armed struggle tactic, but any of the three options can be applied to a given situation. Thus China has far more flexibility in its foreign policy than was the case in the 1960s.

Balance of power diplomacy is primarily concerned with countering the Russian menace and has now gone well beyond the first step of opening communications with the U.S. Peking now has an ambassador posted to the European Economic Community, while backing continued presence of U.S. forces in Western Europe and in any Asian nation (except Taiwan and South Korea) which desires to have them. Meanwhile, China continues to curry relations with East European states such as Romania, which have shown some independence from the Soviet line. Clearly the intent is to focus Moscow's attention on Europe while simultaneously preventing the development of a power vacuum in Asia which the USSR might fill.

Not all of the balance of power strategy is played in the realm of great powers. In May 1975 Teng Hsiao-p'ing visited France and strongly hinted that China would look with disfavor on the reunification of North and South Vietnam, but the Vietnamese ignored China's feelings and joined their nations in 1976. Peking countered by courting the Laotian Premier in his first visit to China, and stepping up naval activity in the South China Sea. China seems to be seeking counterweights to slow the ascendancy of Vietnam in Southeast Asia.

The second major mode of securing China's place in the world is the united front tactic. This is derived from the same theoretical base as PWNL which divides the world into imperialist and socialist camps separated by intermediate zones. Briefly, China is attempting to create a broad united front including both the first and second intermediate zones. PWNL are intended to overthrow governments subservient to imperialism in the first intermediate zone of poor nations. United front tactics seek recognition and cooperation even from "imperialist lackey" governments (e.g., President Marcos of the Philippines). The goal of "surrounding the cities from the countryside" remains the same in PWNL and united front tactics, but the latter emphasizes political and

economic cooperation among third world and second intermediate zone nations—i.e., medium-sized industrialized
states. The target of this strategy has been expanded to
include both capitalist and socialist imperialism, and "great
power hegemony." Until his death, Mao still purported to
believe that "either war will bring revolution, or revolution
will prevent war." However, the definition of revolution has
been expanded to include peaceful economic and political
strategies as well as guerilla movements.

Chou En-lai summarized China's united front position in
his report to the Fourth National People's Congress on
January 13, 1975:

> We should ally ourselves with all the forces in the
> world that can be allied with to combat colonialism,
> imperialism, and above all, super-power hegemonism.
> We are ready to establish or develop relations with all
> countries on the basis of the five principles of peaceful
> coexistence.

> The "third world" is the main force in combating
> colonialism, imperialism and hegemonism. *China is a
> developing socialist country belonging to the third
> world.* We should enhance our unity with the countries
> and peoples of Asia, Africa and Latin America and
> resolutely support them in their struggle to win or
> safeguard national independence, defend their state
> sovereignty, protect their natural resources and develop
> their national economies. . . . We support the countries
> and people of the second [intermediate zone] in their
> struggle against super-power control, threats and bully-
> ing. We support the efforts of West European countries
> to get united in this struggle. We are ready to work
> together with the Japanese government.[16]

Chou's formulation of the policy was the most extreme
statement yet seen since it emphasized China's ties to developing nations over the ideological bonds which are supposed to exist among all communist nations. Chou virtually
moved China out of the socialist camp and into the first

intermediate zone.

The implementation of the united front strategy is most often done in the United Nations where China's official statements have consistently been in defense of the rights of small nations. For example, China supports OPEC and other commodity and resource producers' cartels. It supports 200-mile fishing rights, and in 1972, at the U.N. Stockholm Conference on the environment, Peking sided solidly with the poor nations in opposing international pollution control standards. Such standards were seen as a means to perpetuate the economic advantage of the industrial nations by making new industry more expensive. More recently, China has voiced support for the Panamanian position on the canal issue.

In Asia, in order to curry good state-to-state relations, Peking has begun to tell its overseas Chinese communities that they cannot have dual citizenship, and that Peking would prefer that they should be loyal, law-abiding citizens of the nation in which they reside. This was first stated by Chou En-lai in the case of Malaysia where serious racial tensions have created occasional violence between Chinese and Malays, and where the unsuccessful "people's war" had been fought almost completely by overseas Chinese insurgents.

Both the balance of power diplomacy and especially the international united front tactics require that PWNL be deemphasized in practice, although the rhetoric on the subject continues. Practically any issue of *Peking Review* has news reports of "people's armed forces" victories in Thailand—this, even as relations with Bangkok are normalizing and U.S. forces have been evicted. How can Peking justify improving state-to-state relations on the basis of the five principles of peaceful coexistence while at the same time supporting insurgents? The excuse is an old one used by Lenin and Stalin: when the P.R.C. promises no interference in the internal affairs of another nation, the pledge has no bearing on international communist party relations which are theoretically not part of the governmental apparatus.

A more important and problematic question is: why does Peking continue to support PWNL at all? There are at least three possibilities, none of which are mutually exclusive. First, at present levels of support, PWNL are relatively safe. When China aided black freedom fighters against the remnants of colonialism in Africa, practically everyone applauded except Portugal. When China supports guerilla movements opposed to racist regimes in South Africa and Rhodesia, nobody gets upset except the two states concerned. The second reason is that China has long-standing commitments to insurgent forces which are not easily abandoned. If Peking cut off support to the Thai Patriotic Front and the Communist Party of Thailand, the insurgency would not disappear, it would simply come under the exclusive control of Hanoi, or possibly even obtain help from Moscow. China has long had rivals in the revolutionary game, thus she cannot abandon established PWNL without finding her supporting role usurped by others. The third factor is that PWNL allow China to practice "carrot and stick" diplomacy, especially in Asia. Suppose, for example, that state-to-state relations with Malaysia were to turn sour due to renewed racial violence or other Malaysian actions deemed hostile by Peking. China could then attempt to regenerate the armed struggle tactic in that country in order to pressure the government into policies more amenable to Peking.

It is too soon to determine if the present complex foreign policy will provide China with the security, independence, and international leadership role which it has long sought. One disadvantage of the present stance is that it relegates China to being merely one actor among many. Peking has no more claim to leadership of the third world than does Iran or Brazil. The international economic strategies which Peking supports were begun by others. In the balance of power area, China has not been able to bring international forces to bear which could reduce the Soviet military presence on the northern border. On the other hand, Peking's new diplomacy has made it much easier for the U.S. to quietly phase down its twenty-five-year-old policy of "containing" China. The same friendly face has facilitated normalization of relations with formerly hostile governments. Only Taiwan and South Korea are openly unhappy with the new Asian scene. A return to the primacy of PWNL would probably undo much that has been achieved in Asia; I would venture to predict that the present diplomacy will continue in this post-Mao period and that PWNL will likely remain only one string in China's fiddle.

9

Conclusion

In each chapter I have tried to draw out the significance of
material presented, but the complexity of the PLA calls for a
summary conclusion. Rather than attempting further analysis, this chapter is intended to pull together the various
earlier themes into three different overviews of the Chinese
military system—political, socioeconomic, and national
security.

Political

There are two aspects of this topic which will be dealt with
in turn—Party-army relations and political control within
the PLA. Within the last decade, Party-army relations have
gone through a complete circle. In 1965, the Chinese Communist Party (CCP) was politically supreme; the very concept of a domestic institution challenging the CCP was
nearly inconceivable. Civilian Party secretaries served as
political commissars in the military regions and districts,
giving directives to the PLA. The Central Military Commission (CMC) and the General Political Department stressed
PLA subordination to the requirements of the Party apparatus. During the GPCR, the reverse was true—the Party
machinery in the provinces was stripped of power, even
though the bureaucracy remained mostly intact. Typically,
the Party secretaries were suspended and the bureaucrats
worked on under the supervision of "military control com-

mittees." During the 1968-71 period of political reconstruction, military men held most of the top government and Party posts in the provinces and comprised 46 percent of the Ninth Central Committee. After the Lin Piao affair, the governmental machinery was once again turned over to civilian control. In the provinces, this has been a gradual process which is still going on, but a major advance was made at the end of 1973 when military region commanders were reshuffled and stripped of their civilian posts. PLA membership in the Central Committee was halved during the Tenth Party Congress in 1973 and now has about the same proportion of military members as did the Eighth Central Committee (1956-65).

Besides Central Committee membership, there are other ways in which Party-army relations have returned to the status quo of the early 1960s. The present trend is for civilian Party secretaries to again serve as political commissars in military regions and districts. The PLA is again being told, in even stronger terms than before, that it must serve the Party. Rather than military officers supplanting civilian leaders, as was the case during the GPCR, top Politburo leaders have recently held positions in the CMC and headed the General Political Department. It is not clear whether or not the CMC Control Group has been restored. It provided the president, party secretary general, and the premier with veto power over the decisions of the CMC. At present a Party-army balance seems to have been fully restored. Yet if the Party becomes deeply divided in the succession struggle, the PLA is apt to again wield the political balance of power.

Within the PLA, the system of checks and balances has remained largely intact throughout the last decade with a division of responsibilities between political commissars and commanders. There has also been a continuous issue in the PLA regarding how much emphasis should be placed on political indoctrination relative to technical training. However, this "red vs. expert" conflict does not equate to a commissar vs. commander split. The General Political Department serves the professional interests of the PLA and its commissars seem to function in relative harmony with the commanders. A third chain of command in the logistics system provides an additional check on the power of both commissars and commanders.

Another important balance is the limitations imposed on military regions concerning operational control of troop units. Except for some of the military districts during the height of the GPCR, the regional forces have remained under the control of the military regions and districts while the main force army corps have consistently been under the operational control of the center. Under no circumstances short of complete national political collapse could a military region headquarters create an independent geographic power base.

Three serious political problems within the PLA remain to be solved. First, the promotion system engenders the formation of strong competing cliques; a 1968 decision to break down these "mountain strongholds" by periodic transfer of officers to different units seems not to have been thoroughly implemented. Second, the GPCR revealed a good deal of localism because units had not been moved about. The same 1968 decision called for periodic relocation of troop units. At the end of the GPCR, some army corps were reshuffled, and the Sino-Soviet border clashes resulted in redeployments. However, since the early 1970s, the order of battle has changed very little—there seems to be a good deal of resistance within the PLA to the concept of periodic transfers of officers and units. This could become a significant policy issue which would do much to determine the future political activism of the military. Third, the prestige of the PLA and the wholesale transfers of political power to the military during the GPCR resulted in widespread elitism and some megalomania within the officer corps. Peking has resorted to a long-established approach to this problem, i.e., "sending down" officers to temporarily serve in the ranks. One military district has gone so far as to send officers to communes where, for some months, they work with the peasantry. Despite these intra-army difficulties, it seems that the PLA has been put back in its place and that China is not likely to change into a military dictatorship even in the power struggles which are sure to follow the 1976 demise of Mao Tse-tung.

Socioeconomic

PLA prestige remains high and youth are eager to enlist since military service is one of the best ladders to success. The enviable status of the military personnel engenders one problem, i.e., how to handle demobilized servicemen without creating a disgruntled group of veterans. Peking's approach has been to provide ex-servicemen with responsible jobs, but this causes some resentment among civilians who find their own chances of promotion reduced by the appointment of "outsider" ex-soldiers to cadre positions. However, such friction does not seem to have seriously damaged China's generally good civil-military relations.

Despite Peking's long-standing efforts to portray the PLA as making major contributions to the civilian economy, a close look reveals that this is not the case. Instead, the military reduces as much as possible its cost to the nation by emphasizing self-sufficiency. A good deal of its food requirements are met by crops and animals grown on military bases, and small-scale PLA-run industries reduce the national quartermaster budget. Much of the work done by the service arms (e.g., engineer, signal corps, and railway forces) serves civilian as well as military needs, but China is hardly unique in that regard.

The expansion of the paramilitary production-construction corps from frontier areas to provinces throughout China proved to have been a short-lived experiment. In areas where the commune system is well established and ample manpower is available, production-construction corps (PCC) are an unnecessary drain on the state budget. The expansion of the militia may prove more enduring, although, in the opinion of this writer, the attempts over the last decade to increase its political and control roles have not been very successful. From about 1967-72, the PLA was able to use the militia system to extend and consolidate its political power at local levels. The post-Lin Piao attempt to return the militia to Party control has not fully succeeded except in a few large cities, and unless the post-Mao Party shows unexpected unity and strength, the militia will probably remain an institutional asset of the PLA.

National Security

The PLA is primarily a defensive military force. Except for the nuclear and missile programs, very little effort has gone toward providing China with the capability of projecting its military power abroad. Given the size of the PLA, it could overrun any small country on the periphery of China (Vietnam excepted) but would be unable to operate effectively in noncontiguous nations. The present strategic posture has some similarities to the U.S. in the mid-1950s. Under President Eisenhower, the Strategic Air Command received a disproportionate share of the military budget. As a result, the army languished and the U.S. did not have a "flexible response" capability. In situations such as the Hungarian uprising in 1956, we could threaten nuclear war, bluff, or do nothing. China is in much the same position, but with the added disadvantage that its nuclear capability is still so weak that it barely meets deterrent requirements and cannot function as an offensive threat without placing China in the gravest peril.

The ground forces are large enough and sufficiently well equipped to deter or defend against land invasions of China. However, the air and naval forces could quickly be overwhelmed by a sizeable modern enemy force. A great deal of money and time has been spent with scant results attempting to produce modern fighter-interceptors. The large fleet of guided missile patrol boats and the growing fleet of diesel-powered submarines are vulnerable to electronic countermeasures and antisubmarine warfare respectively. Beginning in 1972, pressing civilian needs have reduced the outsized military budgets of several previous years; thus, with the exception of nuclear weapons and rockets, the military technology gap between China and the superpowers has been growing wider, leaving the nation increasingly vulnerable to sea and air attack. With the phasing down of U.S. military presence in Asia, Peking may well have wished to assume the mantle of dominant military power in that part of the globe, but this will not happen in the foreseeable future.

Appendix:

Infantry Unit Organization Charts

by
Harlan Jencks

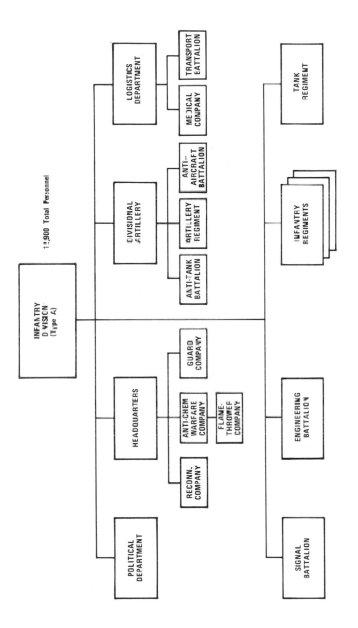

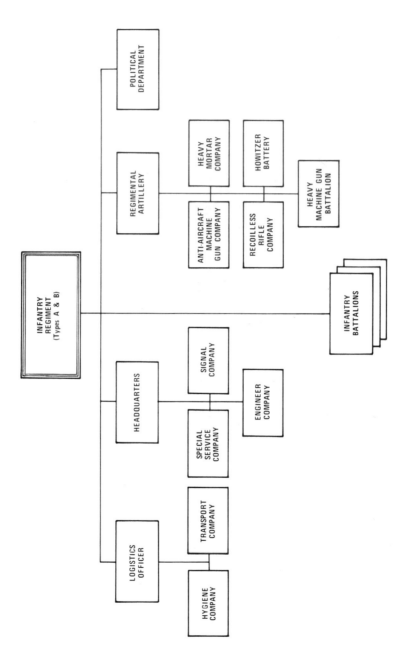

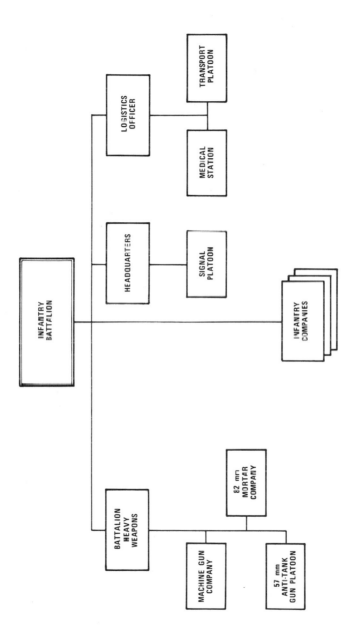

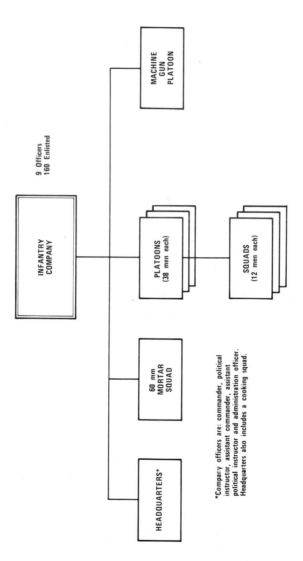

9 Officers
160 Enlisted

INFANTRY COMPANY

HEADQUARTERS*

60 mm MORTAR SQUAD

PLATOONS
(38 men each)

SQUADS
(12 men each)

MACHINE GUN PLATOON

*Company officers are: commander, political instructor, assistant commander, assistant political instructor and administration officer. Headquarters also includes a cooking squad.

Notes

Notes to Chapter 1

1. The low figure is from *Military Balance* (London: Institute of Strategic Studies, 1974). The high figure is from Admiral Thomas H. Moorer, "General Purpose Forces Compared," *Commanders Digest* 15, no. 16 (April 18, 1974).

2. The method used to derive these figures is admittedly crude. We know the ground forces have 37 or 38 army corps, and that they number approximately 50,000 men each for a total of about 1,800,000. There are also around 40 divisions which are independent in the sense that they are supporting units to the basic infantry forces—e.g., artillery, armored, cavalry, and railway divisions plus signal, transport, and engineering regiments. An educated guess is that they total 300,000 personnel. The ground forces also have a large number of regional forces—independent divisions, regiments, and battalions which are at the disposal of military regions, districts, and garrisons. These, plus the special category "border defense forces," number over 1 million. On the eve of the Cultural Revolution in 1966, the People's Armed Police units were absorbed into the regional forces and their number alone accounts for about half of the regional force total.

Estimating the size of the air and naval forces is harder still. The Air Force has about 4000 aircraft and hundreds of airfields and radar stations throughout China. Estimates differ because no one outside China knows how many men are required to fly, service, and provide logistical support for the aircraft; train the personnel; man the radar and antiaircraft systems; staff the headquarters; and provide security. U.S. and British officials are currently using a figure of 220,000. In addition, there are 14 divisions of antiaircraft artillery troops under Air Force control, bringing the total to something over 300,000 men. The naval estimate is derived in the same way. It has about 1500 vessels, most of which are very small, so crew and shore support personnel probably number around

150,000. The Navy also has a shore-based air arm and some on-shore coastal defense responsibilities; therefore its total is estimated at 200,000. The grand total is thus the sum of about 3.2 million ground forces personnel, 300,000 air force, and 200,000 naval, which add up to 3.7 million. This estimate may be slightly conservative since it does not include the Second Artillery rocket and nuclear forces, the numbers of which are unknown, but probably are in the five figure range.

3. All official U.S. estimates claim over four million men in the Soviet military. However, many of those are doing capital construction, land reclamation, and other work similar to China's production-construction corps, which are not counted as part of the regular PLA. The two nations' combat forces are, therefore, about equal in total personnel.

4. Mao's address to the First Plenary Session of the Ninth Party Congress, 1969, as translated in U.S. Department of Commerce, *Translations on Communist China*, Joint Publications Research Service (JPRS hereafter), Washington, D.C., May 21, 1970, JPRS no. 50564, p. 6. Emphasis added.

5. The Canton Military Region served as the command post for the combined arms takeover of the Paracel Islands in 1974.

6. In a 1971 talk, Mao referred to the separation of the political, command, and logistics systems. See *Chinese Law and Government* 5, nos. 3 & 4 (Fall-Winter 1972): 39.

7. Sydney H. Jammes, "The Chinese Defense Burden," in U.S. Congress, Joint Economic Committee, *China: A Reassessment of the Economy*, Washington, D.C., July 1975. The higher estimate is in U.S. Arms Control Disarmament Agency, *World Military Expenditures and Arms Transfers, 1965-74*, Washington, D.C., 1976.

Notes to Chapter 2

1. Strictly speaking, the armed forces departments are controlled by the civil Party committees. However, their functions are in large part military-militia control and training, and a substantial portion of the armed departments staffs are active duty military cadres.

2. *China News Analysis*, Hong Kong (CNA hereafter), February 9, 1973, p. 2.

3. William Heaton, "The Minorities and the Military in China" (Paper presented at the U.S.A.F. Air University conference on The Role of the Military in Communist Societies, Maxwell A.F.B., November 1975).

4. Ibid.

5. Sydney H. Jammes, "The Chinese Defense Burden," in U.S.

Congress, Joint Economic Committee, *China: A Reassessment of the Economy*, Washington, D.C., July 1975.

6. Ibid.

7. Gordon White, "The Politics of Social Stratification in a Socialist Society; the Case of China, 1959-69" (Ph.D. dissertation, Stanford University, 1974), p. 348.

8. Ibid., p. 387.

9. Michel Oksenberg, "Local Leaders in Rural China, 1962-65, Individual Attributes, Bureaucratic Positions and Political Recruitment," in *Chinese Communist Politics in Action*, ed. A. Doak Barnett (Seattle: University of Washington Press, 1969), p. 164.

10. White, "Politics of Social Stratification," p. 369.

11. Ibid. White explores the activities of the veterans' mass organizations during the Cultural Revolution and concludes that they acted as potentially powerful political interest groups. As late as 1974, refugees in Hong Kong reported wall posters in Canton in which veterans complained about insufficient demobilization bonuses and poor job assignments. A general discussion of veterans' groups in the GPCR is in Alan P. L. Liu, *Political Culture and Group Conflict in Communist China* (Santa Barbara: Clio Press, 1976), chapter 7.

12. CNA, October 6, 1972, p. 4.

13. A hero of a border defense unit during the 1969 clashes with the USSR reported that he had never previously heard the sound of artillery and had only once engaged in target practice (*Peking Review*, June 20, 1969, p. 141).

14. A more detailed discussion of the militia is in chapter 7.

15. J. Chester Cheng, ed., *The Politics of the Chinese Red Army* (Stanford, Calif.: Hoover Institution on War, Revolution and Peace, 1966), pp. 374-75.

16. As quoted in John Gittings, "Army-Party Relations in the Light of the Cultural Revolution," in *Party Leadership and Revolutionary Power in China*, ed. John Wilson Lewis (Cambridge University Press, 1970, p. 388.

17. P'eng Chen.

18. Lung Wei-tung, "Wholeheartedly Supporting the Revolutionaries," *Jen-min Jih-pao* [People's Daily] (JMJP hereafter), April 10, 1967, p. 1.

19. Cheng, *Politics of the Chinese Red Army*, p. 565. Liaison stations were established in 1961 among military regions and districts and civil organizations such as colleges, factories, and railway bureaux.

20. *Ching-kang-shan* [Ching-kang Mountains] (Peking), January 11, 1967, translated in American Consulate General, Hong Kong, *Survey of China Mainland Press*, April 6, 1967, p. 19. Hereafter cited as SCMP.

21. Ibid., p. 21.

22. Ralph Powell, "The Role of the Military in China's Transportation and Communication Systems," in U.S. Information Service, Hong Kong, *Current Scene*, February 7, 1972, pp. 5-12. The directive is available in American Consulate General, Hong Kong, *Current Background* (CB hereafter), May 6, 1968, p. 46.

23. JMJP, April 13, 1967, p. 1. "On January 21st and 23rd, Chairman Mao, the Party Central Committee and the Central Military Commission issued the great call for the PLA to support the revolutionary left."

24. JMJP, January 22, 1967, p. 1.

25. In the outpouring of "how-to-do-it" articles in newspapers and other media during March–April 1967, all examples of military work with mass organizations were written by military district officials or leaders of garrisons.

26. JMJP, April 12, 1967; and *Kwang-ming Jih-pao* (Peking), March 25, 1967, p. 1, provide two examples of such activities in military district Party committees.

27. "Students of military academies are free to establish revolutionary ties with localities according to the rules of the CMC, but you must not take part when political struggles are carried out. If you take part, they will think that the PLA is involved and this is undesirable." Yeh Chien-ying, currently minister of National Defense, November 13, 1966, as translated in American Consulate General, Hong Kong, *Selections from China Mainland Magazines* (SCMM hereafter), Supplement, May 8, 1967, p. 36.

28. Chou En-lai told Edgar Snow that two million troops were used in the GPCR (Edgar Snow, *The Long Revolution* (New York City: Random House, 1971), p. 103). The main force units which entered the GPCR were nearly all identified and could not have numbered much over one million. That leaves the other million to be accounted for; the estimated size of the regional forces is about one million.

29. The January 21 directive ordering the PLA into the GPCR stipulated: "counter-revolutionaries and counter-revolutionary organizations which oppose the proletarian revolutionary leftists must be firmly suppressed." CB, May 6, 1968, p. 49.

30. Jurgen Domes, "The Role of the Military in the Formation of Revolutionary Committees, 1967-68," *China Quarterly* 44 (October-December 1970). Prof. Domes provides a province-by-province survey of military reactions to the January 21 and 23 orders.

31. *Ta-p'i T'ung-hsun* [Mass Criticism and Repudiation Bulletin] (Peking), October 5, 1967, translated in SCMP, February 26, 1968, p. 5.

32. The form which that realization took was the January 12 reorganization of the CMC and the January 14 directive ordering the regional PLA to take over the Party communications and

archives—discussed above.

33. Lung Wei-tung, a "responsible person" of the Heilung-kiang Military District, Harbin Radio, October 6, 1967, quoted at greater length in Gittings, "Army-Party Relations."

34. Liang Chi-ch'ing, deputy political commissar, Kiangsu Military District, in JMJP, April 4, 1967.

35. Wang Chia-tao, commander, Heilungkiang Military District, in *Kwang-ming Jih-pao* (Peking), March 25, 1967, as translated in SCMP, April 5, 1967, p. 19.

36. Li Ts'ai-han, commander, Kweichow Military District, in *Cheng-fa Hung Ch'i* [Politics and Law Red Flag] (Peking), no. 6, 1967. Subquotations are the subheads of Li's articles.

37. See CB, May 6, 1968, p. 115, for text of directive.

38. An even larger number of political commissars were removed, but these were Party secretaries who held concurrent PLA positions, thus their removal cannot be definitely attributed to PLA misbehavior.

39. See chapter 4 for more detail.

40. For a detailed account, see Thomas Robinson, "The Wuhan Incident," *China Quarterly* 47 (July-September 1971).

41. For a list of military districts taken over, see chapter 4.

42. Preparatory groups were appointed by the military control committees. They included Party cadres, mass organization representatives, and the PLA. The personnel of the preparatory group usually became the leadership of the revolutionary committee.

43. *Chu-ying Tung-fang-hung* [Pear River Film Studio, East Is Red] (Canton), September 13, 1967, as translated in U.S. Department of Commerce, Joint Publications Research Service (JPRS hereafter), *Communist China Digest*, JPRS no. 43449, November 29, 1967. p. 50.

44. Ibid., p. 49.

45. "Mao's Latest Instructions—September 1967," varying Red Guard versions are translated in *Facts and Features* 1, no. 1 (November 1, 1967): 19; *Communist China Digest* 193, JPRS no. 43903 (January 8, 1968): 44-45; and Chien Yu-shen, *China's Fading Revolution* (Hong Kong: Centre of Contemporary Chinese Studies, 1969), p. 276.

46. *Cheng-fa Hung-ch'i* [Politics and Law Red Flag] (Canton), April 5, 1968, translated in SCMP, May 8, 1968, p. 1.

47. Political rivalries included the 38th Corps versus the Peking Military Region, the 69th Corps vs. the Shansi Military District, the 55th vs. the Kwangsi Military District, naval and air units vs. the Hainan Military District, the 18th Corps vs. the Tibet Military Region, and the 54th Corps vs. the Chengtu Region. For full discussion, see Harvey Nelsen, "Military Forces in the Cultural Revolution," *China Quarterly* 51 (July-September 1972): 459.

48. For example, the former political commissar of the Chengtu

Military Region, Chang Kuo-hua, complained: "Some of the army units . . . are now trying to topple me." Unidentified Red Guard tabloid, translated in SCMP, May 20, 1968, p. 8.

49. New China News Agency (NCNA hereafter), Peking, January 7, 1968, printed in SCMP, January 17, 1968, p. 14.

50. *Kang-pa-i* [Steel August 1st] (Wuhan), June, 1968, as translated in SCMP, July 16, 1968, p. 8. Another reported Mao quote stated: "Since the number of local armed units in our country is large, the various military regions, districts, and army corps should have the duty to help these armed units to rectify their mistakes, publicly commend their achievements, and regard them as brother units." *Hsiao-ping* [Little Soldier] (Canton), April 5, 1968, in SCMP, May 2, 1968, p. 1.

51. See chapter 4, "Recent History," for details.

52. JMJP, October 19, 1967, p. 1, quoting Mao Tse-tung.

53. Translated in SCMP, July 16, 1968, p. 8. The quote is attributed to Wen Yu-ch'eng, then the deputy chief of the General Staff.

54. For details and sources, see Nelsen, "Military Forces," p. 465.

55. CNA, October 6, 1972, p. 4.

56. This author has discovered no reports of independent units relocating in China.

57. Radio Hupeh, June 19, 1972, as translated in *Union Research Service*, Hong Kong (URS hereafter), July 7, 1972, p. 21.

58. Radio Hunan, December 25, 1973, as translated in URS, January 11, 1974, p. 45.

59. See the section in chapter 3 entitled "Recent History of the High Command."

60. Snow, *The Long Revolution*, p. 103.

Notes to Chapter 3

1. U.S. Department of State, *Politico-Military Relationships in Communist China*, prepared for the Bureau of Intelligence and Research by Ralph Powell (Washington, D.C., 1963), pp. 5-6.

2. Along with the Party chairmanship, the premier, and Party secretary general.

3. Yeh Chien-ying, Nieh Jung-chen, and Hsu Hsiang-ch'ien.

4. The probable 1976 membership of the Standing Committee is discussed in the section of this chapter subtitled "Recent History of the High Command."

5. In 1966, former Defense Minister Lin Piao sent a letter to "responsible members" of the CMC. It was addressed only to the vice-chairmen. (Presumably Mao had approved his sending it and thus was not himself an addressee.) Translated in American

Consulate General, Hong Kong, *Survey of China Mainland Press* (SCMP hereafter), June 9, 1967, p. 30.

6. There is a possibility that all military region commanders are members of the full CMC.

7. Notably the Party chairman is excluded from the Control Group, presumably because of this concurrent position as leader of the CMC. *Tzu-liao Ch'uan-chi* [Special Collection of Materials], Canton, translated in American Consulate General, Hong Kong, *Selections from China Mainland Magazines* (SCMM hereafter), October 21, 1968, p. 18.

8. Ibid., p. 26. See also pp. 19, 22, 25, and 67.

9. *Chinese Communist Affairs: Facts and Features* 1, no. 16 (May 29, 1968).

10. Red Guard document, translated in *Issues and Studies* 5, no. 11 (August 1969): 91.

11. In the 1950s, the Inspectorate was a separate department, headed by Yeh Chien-ying.

12. *Wen-i Chan-pao* [Literature and Arts Combat Bulletin] (Peking), March 9, 1968, in SCMP, March 28, 1968, pp. 10-13.

13. Ibid.

14. Courtesy of Professor Jurgen Domes. A highly valuable but difficult to obtain source on organizations in China is *Chung-hua Jen-min Kung-ho-kuo Tsu-chih Jen-min Piao* [Personnel and Organizational Charts of the People's Republic of China], an annually updated internal Japanese government directory.

15. Some Hong Kong analysts feel that this guard unit may be quite large, with responsibilities extending beyond Peking—acting as internal security police for the officer corps. Wan Tung-hsing (known as Mao's bodyguard) is believed to be the commander of the CMC Guard Unit. China News Analysis, Hong Kong (CNA hereafter), March 4, 1974, p. 5. See also, American Consulate General, Hong Kong, *Selections from the People's Republic of China Press* (SPRCP hereafter), May 11, 1975, pp. 162-65.

16. The former chief of the General Staff, Huang Yung-sheng, referred to one of these arms, the engineers, as the "Engineering Corps of the CMC." Red Guard collection of leadership speeches, translated in SCMM, August 6, 1968, p. 17.

17. J. Chester Cheng, ed., *The Politics of the Chinese Red Army* (Stanford, Calif.: Hoover Institution on War, Revolution, and Peace, 1966), pp. 535, 544.

18. "At a CMC meeting in 1962 . . . everyone . . . agreed that a unit should be deployed to a particular section of the border." Red Guard compilation "About the Lo Jui-ch'ing Issue," translated in *Issues and Studies* 5, no. 11 (August 1968): 91.

19. Much of our knowledge is derived from a 1963 document— "The Political Work Regulations for the Chinese People's Liberation Army"—which made its way out of China. Translated in Kau

Yin-mau et al., *The Political Work System of the Chinese Communist Military* (Providence, Rhode Island: East Asia Language and Area Center, Brown University, 1971), pp. 217-323.

20. For a thorough discussion of GPD functions, see Glenn Dick, "The General Political Department" in *The Military and Political Power in China in the 1970's*, ed. William Whitson (New York: Praeger, 1972), pp. 171-182.

21. *Nan-fang Jih-pao* [Southern Daily] (Canton), January 21, 1971, translated in SCMP Supplement, March 12, 1970, p. 13.

22. John Gittings, *The Role of the Chinese Army* (London: Oxford University Press, 1967), p. 110.

23. Dick, "The General Political Department," p. 175.

24. Gittings, *The Role of the Chinese Army*, p. 110.

25. Kau Ying-mao, *The Political Work System of the Chinese Communist Military*, p. 275.

26. Paul Godwin, "The PLA and the Political Modernization of China" (unpublished paper delivered at the U.S. Air University conference on The Role of the Military in Communist Societies, Maxwell AFB, November 1975).

27. Su Yu, Yang Ch'eng-wu, and Lo Jui-ch'ing.

28. John Gittings, "Army–Party Relations in the Light of the Cultural Revolution," in *Party Leadership and Revolutionary Power in China*, ed. John Wilson Lewis (Cambridge University Press, 1970).

29. Richard E. Gillespie and John Sims, "The General Rear Services Department," in *The Military and Political Power in China in the 1970's*, ed. William Whitson (New York: Praeger, 1972).

30. Ibid.

31. A military hero of the Engineering Corps was received and feted in Peking exclusively by GRSD leaders. The tenor of the proceedings strongly implied that the engineers were subordinate to the GRSD. New China News Agency (NCNA hereafter), Peking, October 13, 1967, printed in SCMP, October 18, 1967, pp. 20-21.

32. *Chung-kung Nien-pao*, 1973 [Yearbook on Chinese Communism], book 2 (Taipei: Institute for the Study of Chinese Communist Problems, 1973).

33. *Hung-t'ieh-tao* [Red Railways] (Peking), February 11, 1967, translated in U.S. Department of Commerce, Joint Publications Research Service (JPRS hereafter), *Communist China Digest*, July 31, 1967, no. 188, JPRS no. 42015: 108.

34. American Consulate General, Hong Kong, *Current Background* (CB hereafter), May 6, 1968, pp. 76-77.

35. SCMP, June 3, 1968, p. 8.

36. The overseas arms supply system was analyzed in *Hsing-tao Jih-pao*, Hong Kong, March 28, 1972, in *Translations on the People's Republic of China*, JPRS no. 55816, April 27, 1972, pp. 1-

8. Naval assistance is discussed in Bruce Swanson, "The PRC Navy—Coastal Defense or Blue Water," *U.S. Naval Institute Proceedings* 102, no. 879 (May 1976).

37. *Wen-i Chan-pao*, March 9, 1968, in SCMP, March 28, 1968.

38. *Tzu-liao Ch'uan-chi*, SCMM, October 21, 1968, p. 25.

39. Chou En-lai described a former director of this office as "being in charge of national defense industries." Ibid., p. 18.

40. Ibid. Chou referred to the same former director as having been approved by Defense Minister Lin Piao.

41. Ibid., p. 19.

42. *Tsao-fan Yu-li*, Peking, translated in *Communist China Digest*, JPRS no 42977, October 16, 1967, p. 86.

43. Parris Chang, "China's Military-Industrial Complex and Its Policy Inputs" (paper delivered to the Air University conference on The Role of the Military in Communist Societies, Maxwell Air Force Base, November 1975). At the end of 1975, the respective ministers of the 2nd through 7th Machine Building Ministries were Liu Hsi-yao, Li Chi-tai, Wang Cheng, Li Ch'eng-fang, Pien Chiang, and Wang Yang. All but Liu Hsi-yao are PLA officers.

44. Cheng Chu-yuan, "Growth and Structural Changes in the Chinese Machine Building Industry, 1952-66," *China Quarterly*, no. 41 (January-March 1970): 27. Amended by later information from the Tenth Party Congress.

45. *Tzu-liao Ch'uan-chi*, SCMM, October 21, 1968, p. 10.

46. Wu Yuan-li and Robert Sheeks, *The Organization and Support of Scientific Research and Development in Mainland China* (New York City: Praeger, 1970), pp. 149-51, 253, 260.

47. NCNA, Peking, August 27, 1967, in U.S. Foreign Broadcast Information Service, *Daily Report: People's Republic of China* (FBIS hereafter), August 28, 1967, pp. ccc 3-50.

48. *Tzu-liao Ch'uan-chi*, SCMM, October 21, 1968, p. 20.

49. *Kwang-ming Jih-pao*, Peking, May 8, 1971, p. 2, in *Translations on Communist China*, no. 153 JPRS (July 7, 1971), no. 53542: 12.

50. *Tzu-liao Ch'uan-chi* SCMM, October 21, 1968, p. 13.

51. An additional service arm, the PLA Security Forces Headquarters was abolished on the eve of the GPCR. The security units were amalgamated into the regional forces.

52. Cheng Mien-chih, "The Organization and Equipment of the Chinese Communist Infantry," *Issues and Studies* 3, no. 10: 23. Signal forces have battalion sized units at both corps and division levels.

53. *Chung-kung Nien-pao*, 1973 [Yearbook on Chinese Communism], pp. 53-54. See also, Leo Goodstadt, "Putting the Army in its Place," in *Far Eastern Economic Review*, November 29, 1974.

54. Chang Ta-chih, commander of the Artillery Forces, is presently the only service arm leader on the CMC Standing Com-

mittee.

55. *Aussenpolitick* (Hamburg), February 1972, pp. 66-70, in *Translations on the People's Republic of China*, no. 186, JPRS no. 55616 (April 27, 1972): 14.

56. Lu Cheng-ts'ao.

57. *Hung-t'ieh-tao*, in *Communist China Digest*, no. 188, JPRS no. 42015 (July 31, 1967): 108.

58. *Hung-ch'i T'ung-hsuan* [Red Flag Bulletin] (Canton), June 1968, translated in SCMP, July 8, 1968, p. 4.

59. Charles Horner, "The Production of Nuclear Weapons," in *The Military and Political Power in China in the 1970's*, ed. William Whitson (New York: Praeger, 1972), p. 245.

60. Hsiang Chung-hua and Wang Shu-sheng respectively; *Yomiuri* (Tokyo), Peking dispatch, June 1, 1967, translated in FBIS, June 2, 1967, p. ccc 32.

61. The former commander of the Railway Forces who had operational control over his troops also "repeatedly requested" the CMC to grant him the power to transfer and assign duties to subdivisional officers. Despite the fact that Lu Cheng-ts'ao had more authority within his service than his colleagues, that request was apparently refused. *Hung-t'ieh-tao*, in *Communist China Digest*, no. 188, JPRS no. 42015 (July 31, 1967).

62. Chin Chien-li, "Survey of Artillery and Second Artillery," *Hsing-tao Jih-pao*, Hong Kong, December 29, 30, 31, 1970, January 1, 1971, in *Translations on Communist China*, JPRS no. 52417, February 18, 1971: 18.

63. Thomas H. Moorer, "General Purpose Forces Compared," *Commanders Digest* 15, no. 16 (April 18, 1974): 8.

64. Chin Chien-li, "A Look at Every Aspect of the Chinese Communist Armored Forces," *Hsing-tao Jih-pao*, September 22-26, 1971, in *Translations on the People's Republic of China*, JPRS no. 54447 (November 10, 1971): 10.

65. Cheng Mien-chih, "The Organization and Equipment of the Chinese Communist Infantry."

66. This is assuming 10 tanks per tank company which is the Soviet pattern. Information supplied by Harlan Jencks of the University of Washington.

67. Moorer, "General Purpose Forces Compared."

68. *Chung-kung Nien-pao* 1973 [Yearbook on Chinese Communism], book 2, p. 53. One such Western estimate was printed in *The Far Eastern Economic Review*, November 29, 1974, p. 53.

69. Lan Ching, "Chinese Communist Chemical Defense Forces, *Hsing-tao Jih-pao*, August 25, 26, 27, 1970, in *Translations on Communist China*, no. 132, JPRS no. 52264 (January 27, 1971): 1-7.

70. This is not meant to denigrate China's considerable transportation accomplishments. Road mileage has gone up sixfold since 1949 to 650,000 kilometers, and the truck fleet has been

expanded rapidly over the past decade. Since 1949, railway mileage has doubled to over 40,000 kilometers. Angus Fraser, *The People's Liberation Army* (New York City: Crane Russak & Co., 1973), p. 6.

71. "The Southwest Engineers Detachment [one such paramilitary unit], gave the PLA a bad name." *Hung-t'ieh-tao*, in *Communist China Digest*, no. 188: 108.

72. This point was made by Joseph Heinlein, "The Ground Forces," in *The Military and Political Power in China in the 1970's*, ed. William Whitson (New York: Praeger, 1972), p. 166.

73. Thomas H. Moorer, "People's Republic of China: Strategic Forces," *Commander's Digest* 14, no. 22 (November 29, 1973): 5.

74. *South China Morning Post* (Hong Kong), September 20, 1974 citing *Strategic Survey* (London: Institute of Strategic Studies, 1974).

75. Alice Langley Hsieh, "China's Nuclear Missile Program: Regional or Intercontinental?," *China Quarterly* 45 (January-March 1971), p. 88.

76. U.S. satellite photos spotted an IRBM installation eighty miles from the nearest rail line, according to *Newsweek*, April 14, 1975, p. 15.

77. Statement by former CIA director, William Colby, in U.S. Congress, Joint Economic Committee, *Allocation of Resources in the Soviet Union and China, 1975*, June-July 1975.

78. *Newsweek*, March 1, 1976, p. 65.

79. Alice Langley Hsieh, "China's Nuclear Missile Program," p. 89.

80. The pre-GPCR Standing Committee consisted of Mao Tse-tung as chairman, Lin Piao as first vice-chairman, followed in order of precedence by Ho Lung, Nieh Jung-chen, Lui P'o-cheng, Hou Hsiang-ch'ien, Yeh Chien-ying, Lo Jui-ch'ing, and Hsiao Hua. It was later revealed that Ch'en I was also a member, but his ranking was not announced. Ho Lung, Lo Jui-ch'ing, and Hsiao Hua were dismissed during the GPCR. Although Lo and Hsiao have since been rehabilitated, there is no evidence that they are now serving on the CMC. Lui P'o-cheng retired due to blindness and old age. Mao and Ch'en I died of natural causes and Lin Piao died a political death.

81. Article by Ch'i Pen-yu in *Hung-ch'i*, no. 8, May 23, 1967.

82. *Peking Review*, no. 51 (December 16, 1966): 8.

83. *Chugoku Kenkyo Geppo*, Tokyo, December 1969, in *Translations on Communist China*, JPRS no. 50719 (June 11, 1970): 1-3.

84. This was not a new policy. In 1964, Mao had put forward a national slogan "learn from the PLA." NCNA, May 8, 1967, quoting Mao's May 7 Directive of 1966, in SCMP, May 11, 1967, p. 19.

85. *Hung-ch'i*, no. 8, May 23, 1967, quoting Mao's speech of May 16, 1966; translated in FBIS, August 7, 1967, p. ccc 1. Emphasis

added.

86. CB, May 6, 1968, pp. 34-35.

87. *Jen-min Jih-pao* [People's Daily] (JMJP hereafter), January 2, 1967, quoting *Liberation Army Daily* (LAD hereafter) of the previous day. Translated in SCMP, January 6, 1967, p. 3.

88. LAD, January 12, 1967, as translated in SCMP, January 18, 1967 (emphasis added).

89. This point was made by Ellis Joffe, "The Chinese Army in the Cultural Revolution: The Politics of Intervention," *Current Scene* 8, no. 18 (December 7, 1970).

90. LAD, January 14, 1967, as translated in SCMP, January 18, 1967, p. 1.

91. CB, May 6, 1968, p. 46.

92. *Tokyo Shinbum*, February 4, 1967, reporting Peking wall posters.

93. Compare the CMC directives of January 28, February 8, February 11, and February 16. All are in CB, May 6, 1968, pp. 54-55, 66, 71-72, 78-79.

94. *Yomiuri* (Tokyo), April 13, 1967, reporting Peking wall posters of April 12, translated in FBIS, April 13, 1967, p. ccc 6.

95. Hsieh Fu-chih, Yang Ch'eng-wu, Wu Fa-hsien, and Lin Piao's wife, Yeh Ch'un.

96. Those added were Yan Ch'eng-wu, acting chief of staff, Hsieh Fu-chih, minister of Public Security, Su Yu, in charge of the GPCR in defense industries, and Hsiao Hua, director, GPD. *Kyodo* (Tokyo), April 24, 1967, as translated in FBIS, April 24, 1967, p. ccc 42.

97. Presumably on political issues the votes would have pitted Lin Piao and the other four new members of the CMC against the veteran Marshals, Yeh, Hsu, Ch'en I, and Nieh Jung-chen. The only other members were Mao, the chairman, and Liu Po-ch'eng who was in his eighties, blind, and barely able to walk. Neither Mao nor Liu were presumed to be in regular attendance at CMC meetings.

98. LAD, August 25, 1967, as translated in SCMP, August 31, 1967, p. 25.

99. *Mainichi* (Tokyo), August 9, 1967, translated in FBIS, August 10, 1967, p. ccc 8.

100. *Wen-i Chan-pao* [Literature and Arts Combat Bulletin], March 9, 1968, translated in SCMP, March 28, 1968, pp. 10-13.

101. The central directive of September 5 refers to the earlier order of August 25; see SCMP, September 22, 1967, p. 1.

102. Ibid.

103. "A Circular of the General Office of the Central Committee," September 18, 1967, in SCMP, November 29, 1967, p. 5.

104. "Mao's Latest Instructions," as cited in *Facts and Features* 1, no. 1 (November 1, 1967): 19.

105. *Wen-k'o T'ung-hsun* [Cultural Revolution Bulletin] (Canton), October 9, 1967, as translated in *Communist China Digest* no. 193, JPRS no. 43903 (January 8, 1968): 44-45.

106. Wang Li, Lin Chieh, Mu Hsin, and Kuan Feng.

107. There was an in-depth report on the Wuhan Incident completed in October 1967. It was submitted to the Central CRG. No mention was made of the PLA/CRG although copies were sent to its individual members. *Hung-tien-hsun* [Red Telegram] (Canton), March 1968, in SCMP, April 9, 1968, pp. 1-4.

108. Wu apparently held that post until the spring of 1968 when the new chief of staff, Huang Yung-sheng, took over the reins of the Administrative Committee. Wu remained as a serving member of the committee until his disappearance in 1971.

109. Hsieh Fu-chih headed the group. *Wen-i Chan-pao*, SCMP, March 28, 1968, pp. 11-12.

110. See, for example, Red Guard transcripts of two meetings in the autumn of 1967, in SCMP, January 3, 1968, p. 5, and January 22, 1968, p. 18.

111. Lin Chieh, quoted in *Hsin-chu-ying* [New Pearl River Film Studio] (Canton), August 1, 1968, in SCMP, September 29, 1968, p. 5.

112. Liu Hsien-ch'uan was the sole political survivor on the Administrative Committee. Huang Yung-sheng, Wu Fa-hsien, and Chiu Hui-tso were on the Standing Committee; so, too, was Yeh Ch'un who may have served concurrently as director or secretary to the Administrative Committee.

113. The following discussion is drawn partly from two articles: Philip Bridgham, "The Fall of Lin Piao," *China Quarterly* 55 (July/September 1973); and Harry Harding, "Political Trends in China Since the Cultural Revolution," *The Annals of the American Academy of Political and Social Science*, July 1972.

114. There are other plausible explanations as well. Roger Glenn Brown argues that Mao and Chou En-lai may have provoked the incident in order to maximize the Soviet threat and thus justify their controversial policy of détente with the U.S.; in "Chinese Politics and American Policy: A New Look at the Triangle," *Foreign Policy* 23 (Summer 1976).

115. A detailed analysis of the March 1969 border clashes and ensuing negotiations was done by Thomas Robinson, "The Sino-Soviet Border Dispute," *The American Political Science Review* 66, no. 4 (December 1972): 1175-1202.

116. A. Doak Barnett, *Uncertain Passage* (Washington, D.C.: The Brookings Institution, 1974), p. 85.

117. Namely, Chief of Staff Huang Yung-Sheng; GRSD director, Chiu Hui-tso; Air Force commander Wu Fa-hsien; Navy Political Commissar Li Tso-p'eng; and Lin's wife, Yeh Ch'un. All were members of the CMC Standing Committee. Lin also enjoyed

the political support of the commander and political commissar of the Peking Military Region, respectively, Ch'eng Wei-shan and Li Hsueh-feng.

118. The self-criticisms were probably written by Huang Yung-sheng, Wu Fa-hsien, Ch'iu Hui-tso, Li Tso-p'eng, and Yeh Ch'un. Ch'eng Wei-shan and Li Hsueh-feng also apologized but did not write self-criticisms.

119. Unfortunately, it has not been revealed how many men Mao added nor who they were, but they almost certainly included Li Teh-sheng and Chang Ta-chih. On key policy votes, Lin would then be outvoted with Mao, Yeh Chien-ying, Nieh Jung-chen, Hsu Hsiang-ch'ien, Chang Ta-chih, and Li Teh-sheng, carrying six to five over Lin, Huang, Chiu, Wu, and Li. This is assuming that Lin's wife was not on the Standing Committee. The civilian Party ideologue, Wang Hung-wen, was later (1975) identified as a vice-chairman of the CMC; he might have been added at this earlier period.

120. The three supports and two militaries became a blanket term referring to PLA activities in the civilian polity and economy. Literally, it referred to military support of industry, agriculture, and the "revolutionary left," and military control and training.

121. The quote is also an interesting case of manipulating Mao against himself. Han was not purged following Lin's death, but he was apparently suspended during most of 1972 and was reassigned to the remote Lanchow Military Region in 1974. Radio Fuchow, January 22, 1971, cited in CNA, February 5, 1971, p. 5.

122. The famous statement of the latter is Lin's "Long Live the Victory of People's Wars of National Liberation," September 1965. The text has been reprinted in many publications, including Donald Zagoria's *Vietnam Triangle* (New York: Pegasus, 1967).

123. Roger Glenn Brown, "Chinese Politics and American Policy."

124. Figures are from Byun-joon Ahn, "The Cultural Revolution and China's Search for Political Order," *China Quarterly* 58 (April-June 1974).

125. The PLA's Party organization had been very weak under the previous defense minister, P'eng Teh-huai. (Observation courtesy of Harlan Jencks.)

126. However, as Glenn Dick has noted to this writer, Lo's concepts for the regional forces did tend to undermine Mao's "three tiered" defense structure (militia, regional, and main forces) by effectively degrading the military role of the regional forces.

127. JMJP, November 22, 1968, translated in SCMP, December 4, 1968, p. 2.

128. Data regarding Chinese charges are mostly drawn from a Red Guard compendium of the Lo Jui-ch'ing case, translated in SCMM, January 20, 1969, pp. 1-12.

129. Uri Ra'anan, "Peking's Foreign Policy Debate, 1965-66," in *China in Crisis,* vol. 2, ed. Ho Ping-ti and Tang Tsou (Chicago University Press, 1968), pp. 36-37. On the Lo-Lin foreign policy debate generally, see Zagoria, *Vietnam Triangle.*

130. *Peking Review,* September 3, 1965, analyzed in Edward E. Rice, *Mao's Way* (Berkeley: University of California Press, 1973), p. 234.

131. *Hung-ch'i T'ung-hsun* [Red Flag Bulletin] (Canton), January 1968, translated in SCMP, July 9, 1968, p. 1.

132. *Wen-i Chan-pao* [Literature and Arts Combat Bulletin], March 9, 1968, in SCMP, March 28, 1968, p. 12.

133. *Kung-lien* [Workers Alliance] (Canton), April 1968, in SCMP, May 8, 1968, p. 4.

134. The men in question were Wang Li, Kuan Feng, Lin Chieh, Mu Hsin, and Ch'i Pen-yu. Wang, Kuan, Lin, and Mu were dismissed immediately. Ch'i Pen-yu was staunchly defended by Madam Mao and did not fall until February 1968.

135. *Kung-chiao Hung-ch'i* [Industry and Communications Red Flag] (Canton), October 12, 1967, in SCMP, November 9, 1967, p. 12.

136. *Hung-ch'i T'ung-hsun* in SCMP, July 9, 1968, p. 1.

137. Ibid., p. 2.

138. *Ch'ing-li Chieh-chi Tui-wu* [Purification of Class Ranks], January 1969, in *Translations on Communist China,* JPRS no. 52658 (March 18, 1971): 19-20.

139. *Wen-hui Pao,* February 26, 1968, translated in SCMP, March 25, 1968, p. 11.

140. NCNA, April 22, 1968, quoting an undated editorial of LAD, printed in SCMP, April 26, 1968, pp. 17-19.

141. *Wen-hui Pao,* April 21, 1968, translated in SCMP, May 17, 1968, p. 4.

142. SCMM, October 21, 1968, p. 26.

143. *Ch'ing-li Chieh-chi Tui-wu* in *Translations on Communist China,* no. 140, JPRS no. 52658 (March 18, 1971): 15-16. Lin was speaking on August 10, 1967.

144. *Chugoku Kenkyo Geppo* (Tokyo), December 1969 in *Translations on Communist China,* no. 108, JPRS no. 50719 (June 11, 1970): 1-3.

145. Rice, *Mao's Way,* p. 403.

146. Ibid.

147. *Wen-i Chan-pao* in SCMP, March 28, 1968, p. 12.

148. Ibid.

149. Rice, *Mao's Way,* p. 403.

150. Cited in *Facts and Features* 1, no. 12 (April 3, 1968): 66 (basic source not provided). Emphasis added.

151. *Wen-i Chan-pao* in SCMP, March 28, 1968, p. 12.

152. This point was made by Glenn Dick, in "The General

Political Department," in *The Military and Political Power in China in the 1970's,* ed. William Whitson (New York: Praeger, 1972), p. 178.

153. Li has, however, maintained his positions in the Politburo and CMC.

154. Glenn Dick, "General Political Department," p. 177.

155. *Who's Who in Communist China,* vol. 1 (Hong Kong: Union Research Institute), pp. 20-21.

156. *Ch'ing-li Chieh-chi Tui-wu,* in *Translations on Communist China,* no. 140, JPRS no. 52658 (March 18, 1971): 2.

157. Radio Peking, July 10, 1967, in FBIS, July 12, 1967, pp. ccc 3-10.

158. Richard E. Gillespie and John C. Sims, "The General Rear Services Department," in *The Military and Political Power in China in the 1970's,* ed. William Whitson (New York: Praeger, 1972), p. 205.

159. Red Guard Congress of the China Science and Technology University, "Down with Lo Jui-ch'ing. . .," translated in SCMM, January 20, 1969, p. 7.

160. A summary is provided in CNA, September 10, 1971.

161. Fraser, *The People's Liberation Army,* p. 15.

162. *San-ssu Chan-ch'i* [3rd Headquarters Battle Flag], June 1968, translated in SCMM, August 6, 1968, p. 2.

163. U.S. Congress, Joint Economic Committee Hearings, *Allocation of Resources in the Soviet Union and China,* Document no. 32-730-0 (Washington D.C.: U.S. General Printing Office, April 1974), testimony of William E. Colby, director of CIA.

164. CNA, September 10, 1971.

165. U.S. Congress, *Allocation of Resources,* p. 77.

166. Ibid., p. 47.

167. Ibid., p. 77.

168. Peter L. Sargent and Jack H. Harris, *Chinese Assessment of the Superpower Relationship, 1972-74* (Washington, D.C.: The BDM Corporation, 1975).

Notes to Chapter 4

1. This section is in large part drawn from Cheng Mien-chih, "The Organization and Equipment of the Chinese Communist Infantry," *Issues and Studies* 2, no. 10 (July 1967): 18-25. Mr. Cheng's article is based on captured documents—tables of organization and equipment—brought to Taiwan by defectors in 1965.

2. According to the findings of Captain A.R. Finlayson, type C corps are located in the tropically mountainous provinces of Kwangtung and Yunnan, as well as in Tibet, Szechwan, Shantung, and Kiangsu. From "Command and Control in the Chinese

People's Liberation Army" (Paper presented to the Modern China Seminar, Columbia University, May 1975).

3. The Peking, Tientsin, and Shanghai Garrisons are centrally controlled.

4. Nelsen, "Military Forces in the Cultural Revolution," *China Quarterly* 51 (July-September 1972): 446.

5. Yang Ch'eng-wu, as a deputy chief of staff in 1960, wrote: "In an emergency we must be able to make cross level commands [so that] headquarters can directly command divisions and regiments." J. Chester Cheng, ed., *The Politics of the Chinese Red Army* (Stanford, Calif.: Hoover Institution on War, Revolution and Peace, 1966), p. 544.

6. *Hsin Pei-ta* [New Peking University], January 20, 1967, translated in American Consulate General, Hong Kong, *Current Background* (CB hereafter), August 8, 1968, pp. 3-4.

7. *K'ang Erh-szu*, translated in U.S. Department of Congress, *Communist China Digest*, Joint Publications Research Services (JPRS hereafter), no. 196, JPRS no. 44721 (March 18, 1968): 83.

8. Both the chart and discussion of military region organization are partly derived from Chou Tzu-ch'iang, "An Analysis of the Chinese Communist Military Area System," *Issues and Studies* 8, no. 5 (February 1973): 39-40, 49.

9. Harlan Jencks, "The Politics of Chinese Military Modernization, 1949-77" (Ph.D. dissertation, University of Washington), chapter 6.

10. Ibid.

11. Admiral Thomas H. Moorer, "General Purpose Forces Compared,"*Commanders Digest* 15, no. 16 (April 18, 1974): 8.

12. Ibid.

13. In 1967-68, the U.S. Joint Chiefs of Staff developed a contingency plan for the purpose of cutting off the overland flow of military supplies to North Vietnam. The plan called for U.S. forces to make an amphibious landing, penetrate across Kwangsi Province, cut the rail line to Hanoi, and then hold the territory against counterattack. Fortunately, the plan merely gathered dust in the Pentagon.

14. Perhaps the worst case was the Chengtu Military Region. According to Hsieh Fu-chih, then the minister of Public Security: "The public security organs have become the docile tools [of the Szechuan military leadership]. In Szechuan, 35,000 persons were arrested [to suppress the GPCR there in late 1966 and early 1967]."*Chiu-P'eng Lo Chan-pao* [Drag Out P'eng Teh-huai and Lo Jui-ch'ing Combat Bulletin] (Canton) February 1968. Translated in American Consulate General, Hong Kong, *Survey of China Mainland Press* (SCMP hereafter), March 15, 1968, p. 6.

15. One possible exception was the 38th Corps which may have moved to Peking in early 1967 or, as some observers in Taiwan

believe, as early as July 1966. (*Issues and Studies* 6, no. 12 [September 1970]: 25.) A few relocations also occurred as late as August.

16. See chapter 5, note 25, for a discussion of this point.

17. *New China News Agency* (NCNA hereafter), Peking. February 11, 1969, in SCMP, February 20, 1969, p. 15.

18. Radio Honan, January 1, 1969, as reported in *China News Analysis* (CNA hereafter), Hong Kong, p. 4.

19. *Cheng-fa Hung-ch'i* [Politics and Law Red Flag] (Canton) October 17, 1967, as translated in SCMP, November 30, 1967, p. 6.

20. Kiangsi, Hunan, and Honan.

21. The Sinkiang case was exceptional in that the 9th Air Army commander, Li Chuan-ch'un, did not assume a formal military administrative post in Urumchi, but he did receive his orders direct from Peking and was made a vice-chairman of the Sinkiang Revolutionary Committee when it was finally formed in September 1968. There seems little doubt that Li's Unit 7335 was politically in command of the area. For example, the Civil Aviation General Administration Bureau instructed its subordinates in Sinkiang: "As far as supporting the left is concerned, you should follow Unit 7335." Commander Li received orders directly from the air force chief of staff and at one time was ordered to "handle well the relations with the Sinkiang Military Region Command... paying attention to the methods of handling." Meanwhile, the commander of the Region, Wang En-mao, spent much of the Cultural Revolution in Peking. See CB, June 17, 1968, pp. 14, 16. See also SCMP, February 28, 1968, pp. 13-14.

22. *Tokyo Shimbun*, August 22, 1967, as translated in U.S. Foreign Broadcast Information Service, *Daily Report: People's Republic of China* (FBIS hereafter), August 22, 1967, pp. ccc 2-3. See also FBIS, August 23, p. ccc 2.

23. *Ke-t'i T'ung-hsun* [Bulletins from All Parts of the Country] (Dairen), September 13, 1967, in SCMP, December 15, 1967, p. 9.

24. *Kwangchow Hung-szu and Wuhan Hsien-hua Kung*, combined issue, Canton editon, August 21, 1967, as translated in *Communist China Digest* 191, JPRS no. 43204 (October 30, 1967), 75.

25. *Facts and Features* 1, no. 25 (August 7, 1968): 3.

26. Chekiang Daily, editorial broadcast on the provincial radio service; translated in FBIS, December 5, 1967, pp. ddd 12-14.

27. *Pei-hang Hung-ch'i* [Peking Aviation Institute Red Flag], no. 47, in *Facts and Features* 1, no. 26 (October 1968): 19-23. See also American Consulate General, Hong Kong, *Selections from China Mainland Magazines* (SCMM hereafter), January 20, 1969, pp. 25-30.

28. *Shou-tu Hung-wei-ping* [Capital Red Guards] (Peking), September 12, 1968, as cited in Chien Yu-shen, *China's Fading Revolution* (Hong Kong: Hong Kong Center of Contemporary

Chinese Studies, 1969), p. 203. See also SCMP, July 9, 1968, pp. 1-3 and SCMP, August 29, 1968, pp. 3-7.

29. The first two of the three measures mentioned are discussed in chapter 2. Lin's efforts to resolve conflict among army corps in Hopeh and Shansi are in his April 9, 1968 Directive—SCMP, August 10, 1968, pp. 8-11.

30. Mao Tse-tung told Red Guard representatives that the revolutionary rebels had failed and that their services would no longer be needed. A complete transcript of the July 28 meeting is in *Mao Tse-tung Ssu-hsiang Wan-sui* [Long Live the Thoughts of Mao Tse-tung], vol. 1 (Taipei: Institute of International Relations, 1974), pp. 687-716—a reprint of a book originally printed in the People's Republic of China.

31. Nelsen, "Military Forces in the Cultural Revolution," p. 465.

32. For example, the 47th Corps in Hunan was moved north and no unit was dispatched to take its place. The 43rd Corps was removed from Hainan Island to the Wuhan Military Region— again with no replacement. The Peking Military Region gained at least two additional corps—the 27th and 28th, from Kiangsu and Fukien respectively. Those moves to the capital region may have been related to Mao's maneuvering against Lin Piao in 1971. Since that time, they have remained to strengthen the defenses of North China against possible Soviet attacks. Michael Pillsbury, "Patterns of Chinese Power Struggles" (paper delivered to the Seminar on Modern China, Columbia University, March 24, 1974).

33. *Tzu-liao Ch'uan-chi*, in SCMM, August 6, 1968, p. 13.

34. *Wen-i Chan-pao* [Literature and Arts Combat Bulletin], March 9, 1968, in SCMP, March 28, 1968, pp. 10-13.

35. The three supports were support to agriculture, industry, and the revolutionary left; the two militaries were military control and military training of civilians.

36. See chapter 3, p. 89.

37. *Red Flag*, August 7, 1971, as translated in CNA, October 1, 1971, pp. 2-3.

38. *Hsing-tao Jih-pao*, September 21, 1973.

39. Mao's address to the Second Plenum of the Ninth Party Congress, 1970, as translated in CNA, October 6, 1972, p. 4.

40. Specifically, the PLA was charged with not observing the first of the "three great disciplines," and the first and fifth of the eight points meant to guide military behavior. Ibid., p. 5.

Notes to Chapter 5

1. *Selected Works of Mao Tse-tung*, vol. 4 (Peking: Foreign Languages Press, 1961), pp. 363-64.

2. Bernhard Grossman, "The PLA: Economic Aspects," in *The Role of the PLA*, vol. 1, Proceedings of a conference of the same name sponsored by the Centre D'Etude Du Sud-est et de L'Extrême Orient, Brussels, June 17, 1969.

3. *Jen-min Jih-pao* [People's Daily] (JMJP hereafter), January 9, 1961, calculation courtesy of Professor Jurgen Domes.

4. Ralph Powell, "Soldiers in the Chinese Economy," *Asian Survey* 11, no. 8 (August 1971): 743.

5. Radio Nanchang, Kiangsi Provincial Service, in U.S. Foreign Broadcast Information Service, *Daily Report: People's Republic of China* (FBIS hereafter), February 12, 1975. The same report mentions that the Kiangsi Military District contributed 134,000 workdays in "socialist construction." Even if all of that work was strictly nonmilitary-related, it would amount to less than one week per year per man (based on an estimate that the military district has about 20,000 troops).

6. In the words of Lin Piao: "It is a good way to rotate the troops for construction, production and training." *Pei-hang Hung-ch'i* [Peking Aviation Institute Red Flag], no. 47, n.d., as translated in *Facts and Features* 1, no. 26 (October 16, 1968): 19-23.

7. Radio Chengtu, August 2, 1974, in FBIS, August 5, 1974, pp. J 2-3.

8. The Military Service Law is printed in American Consulate General, Hong Kong, *Current Background* (CB hereafter), February 16, 1955.

9. Parris Chang, "Political Profiles: Wang Hung-wen and Li Teh-sheng," *China Quarterly* 57 (January-March 1976): 119n.

10. The directive is translated in CB, May 5,1968, pp. 54-55.

11. Ibid.

12. *Kwang-chow Hung-wei-ping* [Canton Red Guard], September 5, 1968, in American Consulate General, Hong Kong, *Survey of China Mainland Press* (SCMP hereafter), December 11, 1968, pp. 1-4.

13. *Hung-ssu T'ung-hsun* [Red Bulletin] (Canton), July 7, 1968, in American Consulate General, Hong Kong, *Selections from China Mainland Magazines* (SCMM hereafter), August 6, 1968, p. 17.

14. *T'ien-shan Feng-huo* [Heavenly Mountains Beacon Fire], January 15, 1968, in CB, June 17, 1968, pp. 3-4.

15. In addition to the above-mentioned attack on Commander Wang by a deputy political commissar of the Sinkiang Region, Deputy Commander Li Ying-hsi and Deputy Political Commissar Chang Kwang-ts'ai attacked the commander of the Wuhan Military Region, Ch'en Tsai-tao. In the Canton Region, it was Hsiang Wei and Chiang Min-feng, respectively the director and deputy director of the region's political department, who attacked Commander Huang Yung-sheng. In Tibet, Deputy Commander Tseng Yung-ya supported Red Guards who were attacking the regional

commander, Chang Kuo-hua. Respective references are in SCMP, April 30, 1968, pp. 2-13; U.S. Department of Commerce, *Translations on Communist China,* Joint Publications Research Service (JPRS hereafter),JPRS no. 47701 (March 24, 1969): 35-38, and *Communist China Digest,* JPRS no. 44471 (March 18, 1968): 109-12.

16. Tseng Yung-ya remained a frustrated subordinate of Chang Kuo-hua in Tibet when that area became subordinate to the Chengtu Military Region—probably in 1968 or early 1969.

17. Radio Kiangsu, January 15, 1973, cited in Wang Shuan-chi, "Mao Tse-tung's Current Problems Within the Army," *Studies on Chinese Communism* 8, no. 10 (October 1974): 9.

18. Wang Hung-wen quoting Mao in January 1974; *China News Analysis* (CNA hereafter), January 10, 1975, p. 6.

19. American Consulate General, Hong Kong, *Selections from the People's Republic of China Press* (SPRCP hereafter), December 5, 1974, p. 59.

20. *Hsin Pei-ta,* January 20, 1967, in CB, August 8, 1968, pp. 3-4.

21. *K'ang Erh-szu* (Wuhan), September 1, 1967, in *Communist China Digest* no. 196, JPRS no. 44721 (March 18, 1968): 83.

22. Edgar Snow, *The Long Revolution* (New York City: Random House, 1971), pp. 112-113.

23. Chou En-lai remarked upon Yang Ch'eng-wu's dismissal as follows: "No matter from which base our Party members and armed forces units come, aren't you all children of the working people? Aren't you all soldiers of Chairman Mao? Why make a distinction among yourselves?" (As translated in SCMP, May 1, 1968, p. 7) Another charge against Yang was that he was trying to get rid of military region commanders who did not belong to his clique. Also, regarding the military unit basis of PLA factionalism, Chou En-lai asked ironically: "Does the 189th Division (Yang's old unit) feel despondent now that it is not under Yang Ch'eng-wu? (SCMM, January 20, 1969, p. 27) Following the purge of Ho Lung (a former CMC vice-chairman), Lin Piao was quoted as having said: "He is an infamous bandit. He eats and eats but never works. He invites many people to his home to make leaders his puppets. He has many of his puppets in all departments of the PLA." (Peking wall posters reported in *Akhata* (Tokyo), November 23, 1967, translated in FBIS, December 8, 1967, p. ccc 10)

24. "Chairman Mao has instructed that military cadres must be transferred to other posts and the armed forces units must also be dispatched to other places," deputy chief of staff Wen Yu-ch'eng as translated in SCMP, July 16, 1968, p. 8.

25. Of the units relocated, two are descended from the 2nd Field Army, three from the 3rd, six from the 4th, and one from the North China units of Nieh Jung-chen. Had some sort of balance of power among the field armies been operative in 1967, Nieh's units should

have been much better represented in the army's new political role. In fact, such a balance of power did not exist. The 1st Field Army of Ho Lung and P'eng Teh-huai has been represented by only one corps for seventeen years. Its performance during the GPCR was exemplary. Several of the corps leaders who performed well for Mao and Lin were from supposedly hostile factions. For example, 12th Corps Commander Li Teh-sheng did so well in Anhui that he was later promoted to director of the General Political Department. Yet he is a "professional" soldier of the "Liu Po-ch'eng faction" which was supposedly opposed to Maoist military doctrine. There are similar examples of excellent behavior for units of the Ch'en I and Nieh Jung-chen "factions." Conversely, probably the worst-behaved corps during the GPCR was the 54th—a "Lin Piao unit."

26. *Tung-fang Tien-hsun* [East is Red Telegram] (Canton), July 1968, as translated in *Communist China 1968* (Hong Kong: Union Research Institute, 1969), p. 215.

27. Ward Just, *Military Men* (New York: Alfred Knopf, 1970), pp. 136-38.

28. *Tzu-liao Ch'uan-chi*, in SCMM, October 21, 1968, p. 25.

29. This judgment is admittedly drawn from a very limited evidential base—i.e., an interview with a former PLA officer in Hong Kong and the personal account of another former officer, Chin Chien-li, in *Pei-kuo Chien-wen-lu* [Odyssey in North China] (Hong Kong: Union Press, 1973), pp. 293-95. Probably more important is the negative evidence—the resolution of conflict between commanders and political commissars is a very uncommon subject even in the uncensored Chinese media such as Red Guard journals and CMC *Work Bulletins*.

30. William Whitson, *The Chinese High Command* (New York City: Praeger, 1973), epilogue.

31. Radio Sian, November 15, 1974, in FBIS, November 21, 1974, pp. M 5-6.

32. *Kang-pa-i T'ung-hsun* [Steel August 1st Bulletin] (Canton), June 1968, in SCMP, July 16, 1968, p. 11.

33. Both cases are cited in CNA, August 15, 1975, p. 7.

34. See, for example, New China News Agency (NGNA hereafter), Peking, February 23, 1975, in FBIS, February 25, 1975, p. M 1.

Notes to Chapter 6

1. *Chung-kung Nien-pao*, 1973 [Yearbook on Chinese Communism], book 2 (Taipei: Institute for the Study of Chinese Problems, 1973), p. 53.

2. *Issues and Studies* 10, no. 11 (August 1974): 96-97.

3. Ibid.

4. There were only six air districts; the change was made around 1970.

5. There are exceptions to this general guideline, e.g., Sinkiang has an air army even though it is not an air district. On the other hand, a few districts have no air armies. *Chung-kuo K'ung-chun Chan-chi Te-ch'i* [Special Compilation on China's Fighting Aircraft] (Hong Kong: Arms of the World Publishing Co., 1974), p. 18.

6. In Tsinghai Province, twenty-four persons were stranded on a large lake when the winter ice broke up in 1969. The provincial revolutionary committee notified the "proletarian headquarters" in Peking and "a notice ordering aircraft to be sent to rescue the men was issued two hours later." Apparently the air force officers within the province and air district did not have the authority even to dispatch unarmed rescue aircraft in case of an emergency. New China News Agency (NCNA hereafter), Sining, Tsinghai, March 7, 1969, in American Consulate General, Hong Kong, *Survey of China Mainland Press* (SCMP hereafter), March 13, 1969, p. 15.

7. *Chung-kung Nien-pao*, 1973, p. 54.

8. Chinese Nationalist analysts claim six divisions, ibid. Personnel of the 15th Corps wear army uniforms and seem to be treated much as any other army corps except for specialized training and equipment.

9. In recent years China has purchased modern jet transports for its civil aviation fleet. (The suppliers have been the U.S., Great Britain, and the USSR.) These aircraft increase the airlift capability in wartime, but are not suited to paradrop operations.

10. Richard Bueschel, *Communist Chinese Air Power* (New York City: Praeger, 1968), p. 68.

11. The Soviet sale of helicopters to China in 1974 might eventually be remembered as a significant good will gesture aimed at reducing Sino-Soviet tensions. China later reciprocated by releasing a captured Soviet helicopter crew.

12. Congressional testimony of U.S. Secretary of Defense, James Schlesinger, reported in the *Hong Kong Standard*, February 13, 1975, p. 1.

13. Angus Fraser, *The People's Liberation Army: Communist China's Armed Forces* (New York City: Crane and Russack, 1973), p. 11.

14. Sydney Jammes, "The Chinese Defense Burden," in U.S. Congress, Joint Economic Committee, *China: A Reassessment of the Economy*, Washington, D.C., July 1975.

15. *Newsweek*, August 5, 1974, p. 15.

16. Richard Bueschel, *Communist Chinese Air Power* (New York City: Praeger, 1968), p. 153.

17. For over a decade, the PLAAF has had radar-guided air-to-air missiles. They may now also have infrared, heat-seeking ver-

sions.

18. Radio Peking, August 8, 1967, in U.S. Foreign Broadcast Information Service, *Daily Report: People's Republic of China* (FBIS hereafter), August 9, 1967, p. ccc 2.

19. Radio Shanghai, February 1, 1967, in FBIS Supplement; "Material on the Great Proletarian Cultural Revolution," vol. 4, 1967, p. 19.

20. Radio Hupeh, May 18, 1969, in FBIS, May 28, 1969, p. D 17.

21. *T'ien-shan Feng-huo* [T'ien Mountain Beacon Fire], January 15, 1968, in SCMP Supplement, February 12, 1968, p. 18.

22. *Chung-ta Chan-pao* [Chung-shan University Combat News] (Canton), August 7, 1968, in SCMP, January 17, 1969, p. 9.

23. See Red Guard documents in SCMP, August 7, 1968, p. 10, and SCMP, April 2, 1969, p. 5.

24. *Chekiang Jih-pao* editorial, broadcast by Radio Chekiang, translated in FBIS, December 5, 1967, pp. ddd 12-14.

25. They simply flew their planes to new bases; ground-based equipment remained in place.

26. *Issues and Studies* 10, no. 11 (August 1974): 99-103.

27. William Colby, Congressional testimony, in U.S. Congress, Joint Economic Committee, *Allocation of Resources in the Soviet Union and China* (Washington, D.C.: April 12, 1974), pp. 76-77.

28. Recently published estimates range from a low of 170,000 in John E. Moore, ed., *Jane's Fighting Ships, 1974-75* (London: S. Low, Marston , 1975), to a high of 300,000 (*Chung-kung Nien-pao*, 1973).

29. Lo Jui-ch'ing directed the Fuchow Military Region, rather than the East Sea Fleet, to take the initiative in naval actions in the Taiwan Straits. The "Fukien Front" of the Fuchow Military Region (opposite Taiwan) has been on a war footing for many years. Seemingly, on the basis of Lo's directive, the regional headquarters controls naval forces in the Straits. Uri Ra'anan, "Peking's Foreign Policy Debate," in *China in Crisis*, vol. 2, ed. Ho Ping-ti and Tang Tsou (Chicago University Press, 1968), pp. 36-37.

30. *Chung-kung Nien-pao*, 1973, p. 55.

31. Defense Intelligence Agency statement in U.S. Congress, Joint Economic Committee, *Allocation of Resources in the Soviet Union and China, 1975*, Washington, D.C., July 1975, p. 117.

32. Moore, *Jane's Fighting Ships, 1975-76*, p. 81. See also Thomas H. Moorer, "General Purpose Forces Compared—U.S., Russia and China," *Commander's Digest* 15, no. 16 (April 18, 1974): 13-14.

33, During the height of the U.S. involvement in the Vietnam war, many of the bombing missions were launched from "Yankee Station"—an area in the Gulf of Tonkin where large aircraft carriers cruised for months at a time. The North Vietnamese attempted to obtain Osa/Komar missile patrol boats, presumably in order to attack Yankee Station. Both Russia and China refused to supply North Vietnam with the vessels, probably realizing that if a U.S. aircraft carrier were to be successfully attacked with boats supplied from either nation, the Vietnam war might have grown into a wider and much more destructive conflict.

34. *The Christian Science Monitor*, January 21, 1974, p. 2.

35. The navy was rather dilatory in this matter. The kidnapping took place in the predawn hours of July 20, yet it was not until 4:00 p.m. that the East Sea Fleet issued a statement supporting the kidnap victims. *Wuhan K'ang-erh-szu*, August 22, 1967, in U.S. Department of Commerce, *Communist China Digest*, Joint Publications Research Service, no.194 (JPRS hereafter), JPRS no. 44241 (February 5, 1968): 138.

36. *Issues and Studies* 10, no. 12 (November 1973): 32.

37. Jammes, "The Chinese Defense Burden."

Notes to Chapter 7

1. One of many references to militia cadres is in *Union Research Service*, Hong Kong (URS hereafter), July 6, 1973, p. 16.

2. In 1974, Sinkiang claimed that 25 percent of the population there was enrolled in the militia—probably the highest percentage claim since the days of the Great Leap Forward. Radio Sinkiang, November 8, 1974, cited in *China News Summary*, Hong Kong (CNS hereafter), November 13, 1974, p. 7.

3. A Nationalist study asserts that one-fourth of all militia are "basic" or "backbone" units, but there is probably a good deal of regional and local variation. *Fei-ching Yueh-pao*, April 30, 1970, in U.S. Department of Commerce, *Translations on Communist China*, Joint Publications Research Service (JPRS hereafter), no. 111, JPRS no. 50926 (July 10, 1970): 13.

4. Edgar Snow, *The Long Revolution* (New York City: Random House, 1971), p. 109.

5. Radio Anhui, September 22, 1971, as translated in URS 65, no. 3: 32.

6. *Chung-kung Nien-pao*, 1974 [Yearbook on Chinese Communism] (Taipei: Institute for Study of Chinese Problems, 1973), sec. 2, p. 68.

7. Radio Shensi, November 4, 1974, translated in CNS, November 13, 1974, p. 6.

8. In Shanghai and Peking, Politburo-level Party leaders are in charge of the militia commands, which is indicative both of the importance placed on building up the urban militia and strong Party leadership over it.

9. J. Chester Cheng, *The Politics of the Chinese Red Army* (Stanford, Calif.: Hoover Institute on War, Revolution and Peace,

1966), p. 47.

10. Radio Hupeh, September 30, 1973, translated in URS, October 2, 1973, p. 4.

11. For PADs as "advisors," see URS, ibid., p. 12. For a typical military district order ignoring the Party role, see Hupeh M.D. order, broadcast over the domestic service, Peking, November 21, 1975, in U.S. Foreign Broadcast Information Service, *Daily Report: People's Republic of China* (FBIS hereafter), November 26, 1975, p. H 2.

12. *Nan-fang Jih-pao* [Southern Daily] (Canton), September 19, 1973, cited in URS, October 19, 1973, p. 72.

13. In 1973, a Hupeh commune had sixty-four ex-soldiers. Sixty-one had been appointed as militia cadres. Radio Hupeh, June 18, 1973, translated in URS, July 6, 1973, p. 21.

14. American Consulate General, Hong Kong, *Survey of China Mainland Press* (SCMP hereafter), November 30, 1967, p. 10.

15. *Chung-kung Nien-pao,* 1974, sec. 2, p. 58.

16. Radio Sinkiang, November 8, 1974, translated in CNS, November 7, 1974, p. 7.

17. Those priorities have been necessitated in part by recent expansion in militia forces—Sinkiang claimed in 1974 that its militia had doubled in size since 1965. Ibid.

18. Radio Fukien, June 19, 1972, cited in URS, July 7, 1972, p. 27.

19. Radio Hunan, September 13, 1966, as cited in *Fei-ch'ing Yueh-pao,* April 30, 1970, pp. 61-66. See *Translations on Communist China,* no. 111, JPRS no. 50926 (July 10, 1970): 13.

20. Radio Shanghai, September 12, 1974, as translated in CNS, November 13, 1974, p. 1.

21. *Liberation Army Daily* (LAD hereafter) editorial, March 17, 1967, translated in *Communist China Digest,* no. 184, JPRS no. 41147 (May 25, 1967): 30.

22. LAD, August 6, 1967, as translated in SCMP, August 25, 1967, p. 8.

23. The Minister was Hsieh Fu-chih. *Chiu P'eng Lo Chan-pao* [Drag Out P'eng Teh-huai and Lo Jui-ch'ing Combat News] (Peking), February 1968, as translated in SCMP, March 15, 1968, pp. 5-7.

24. See American Consulate General, Hong Kong, *Current Background* (CB hereafter), May 6, 1968, pp. 135-36 for the complete text of the directive.

25. *Sankei* (Tokyo), August 12, 1967, quoting Peking wall posters, translated in FBIS, August 14, 1967, p. ccc 15.

26. The city was Chengtu, Szechwan. From an unidentified Red Guard circular, translated in SCMP, November 6, 1967, p. 10.

27. *Kwangchow Kung-jen* [Canton Workers], no. 34, n.d., translated in SCMP, June 28, 1968, pp. 12-16.

28. Cited in Chien Yu-shen, *China's Fading Revolution* (Hong Kong: Centre of Contemporary Chinese Studies, 1969), pp. 38-39.

29. *Chan Kwangtung* [Fighting Kwangtung] (Canton), July 10, 1968, as translated in SCMP, April 2, 1969, p. 7.

30. *Hsi-chiang Nu-t'ao* [Angry Waves of the West River] (Wuchow, Kwangsi), June 1968, in SCMP, July 23, 1968, pp. 16-18.

31. *Jen-min Jih-pao* [People's Daily] (JMJP hereafter), August 3, 1968, as translated in SCMP, August 14, 1968, p. 5.

32. Information courtesy of Anita Ch'an, University of Sussex, who interviewed refugees in Hong Kong during 1974-75 partly with the intent of discovering how the justice system has functioned since the GPCR.

33. Margaret Jones, "Crime and Punishment in China," *National Times* (Sydney), reprinted in *Atlas*, September 1975, pp. 19-21.

34. "An extensively armed working class can play a greater role in opposing capitalist restoration internally." *Studies in Criticism*, September 1973, cited in CNS, No. 499, November 22, 1973, pp. 4-5.

35. The largest actual work units are regiments. However, mention has been made of "PCC Army Groups"—apparently one per military region—but this echelon is undoubtedly an administrative convenience rather than a meaningful military unit.

36. Edgar Snow, *The Long Revolution*, pp. 112-113.

37. *Hsing-tao Jih-pao* (Hong Kong), October 18, 1971, in *Translations on the People's Republic of China*, no. 167, JPRS no. 54616 (December 6, 1971): 4.

38. Inner Mongolia Radio, cited in *China News Analysis*, Hong Kong (CNA hereafter), February 16, 1973, p. 3.

39. Pai Ch'ung-te, "The Production-Construction Corps—a Survey," *Issues and Studies* 10, no. 2 (November 1973): 45-61.

40. Ibid.

41. Interview with refugee who formerly worked on a Hainan rubber plantation, Hong Kong, 1974.

42. Even a hostile analysis in *Chung-kung Yeh-chiu* (Taipei) admits this and provides interesting production claims from an October 1965 JMJP article. According to the latter, 10 million *mou* (about 1.6 million acres) of wasteland had been reclaimed and 100 state farms organized. The well-established farms and enterprises are run similarly to those in interior provinces, with part of the production going to the state and the remainder providing for the operating costs, wages, and investments of the factory or farm. See *Translations on Communist China*, no. 108, JPRS no. 50719 (June 11, 1970): 25.

43. William R. Heaton Jr., "The Minorities and the Military in China" (paper presented at the U.S. Air University conference on The Role of the Military in Communist Societies, Maxwell Air

Force Base, November, 1975).

Notes to Chapter 8

1. Rosa Luxemburg predicted prior to World War I that competition among imperialist nations for colonies, raw materials, and
markets abroad would lead to world war. She believed that war
among the imperialists would cause the collapse of capitalism
rather than the longer process of nationalistic awakening in Asia,
Africa, and Latin America. Her concepts are still reflected in
official Chinese pronouncements (e.g., the lead-in quotation for
this chapter). Peking sees socialist imperialism, led by the USSR,
and capitalist imperialism as irreconcilable competitors which
may well precipitate a devastating world war. From its ashes would
arise the "true" revolution. However, Peking would much rather
have revolutions develop in third world nations which would
preempt world war by undermining imperialisms of all kinds.

2. *Selected Works of Mao Tse-tung*, vol. 4 (Peking: Foreign
Languages Press, 1961), pp. 99-100.

3. "Long Live the Victory of People's War," *Peking Review*, no.
36, (1965).

4. Peter Van Ness, *Revolution and Chinese Foreign Policy*
(Berkeley: University of California Press, 1970), pp. 95-98. Professor Van Ness uses the example of French Somaliland where there
was an active anticolonial insurgency in the mid-1960s. Peking
refused to recognize or assist this movement because France had
extended diplomatic recognition to the P.R.C. and had adopted a
diplomacy independent from the U.S. line.

5. This was apparent in the strong, though abortive, efforts of
China to convene a Second Afro-Asian People's Solidarity Confer-
ence in Algeria, and in the main themes emphasized during Chou's
African trips.

6. Nkrumah was in Peking, receiving the full red carpet treatment when he was overthrown in February 1966. Ben Bella was
ousted just prior to the scheduled convening of the Chinese
sponsored Second Afro-Asian Conference which was to meet in
Algiers. China was attempting to form a united front among the
poor nations against both U.S. imperialism and Soviet great power
hegemony. The conference was never convened.

7. Thakin Than Tun, *New York Times*, November 1, 1968, p. 5.

8. Melvin Gurtov, *China and S.E. Asia: The Politics of Survival*
(Baltimore: Johns Hopkins University Press, 1971), p. 39. However, another source showed continuous growth of insurgent
forces—*Yearbook on International Communist Affairs* (Stanford,
California: Hoover Institute on War Revolution and Peace, published annually).

9. The 1975 Thai Prime Minister Kukrit Pramog told an American editor that the D.R.V. was the new leader in Southeast Asia and that it was supporting an insurgency along the Viet-Thai border. The prime minister did not mention any current Chinese support for the insurgents. *St. Petersburg Times*, July 14, 1975, p. 3.

10. *New York Times*, July 25, 1969, cited in Allen S. Whiting, "The Use of Force in Foreign Policy by the P.R.C.," *The Annals of the American Academy of Political and Social Sciences*, July 1972.

11. In the Brezhnev Doctrine, the USSR allocated to itself the right to interfere in the internal affairs of socialist states in order to prevent major deviations. It was used to justify the occupation of Czechoslovakia.

12. Robert M. Field, "Some Overlooked National Product Data," *China Quarterly* 59 (July/September 1974); and Alexander Eckstein, "Economic Growth and Change in China," *China Quarterly* 54 (April/June 1973).

13. *Peking Review*, July 2, 1971, p. 21.

14. *New China News Agency*, Peking (NCNA hereafter), July 31, 1971, translated in U.S. Foreign Broadcast Information Service, *Daily Report: People's Republic of China*, August 2, 1971, pp. A5-7.

15. *Red Flag*, November 9, 1971, as cited in Philip Bridgam, "The Fall of Lin Piao," *China Quarterly* 55 (July/September 1973): 446.

16. NCNA, January 20, 1975. Emphasis added.

Selected Bibliography

Primary Sources and Documentary Compilations

American Consulate General, Hong Kong. *Current Background*. May 6, 1968.

Asia Research Centre. *The Great Cultural Revolution in China*. Rutland, Vermont: Charles E. Tuttle Co., 1968.

Cheng, J. Chester, ed. *The Politics of the Chinese Red Army*. Stanford, California: Hoover Institution on War, Revolution and Peace, 1966.

Hung Ch'i [Red Flag], Peking.

Jen-min Jih-pao [People's Daily], Peking.

Kau, (Michael) Ying-mao. *The Lin Piao Affair*. White Plains, New York: International Arts and Sciences Press, 1975.

Kau, Ying-mao. *The People's Liberation Army and China's Nation Building*. White Plains, New York: International Arts and Sciences Press, 1973.

Kau, Ying-mao, ed. *The Political Work System of the Chinese Communist Military*. Providence, Rhode Island: East Asia Language and Area Center, Brown University, 1971.

Mao Tse-tung. *Selected Works of Mao Tse-tung*. 4 volumes. Peking: Foreign Languages Press, 1961-65.

Peking Review, Peking.

Schram, Stuart. *Chairman Mao Talks to the People: Talks and Letters, 1965-71*. New York City: Random House, 1974.

Union Research Institute. *The Case of P'eng Teh-huai, 1959-68*. Hong Kong: Union Research Institute, 1968.

Union Research Institute. *Chinese Communist Party Documents of the Great Proletarian Cultural Revolution, 1966-67*. Hong Kong: Union Research Institute, 1968.

U.S. American Consulate General, Hong Kong. *Current Background*. Hong Kong.

U.S. American Consulate General, Hong Kong. *Selections from China Mainland Magazines*. Hong Kong.

U.S. American Consulate General, Hong Kong. *Survey of China Mainland Press*. Hong Kong.

U.S. American Consulate General, Hong Kong. *Survey of People's Republic of China Press*. Hong Kong.

U.S. Department of Commerce. *Communist China Digest*. Washington, D.C.: Joint Publications Research Service.

U.S. Department of Commerce. *Translations on Communist China*. Washington, D.C.: Joint Publication Research Service.

U.S. Department of Commerce. *Translations on the People's Republic of China*. Washington, D.C.: Joint Publications Research Service.

U.S. Foreign Broadcast Information Service. *Daily Report: People's Republic of China*. Washington, D.C.

Books

Barnett, A. Doak. *Uncertain Passage*. Washington, D.C.: Brookings Institution, 1974.

Bueschel, Richard. *Communist Chinese Air Power*. New York City: Praeger, 1968.

Chien Yu-shen. *China's Fading Revolution*. Hong Kong: Hong Kong Centre of Contemporary Chinese Studies, 1969.

Corr, Gerard H. *The Chinese Red Army*. New York City: Schocken Books, 1974.

Ebon, Martin. *Lin Piao*. New York City: Stein and Day, 1970.

Fraser, Angus M. *The People's Liberation Army*. New York City: Crane, Russak and Co., 1973.

Gittings, John. *The Role of the Chinese Army*. London: Oxford University Press, 1967.

Griffith, Samuel B. *The Chinese People's Liberation Army*. New York City: McGraw-Hill, 1967.

Gurtov, Melvin. *China and Southeast Asia: The Politics of Survival*. Baltimore: Johns Hopkins University Press, 1971.

Hoover Institution on War, Revolution and Peace. *Yearbook on International Communist Affairs, 1975*. Stanford, California: Hoover Institution on War, Revolution and Peace.

Institute of International Relations. *Chung-kung Nien-pao* [Yearbook on Chinese Communism]. Taipei: Institute of International Relations, 1973, 1974.

Institute of Strategic Studies. *The Military Balance, 1975*. London: Institute of Strategic Studies, published annually. Supplemented each spring by *Strategic Survey*.

Joffe, Ellis. *Party and Army: Professionalism and Political Control in the Chinese Officer Corps*. Cambridge, Mass.: Harvard University Press, 1967.

Johnson, Chalmers. *Autopsy on People's Wars*. Berkeley, University of California Press, 1973.

Liu, Alan P. L. *Political Culture and Group Conflict in Communist China*. Santa Barbara, California: Clio Press, 1976.

Moore, John E., ed. *Jane's Fighting Ships, 1975-76*. London: S. Low, Marston and Co., 1975.

Powell, Ralph L. *Politico-Military Relationships in Communist China*. Washington D.C.: U.S. Department of State, Bureau of Intelligence and Research, 1963.

Rice, Edward E. *Mao's Way*. Berkeley: University of California Press, 1972.

Sargent, Peter L., and Harris, Jack H. *Chinese Assessment of the Superpower Relationship, 1972-74*. Washington, D.C.: BDM Corporation, 1975.

Snow, Edgar. *The Long Revolution*. New York City: Random House, 1971.

Union Research Institute. *Who's Who in Communist Chi-*

na. Hong Kong: Union Research Institute, 1969.

U.S. Arms Control and Disarmament Agency. *World Military Expenditures and Arms Transfers, 1965-74.* Washington, D.C.: 1976.

U.S. Congress, Joint Economic Committee. *Allocation of Resources in the Soviet Union and China.* Washington, D.C., 1975.

Van Ness, Peter. *Revolution and China's Foreign Policy.* Berkeley: University of California Press, 1973.

Whitson, William. *The Chinese High Command.* New York City: Praeger Press, 1973.

Whitson, William. *The Military and Political Power in China in the 1970s.* New York City: Praeger, 1972.

Wu Yuan-li, and Sheeks, Robert. *The Organization and Support of Scientific Research and Development in Mainland China.* New York City: Praeger, 1970.

Zagoria, Donald. *Vietnam Triangle.* New York City: Pegasus, 1967.

Articles, Papers, and Dissertations

Ahn, Byun-joon. "The Cultural Revolution and China's Search for Political Order." *China Quarterly* 58 (April-June 1974).

Bobrow, Davis B. "The Good Officer: Definition and Training." *China Quarterly* 18 (April-June 1964).

Bridgham, Philip. "The Fall of Lin Piao." *China Quarterly* 55 (July-September 1973).

Brown, Roger G. "Chinese Politics and American Policy: A New Look at the Triangle." *Foreign Policy* 23 (Summer 1976).

Chang, Parris. "The Changing Pattern of Military Participation in Chinese Politics." *Orbis* 16, no. 7 (Fall 1972).

Chang, Parris. "China's Military." *Current History.* September 1974.

Chang, Parris. "China's Military-Industrial Complex and Its Policy Inputs." Paper presented to the U.S. Air University conference on The Role of the Military in Communist Societies, November 1975, at Maxwell Air Force Base.

Cheng Chu-yuan. "Growth and Structural Change in the

Chinese Machine Building Industry, 1952-66." *China Quarterly* 41 (January-March 1970).

Cheng Mien-chih. "The Organization and Equipment of the Chinese Communist Infantry." *Issues and Studies* 3, no. 10 (July 1967).

Chou Tzu-ch'iang. "An Analysis of the Chinese Communist Military Area System." *Issues and Studies* 8, no. 5 (February 1973).

Domes, Jurgen. "Generals and Red Guards." *Asia Quarterly* (Brussels) 1, nos. 1 & 2 (1971).

Domes, Jurgen. "The Role of the Military in the Formation of Revolutionary Committees, 1967-68." *China Quarterly* 44 (October-December 1970).

Finlayson, Andrew R. "Command and Control in the Chinese People's Liberation Army." Paper presented at the Modern China Seminar, May 1975, at Columbia University.

Gittings, John. "Army-Party Relations in the Light of the Cultural Revolution." In *Party Leadership and Revolutionary Power in China.* Edited by John Wilson Lewis. London: Cambridge University Press, 1970.

Godwin, Paul. "The People's Liberation Army and the Political Modernization of China." Paper presented at the U.S. Air University conference on the Role of the Military in Communist Societies, November 1975, at Maxwell Air Force Base.

Grossman, Bernhard. "The People's Liberation Army: Economic Aspects." *The Role of the People's Liberation Army.* Vol. 1. Proceedings of a conference of the same name sponsored by the Centre d'Etude du Sud-est et de l'Extrême Orient, Brussels, June 17, 1969.

Harding, Harry. "Political Trends in China Since the Cultural Revolution." *The Annals of the American Academy of Political and Social Science* 402 (July 1972).

Heaton, William. "The Minorities and the Military in China." Paper presented at the U.S. Air University conference on The Role of the Military in Communist Societies, November 1975, at Maxwell Air Force Base.

Hsieh, Alice Langley. "China's Nuclear Missile Program: Regional or Intercontinental?" *China Quarterly* 45

(January-March 1971).

Jammes, Sydney H. "The Chinese Defense Burden." In *China: A Reassessment of the Economy*. Washington, D.C.: U.S. Congress, Joint Economic Committee, 1975.

Jencks, Harlan. "The Politics of Chinese Military Modernization, 1949-77." Ph.D. dissertation, University of Washington.

Joffe, Ellis. "The Chinese Army in the Cultural Revolution: The Politics of Intervention." *Current Scene* 8, no. 18 (December 7, 1970).

Moorer, Thomas H. "General Purpose Forces Compared: U.S., U.S.S.R., China." *Commanders Digest* 15, no. 16 (April 18, 1974).

Nelsen, Harvey. "Military Bureaucracy in the Cultural Revolution." *Asian Survey* 14, no. 4 (April 1974).

Nelsen, Harvey. "Military Forces in the Cultural Revolution." *China Quarterly* 51 (July-September 1972).

Pai Cheng-te. "The Production-Construction Corps: A Survey." *Issues and Studies* 10, no. 2 (November 1973).

Pillsbury, Michael. "Patterns of Chinese Power Struggles." Paper given at the Modern China Seminar, March 1974, at Columbia University.

Powell, Ralph. "The Party, the Government and the Gun." *Asian Survey* 10, no. 6 (June 1970).

Powell, Ralph. "The Role of the Military in China's Transportation and Communications Systems." *Current Scene* 10, no. 2 (February 7, 1972).

Powell, Ralph. "Soldiers in the Chinese Economy." *Asian Survey* 11, no. 8 (August 1971).

Ra'anan, Uri. "Peking's Foreign Policy Debate, 1965-66." in *China in Crisis*, Vol. 2. Edited by Ho Ping-ti and Tang Tsou. Chicago: Chicago University Press, 1968.

Robinson, Thomas. "The Sino-Soviet Border Dispute." *American Political Science Review* 66, no. 4 (December 1972).

Robinson, Thomas. "The Wuhan Incident." *China Quarterly* 47 (July-September 1971).

Ryan, Deidre Mead. "The Decline of the Armed Struggle Tactic in Chinese Foreign Policy." *Current Scene* 10, no. 12 (December 1972).

Swanson, Bruce. "The People's Republic of China Navy—

Coastal Defense or Blue Water." *U.S. Naval Institute Proceedings* 102, no. 879 (May 1976).

White, Gordon. "The Politics of Social Stratification in a Socialist Society: The Case of China, 1959-69." Ph.D. dissertation, Stanford University, 1974.

White, Lynn T. "The Liberation Army and the Chinese People." *Armed Forces and Society* 1, no. 3 (Spring 1975).

Whiting, Allen S. "The Use of Force in Foreign Policy by the People's Republic of China." *The Annals of the American Academy of Political and Social Science* 402 (July 1972).

Periodicals

China News Analysis. Hong Kong.

China News Summary. Hong Kong, British Regional Information Service.

China Topics. Hong Kong, British Regional Information Service.

Chinese Communist Affairs: Facts and Features. Taipei (ceased publication ca. 1968).

Chung-kung Yen-chiu [Studies on Chinese Communism]. Taipei.

Current Scene. Hong Kong, U.S. Information Service.

Far Eastern Economic Review.

Fei-ch'ing Yueh-pao [Chinese Communist Affairs Monthly]. Taipei.

Issues and Studies. Taipei.

Union Research Service. Hong Kong.

Index